PAUL THE DEACON

HISTORY OF THE LOMBARDS

TRANSLATED BY

WILLIAM DUDLEY FOULKE, LL.D.

EDITED, WITH INTRODUCTION BY

EDWARD PETERS

UNIVERSITY OF PENNSYLVANIA PRESS

PHILADELPHIA

Originally published in 1907 by the University of Pennsylvania as *History of the Langobards.*

Introduction and Appendix copyright © 1974 by the University of Pennsylvania Press, Inc.

Library of Congress Catalog Card Number : 74–16829
ISBN (cloth) : 0–8122–7671–X
ISBN (paper) : 0–8122–1079–4

Printed in the United States of America

TABLE OF CONTENTS.

A NOTE ON THE TITLE
OF THIS REPRINT EDITION.

Although the Latin title of Paul's *History* is the *Historia Langobardorum* and William Dudley Foulke translated it as *The History of the Langobards,* modern usage favors *The History of the Lombards,* and I have used the more recent style. The running heads of the text, of course, retain Foulke's usage, but this should be a minor inconvenience. For a discussion of the question of Langobarn/Lombard usage, see Thomas Hodgkin, *Italy and Her Invaders,* Vol. VI, *The Lombard Invasion* (Oxford, 1895), pp. 174–175.

EXPLANATION OF REFERENCES.

"Waitz" indicates the edition of "Pauli Historia Langobard-orum" in "Monumenta Germaniae, Scriptores Rerum Lango-bardicarum," from which this translation is made, and unless otherwise stated, the matters referred to will be found in connec-tion with the book and chapter (the page not being given) corre-sponding to those of this translation.

"Abel" refers to the German translation entitled "Paulus Diakonus und die übrigen Geschichtschreiber der Langobarden," by Dr. Otto Abel." (Second edition revised by Dr. Reinhard Jacobi, Leipsic, 1888; published as Vol. 15 of the series "Geschichtschreiber der deutschen Vorzeit," and the matters referred to, unless otherwise stated, will be found either in the text or notes of the book and chapter corresponding to those of this translation.

"Giansevero" indicates the Italian translation entitled "Paolo Diacono, Dei Fatti de' Langobardi," by Prof. Uberti Giansevero (Cividale, 1899), and the matters referred to will be found in the book and chapter corresponding to those of this translation.

"Bethmann" unless otherwise stated refers to one of his articles, "Paulus Diakonus Leben." "Paulus Diakonus Schriften," "Die Geschichtschreibung der Langobarden," contained in the tenth volume of the "Archiv der Gesellschaft für ältere deutsche Geschichtkunde" (Hanover, 1849).

"Jacobi" refers to "Die Quellen der Langobardengeschichte des Paulus Diaconus. Ein Beitrag zur Geschichte deutscher His-toriographie," by Dr. R. Jacobi (Halle, 1877).

"Mommsen" to an article "Die Quellen der Langobarden-geschichte des Paulus Diaconus" by Th. Mommsen in volume V,

EXPLANATION OF REFERENCES.

p. 53, of the "Neues Archiv der Gesellschaft für ältere deutsche Geschichtskunde" (Hanover, 1879).

"Hartmann" to the second volume of "Geschichte Italiens im Mittelalter," by Ludo Moritz Hartmann, being the 32d work of the series "Geschichte der europaischen Staaten," edited by Heeren, Ukert, Giesebrecht and Lamprecht (Gotha, 1903).

"Dahn" to "Paulus Diaconus," by Felix Dahn, Part I (Leipsic, 1876).

"Hodgkin" to "Italy and her Invaders," by Thomas Hodgkin (Clarendon Press, 1895).

"Zeuss" to "Die Deutschen und die Nachbarstämme," by Kaspar Zeuss (Göttingen, 1904).

"Schmidt" to "Zur Geschichte der Langobarden," by Dr. Ludwig Schmidt (Leipsic, 1885).

"Pabst" to "Geschichte des langobardischen Herzogthums" in Vol. II, p. 405, "Forschungen zur deutschen Geschichte," (Göttingen, 1862.)

"Bruckner" to "Die Sprache der Langobarden," by Wilhelm Brückner (Quellen und Forschungen, Part 75, Strasburg, 1895).

"Koegel" to "Geschichte der deutschen Litteratur," by Rudolf Koegel, Vol. I, Part 1 (Strasburg, 1894).

"Wiese" to "Die aëlteste Geschichte der Langobarden," by Robert Wiese (Jena, 1877).

INTRODUCTION.

PAUL THE DEACON, THE LOMBARDS, AND A SOMETIME MEDIEVALIST FROM INDIANA

"The translation of Paul the Deacon has just come, and I have already begun to read it. It is such a pleasure to have friends who do such things as you do! What a delightful old boy the Deacon was; and what an interesting mixture of fact and fable he wrote!"

—Theodore Roosevelt to William Dudley Foulke, 1907

The route from the court of Charlemagne and the monastery of Monte Cassino, where Paul the Deacon wrote his *History of the Lombards* late in the eighth century, to the circle of government officials and confidants around Theodore Roosevelt, where Paul's *History* found its first English translator, is long, circuitous, often improbable, and remarkably ill-lit. There are few reliable guides to the history of the idea of, and interest in, the Middle Ages. Nor is there much in the way of explanation, except his own, as to why William Dudley Foulke, lawyer, newspaper publisher, Progressive Republican state legislator, Civil Service Commissioner, and sometime man of letters in Indiana and Washington, D.C., decided to translate Paul the Deacon's remarkable *History*:

I had come across an attractive book written in Latin by Paul the Deacon, a Benedictine monk, during the reign of

(vii)

Charlemagne, "The History of the Langobards." In his garrulous story-telling he seemed to me a sort of medieval Herodotus. . . . Quite apart from its value as a source of medieval history, Paul's quaint and simple narrative has a charm of its own and is fitted for the entertainment of the general reader as well as of the student.[1]

Foulke's final decision, as described in his 1922 autobiography, was made as an alternative to his first choice, a history of Venice, a subject too vast and complicated as Foulke sadly observed. Except for some undistinguished translations of Petrarch's lyrics, the translation of Paul the Deacon was Foulke's only excursion into early European history, and yet he fails to find a notice in the only standard account of the development of medieval studies in the United States even though his translation of Paul the Deacon has remained the only one in English.[2]   Rather than the amateur of letters and history that he makes himself out to be, Foulke took his task seriously and went for his notes and commentary to the best German scholarship of the late nineteenth century.   Therefore, Paul's *History of the Lombards* and his first English translator both deserve to be reintroduced to a public ideally composed of both general readers and students.

[1] William Dudley Foulke, *A Hoosier Autobiography* (New York, 1922), pp. 209–210.   See also the *Dictionary of American Biography,* Vol. XXI, Supplement One (New York, 1944), pp. 314–315.

[2] The standard account is Hans Rudolf Guggisberg, *Das europäische Mittelalter im amerikanischen Geschichtsdenken des 19. und des frühen 20. Jahrhunderts* (Basel and Stuttgart, 1964).   See also John Higham, Leonard Krieger, and Felix Gilbert, *History: the Development of Historical Studies in the United States* (Englewood Cliffs, 1965).

I

The Lombard invasion of Italy in 568 followed hard upon the Ostrogothic occupation after 491, the devastating and implacable war waged by imperial armies to destroy the Ostrogothic kingdom, and a heavy–handed and rapacious imperial peace. Burdensome exactions were collected by a series of imperial governors far enough removed from the imperial court at Constantinople to wield great power, yet sufficiently identified with imperial policy to generate bitter resentment against both the Enmpire and themselves on the part of the population of Italy. The Lombards, the last of the migrating Germanic peoples to enter the western part of the old Roman Empire, had migrated southwards from the valley of the lower Elbe. They ventured first into the lands north of the Danube and then, in the first quarter of the sixth century, across the Danube into the old province of Pannonia. There, stopped by the Ostrogothic kingdom in Italy, as well as Byzantine imperial strength and diplomacy in the east, and made uneasy by the presence of other migrating peoples (the Gepids and the powerful Avars), the Lombards stayed for half a century. With the collapse of the Ostrogoths, the resultant Byzantine imperial occupation, and the annihilation of the Gepids by joint Lombard–Avar forces, the Lombards moved southwest into Italy under their king, Albion. From 568, until the fall of the Lombard kingdom in Italy to the armies of Charlemagne in 774, Lombard power expanded slowly and irregularly throughout northern Italy and into the two great duchies of Spoleto and Benevento to the east and south of Rome. Only Rome itself and the coastal lands around the imperial capital of Ravenna in the northeast, and around Genoa in the west, eluded Lombard domination for any length of time. By the middle of the eighth century, with the fall of Ravenna and the increasing Lombard pressures on Rome, the Lombard kingdom wholly dominated the north of the peninsula, while the Byzantine forces held the south. This division survived Charlemagne's conquests, the raids of the Arabs in the ninth and early tenth centuries, and the Norman invasions of south Italy in the eleventh and twelfth centuries. In addition, it played an important part in the later history of Italy, contributing to the many differences between the north and the south and shaping the culture out of which emerged the Italian communes of the north in the tenth, eleventh and twelfth centuries.[3]

Upon their arrival in Italy the Lombards were Arian Christians, grouped into clans under war–leader kings, and sharing many of the characteristics of migratory Germanic and Asiatic peoples between the second and the seventh centuries. The physical facts of migration and warfare, cultural and religious change, new circumstances of economic dependence and independence, and the acquisition of new wealth all contributed to the instability of traditional Lombard society. Not until the seventh century did a monarchy begin to impose a central authority over the dispersed and localised Lombard clans and their "dukes." Around the Lombard–controlled lands of northern and central Italy, moved the forces of a world they knew little about— Byzantine diplomacy among the Franks and Burgundians in Gaul attempted to raise a force to dislodge the Lombards; the papacy in Rome remained loyal to the Empire, and a series of popes beginning with Pelagius II (579–589) at-

---

[3] There is an extensive bibliography and a good analysis of Lombard society and law in Katherine Fischer Drew, *The Lombard Laws* (Philadelphia, 1973).

tempted, sometimes reluctantly, to mediate between Pavia (the Lombard capital) and Constantinople, and Ravenna. The conversion of the Lombards to orthodox Christianity took nearly a century, and the Lombards had entered the economic community of the Byzantine–dominated Mediterranean long before they captured imperial Ravenna in 751—and they remained in it long after. Problems in papal–imperial relations dominated the mid–eighth century, and when Lombard pressures on Rome itself mounted after the fall of Ravenna, the popes turned to the Franks in Gaul for aid. The papal relations with the Franks between 751 and 774 paved the way not only for the destruction of the Lombard kingdom, but also for the formation of the papal states in central Italy, the revival of the Roman imperial title in the west under Charlemagne in 800, the increasing role of Italy in trans-alpine political affairs, and the growing estrangement between the Greek East and the Latin West.

II

Paul the Deacon was born around 720 to Warnefridus and Theudelinda, Lombards of sufficiently prominent status as to have their son educated by the grammarian Flavianus, possibly at the royal Lombard court of Pavia itself. The survival of traditions of literacy, of antique educational practices, and of physical and cultural legacies from antiquity contributed much to the intellectual conditions of eighth–century Italy and shaped the education of Paul himself. Under the patronage of King Liutprand (712–744), perhaps the most powerful of the Lombard kings, the centralization of royal power and the patronage of religious figures contributed to the favor shown to teachers and scholars, laymen as well as clergy. Paul himself appears to have served as a lay tutor to Adelperga, the daughter of King Desiderius (756–774) and wife of Arichis, Duke of Benevento. Paul had learned Latin and Greek letters under Flavianus, and he may have filled other official duties besides that of tutor. With the fall of the Lombard kingdom in 774, Paul entered the monastery of Monte Cassino, perhaps unwillingly, where he remained until 783. In 776, Paul's brother, Arichis, and other Lombard nobles revolted against Charlemagne. The revolt was suppressed, and Arichis was imprisoned. Paul wrote to Charlemagne himself in 782, requesting release from the cloister, and in 783 he travelled across the Alps to plead his brother's cause personally before the King of the Franks. Sometime between 785 and 787 Paul returned to Monte Cassino, where he remained until his death, around 799.

Paul's earliest literary works, verses to Adelperga and Arichis of Benevento, as well as several historical works, suggest the high literary level of eighth–century Italy. When Paul arrived at Charlemagne's court in 783, his experience at the courts of Pavia and Benevento, and his obvious literary gifts, greatly impressed the king of the Franks, who himself was in the process of surrounding himself with learned scholars from all parts of his dominions and beyond. Peter of Pisa and Paulinus of Aquileia also travelled from Italy to Charles' court and remained for long periods. Alcuin from England, Theodulf the Visigoth from Spain, Dicuil from Ireland, and others surrounded Charlemagne between 775 and 805. Paul's ostensible mission, the restoration of his brother's freedom and estates, appears to have been ultimately, but not immediately successful. Consequently, Paul remained at the king's court, an impressive figure even by the standards of that learned group, probably performing the wide variety of miscellaneous duties that Charles, with his widening conception of royal responsibility, required. He tutored Charles' daughter, Rotrud, in elementary Greek, in anticipation of her marriage to Constantine VI of Constantinople (a marriage that ultimately never took place). At the request of Angilram, Bishop of Metz and archchaplain of Charlemagne's court, Paul composed the *History of the Bishops of Metz,* an important document in the history of ecclesiastical biography. Several of his exchanges of verse with other members of the court circle survive.

Upon Paul's return to Monte Cassino, his interests appear to have become more deeply spiritual. He worked briefly upon an edition of the letters of Pope Gregory the Great (590–604) for his friend Adalhard (Abbot of Corbie); wrote a *Life* of Gregory; a commentary on the *Rule* of St. Benedict that later influenced other commentaries during the Benedictine reforms of the early ninth century; composed two volumes of *Homilies* that Charlemagne later recommended to his own clergy for use in the Frankish church; and, as his last work, the *History of the Lombards.*

III

Among the many transformations of Germanic societies that followed their migration into the old Roman world, the development of written law codes and the idea of national histories are two of the most striking. Influenced by Roman jurists, ecclesiastical and lay, the written law codes of the Visigoths, Ostrogoths, Burgundians, Lombards, Franks, and Anglo–Saxons are important documents not only of legal, but of social, cultural, and intellectual change as well.

From the early sixth century, when the Roman aristocrat Cassiodorus composed the first version of his *Gothic History,* to the last years of the eighth, when Paul the Deacon stopped his *History of the Lombards,* the transformation of tribal legends and folklore into organized historical narratives served to join the Germanic migrants and their descendants to the cultural as well as the physical history of the new world into which they had come. During the sixth, seventh, and eighth centuries the existence of such histories served to provide an expanded intellectual framework for explaining to the descendents of the migrating peoples their place in the new world. The histories drew upon both tradition and new conceptions of time and the nature of Christian Germanic societies. The earliest examples of this important genre—Jordanes' *History of the Goths,* Gregory of Tours' *History of the Franks,* and Isidore of Seville's *History of the Goths, Vandals and Suevi*—offered far more than simple continuations of late Roman history. They suggest a pattern and a meaning, invested with Christian morality, greater and more significant than the early heroic songs and legends. The later examples, Bede's *History of the English Church and People* and Paul the Deacon's *History of the Lombards,* are somewhat more complex. For Bede, the significant *fact* in the history of England was the Christianization of Celts and Germans both, and the only meaningful *history* that England possessed was the account of this process. After Bede, one of the greatest historians of any period, older styles of national history could not be duplicated. Thus, when Paul the Deacon undertook to write the history of his own people, he wrote in a tradition that had already been transformed by Bede, and he wrote at the end of a life that had witnessed many of the most important affairs in the western world: the flowering of

Lombard culture and society under Luitprand; the life of the courts at Pavia and Benevento; the beginnings of what has come to be called "the Carolingian Renaissance" under Charlemagne; the religious and literary revival in Gaul, Britain, and Italy in the eighth century; and the complex affairs of diplomacy and politics that had weakened the Byzantine hold on Italy, destroyed the Lombard kingdom, and propelled Charlemagne to the eve of his imperial coronation in 800. Moreover, Paul was an astute and emotional observer, personally touched by many of these events and personally acquainted with many of their participants. He possessed a deep affection for his own people, certainly as great as that which he felt for Charlemagne, probably greater. Although the variety of materials with which he had to work were inadequate, Paul did have several decades as a historical writer already behind him, as well as the experience of a lively literary culture in Italy and Gaul to support his efforts. He recognized Charlemagne's own spiritual claims to hegemony in the Latin and Germanic Christian world, but he also respected the spiritual traditions of the Lombards. It is in Paul's ability to write a national history of a single people—weaving in the major strands from the Byzantine and Frankish worlds outside, focusing upon the Christianization and spiritualizing of the Lombard people, and aware of the richness of ecclesiastical history— that his value lies. It appears that Paul died before he could finish his history (the work extends only to the reign of Liutprand), but it is possible that just as he described the dissolution of western Roman imperial power in Italy into a vigorous Lombard monarchy, so might he have focused on the reduction of the Lombard monarchy in its turn to the greater spiritual legitimacy of Charlemagne and an enlarged concept of a new western Christian community.

The *History of the Lombards,* which exists in more than one hundred manuscripts and many modern editions from the sixteenth century on, is divided into six books. The first book describes the origin and early wanderings of the Lombards down to the sixth century. The second deals with the Lombard entry into Italy and the abolition of the migration–monarchy of Alboin and his successor Cleph. Book three deals with the period of ducal autonomy, the difficulties of regionalism, and ends with the establishment of the monarchy under Authari and Theudelinda. Authari, Theudelinda, and Theudelinda's second husband (Authari's successor) Agilulf, comprise three of the most attractive characters in this history, and their careers serve as a kind of pivot upon which Lombard history turns to the monarchical state. Books Four, Five, and Six continue the history of the monarchy, but they are interspersed with information of the wider world, from Constantinople to Spain, which Paul considers important in the history of the seventh and eighth centuries.

A glance on Paul's slim sources for Lombard history makes his achievement even more remarkable.[4] The documents known as the *Origo Gentis Langobardorum* and the lost history of the Lombards by Secundus of Trent offered him little with which to work, but his literary skill, erudition, and cosmopolitan vision produced a work that is, in its way, as great as Bede's and as colorful and lively as that of Gregory of Tours. Where his work is weakest is precisely upon exact points of chronology, and although the Latin of his *History* is far simpler than he could have made it, Paul's portraits of individuals and scenes possess both strength and sophistication. From the meticulous description of the prov-

---

[4] See Appendix for the *Origo Gentis Langobardorum.*

inces of Italy (II, 15–24) to the dramatic escape of the young Grimoald from the Avars (IV, 37), Paul's pace varies. Episodes of great clarity and effect pass alongside the invasions of Arabs, Avars, Byzantines, Franks, the affairs of the papacy, bishops, monasteries, and the constant intrusion of the supernatural world into the affairs of humans in the shape of omens, miracles, and divine retribution. Only in the last book does the style lag, and that is perhaps because Paul himself was dying and did not have time to revise and polish his work. For five full books, however, and in parts of the sixth, the *History of the Lombards* constitutes one of the most important literary sources for the early history of Europe, and the vision and energy of its author makes it, despite its apparent simplicity, the most complex of the histories of the Germanic peoples between the sixth and the ninth centuries.[5]

IV

Paul the Deacon's English translator, William Dudley Foulke, is a man in many ways as interesting as Paul himself. Of all the chapters in the intellectual history of the United States during the second half of the nineteenth and first few decades of the twentieth centuries, one of the most perplexing is the story of the change in American attitudes toward the European Middle Ages. From the pure Enlightenment scorn of Thomas Jefferson, who denounced "barbarism and despotism" on the one hand and "monkish

[5] A good recent series of studies on the problems of early medieval historiography is *La Storiografia Altomedievale*, 2 vols., *Settimane di studio del centro italiano di studi sull'alto Medioevo* (Spoleto, 1970).

ignorance and superstition" on the other, to the first seminar in medieval history at an American university, that of Henry Adams at Harvard in 1897, the story is varied, picturesque, surprising, and wholly unpredictable. And even now it is difficult to see where William Dudley Foulke fits in.

Foulke was born in New York in 1848. His father, a Hicksite Quaker school director, was independently wealthy, enabling Foulke to attend and graduate from Columbia in 1869. Two years later, in 1871, he received his law degree, also from Columbia. Foulke practised law in New York until 1876, when, following his marriage, he moved with his wife to her own state of Indiana, settling near his in–laws' estate in Richmond. From 1883 to 1885 Foulke was an Indiana state senator, and throughout the last two decades of the century played an important part in reform politics. At various times, usually with great dedication and consistency, he supported such Progressive movements as prison and civil service reform, equal rights for married women, women's suffrage, and voter registration. Although he was a Republican, he frequently voted against his party when he thought it in the wrong, and he became a life–long friend of Theodore Roosevelt, eventually serving in Roosevelt's old seat on the Civil Service during Roosevelt's presidency in 1901. In 1891 Foulke accepted the presidency of Swarthmore College, although he could not fulfill his commitment because of pressing family affairs in Indiana. He translated Paul the Deacon's *History,* he tells us, in 1904, disappointed at finding the prospect of writing the history of Venice too time–consuming. In addition, Foulke wrote many poems, occasional literary pieces, speeches, and pamphlets for various causes. With that curious, unpredictable curiosity he shared with many late nineteenth–century American business, professional, and political figures, Foulke was led to Paul the Deacon apparently by sheer accident. He then translated the work and happily found a publisher in the Pennsylvania series *Translations and Reprints,* itself begun in 1894. Foulke's autobiography, written in 1922, reveals a confidence and discretion that perhaps makes his life and career seem less remarkable than they were. He moved with ease through New York, Columbia University, Indiana, Washington, Paris, Rome, and Venice. Nothing he did appeared to him to call for particular notice, and his own account of his translation occupies but a few lines in a minor chapter of his autobiography. His translation, however, was good and careful, no small achievement in a period when medieval Latin was still a recondite specialty and extensive translations from early medieval source materials were extremely rare. Virtually single–handedly, in a field where even professional scholars were walking gingerly, Foulke picked up an interesting book, decided to translate it and did, displaying in this, as in his many other activities, intelligence, diligence, erudition, and remarkable far–sightedness. No one has felt the compulsion to improve his work in nearly seventy years. That is eloquent testimony to a translator's work, and with the publication of Professor Katherine Fischer Drew's translation of *The Lombard Laws* in 1973 it seems a useful and enjoyable task to reissue Foulke's translation of the other major literary source for Lombard history.

V

This reprint edition contains the complete translation of the *History of the Lombards* by William Dudley Foulke,

published in the University of Pennsylvania series *Translations and Reprints From the Original Sources of European
History* in 1907. Omitted from this edition are Foulke's
Introduction; Appendix I, "Ethnological Status of the
Lombards"; Appendix II, "Sources of Paul's *History of
the Langobards*"; Appendix III, "Paul the Deacon's Hymns
in Honor of St. Benedict." There are more recent discus-
sions of the topics of the first two appendices available.
The Index is also omitted.

Thomas Hodgkin, *Italy and Her Invaders,* 8 vols. (Oxford, 1880–1899), is still the standard history in English
for the period covered by Paul's *History.* Donald Bullough,
"Germanic Italy: The Ostrogothic and Lombard Kingdoms," in David T. Rice, ed., *The Dark Ages* (London,
1965), pp. 157–174 offers a brief up–to–date treatment with
excellent illustrations. J K. Hyde, *Society and Politics in
Medieval Italy* (New York, 1973) is good, but slight on the
Lombard period. Peter Llewellyn, *Rome in the Dark Ages*
(New York, 1970) is excellent generally and has much on
Lombard history, particularly from the interesting Roman
viewpoint.

Katherine Fischer Drew, *The Lombard Laws* (Philadelphia, 1973) offers an excellent translation of the important law code, a good detailed introduction, and an
extensive bibliography. G. Barni and G. Fasoli, *L'Italia
nell'alto Medioevo* (Turin, 1971) is a well–illustrated social
and cultural history in the series *Società e Costume.* When
it appears, Donald Bullough's volume in the *General History of Europe* series, ed., Denys Hay should be the best
general work on the period for English readers. Until
then, the *Cambridge Medieval History,* Vol. III (Cam-

bridge, 1926), Chapter 8 by L. M. Hartmann, "Italy under the Lombards," is a good brief treatment by a great master. There is a brief account of Paul the Deacon in M. L. W. Laistner, *Thought and Letters in Western Europe, A.D. 500 to 900* (2nd ed., London, 1957) and some account of Paul as a poet in F. J. E. Raby, *A History of Christian Latin Poetry* (Oxford, 1953). For the general period, see Donald Bullough, *The Age of Charlemagne* (New York, 1966).

In Italian, particularly important modern studies are those of G. P. Bognetti, *L'Età Longobarda* (Milan, 1968) and A. Tagliaferri, ed., *Problemi della civiltà e dell'economica longobarda* (Milan, 1964). An old work that sets Paul in the tradition of early medieval chronicles is Ugo Balzani, *Early Chroniclers of Europe: Italy* (London, 1883). Recent German scholarship may be seen in Jörg Jarnut, *Prosopographische und sozialgeschichtliche Studien zum Langobardenreich in Italian* (Bonn, 1972). Most modern scholarship is fully listed in W. Levison and H. Löwe, *Deutschlands Geschichtsquellen im Mittelalter,* Bd. II, (Weimar, 1953), pp. 203–224.

Because this reprint edition omits parts of the original introduction and the Appendices, some of the references in Foulke's footnotes will obviously be inapplicable. Following this Introduction is an "Explanation of References" from the original edition indicating shortened abbreviations in the notes.

EDWARD PETERS
PHILADELPHIA, 1974

PAUL THE DEACON'S HISTORY OF THE LANGOBARDS.

BOOK I.

CHAPTER I.

The region of the north, in proportion as it is removed from the heat of the sun and is chilled with snow and frost, is so much the more healthful to the bodies of men and fitted for the propagation of nations, just as, on the other hand, every southern region, the nearer it is to the heat of the sun, the more it abounds in diseases and is less fitted for the bringing up of the human race. From this it happens that such great multitudes of peoples spring up in the north, and that that entire region from the Tanais (Don) to the west[1] (although single places in it are designated by their own names) yet the whole is not improperly called by the general name of Germany.[2] The Romans, however, when they occupied

[1] Paul's designation of the whole region from the Don to the west, as Germany, which is wholly incorrect, appears, according to Mommsen (p. 61), to have come from his misinterpretation of the words of his authority, Isidore of Seville.

[2] Paul appears to deduce the name "Germany" from *germinare* to germinate. Cf. Isidore, Etym., XIV, 4, 2. This fanciful derivation is quite different from that given by Tacitus (Germania, II), who derives it from the name of a single tribe afterwards called the Tungrians, who were the first to cross the Rhine and drive out the Gauls.

those parts, called the two provinces beyond the Rhine, Upper and Lower Germany.[1]　From this teeming Germany then, innumerable troops of captives are often led away and sold for gain to the people of the South. And for the reason that it brings forth so many human beings that it can scarcely nourish them, there have frequently emigrated from it many nations that have indeed become the scourge of portions of Asia, but especially of the parts of Europe which lie next to it.　Everywhere ruined cities throughout all Illyria and Gaul testify to this, but most of all in unhappy Italy which has felt the cruel rage of nearly all these nations.　The Goths indeed, and the Wandals, the Rugii, Heroli, and Turcilingi,[2] and also other fierce and barbarous nations have come from Germany.　In like manner also the race of

[1] "Beyond the Rhine" means in this case on the left bank of the Rhine.　The dividing line between Upper and Lower Germany ran a little below the junction of the Rhine with the Moselle. Mogontiacum (Mayence) was the capital of Upper Germany, and Vetera (Birten) near Wesel, of Lower Germany.　(Mommsen's Geschichte des romischen Reichs, V, pp. 107–109).　Although these two provinces included at various times more or less territory on the east side of that river, it was only a small part of Germany which was thus occupied by the Romans.　Germania Magna, or Great Germany, east of the Rhine, remained independent.

[2] The Rugii and Turcilingi were tribes first mentioned as inhabiting the shores of the Baltic sea (Zeuss, 154–155).　They were subsequently found in the army of Attila and afterwards dwelling on the Danube.　The Heroli were a migratory people appearing at different times in various parts of Europe (Zeuss, 476).　All three of these tribes were among the troops of Odoacar in Italy. As to the Heroli and Rugii see infra, chs. 19 and 20,

Winnili, [1] that is, of Langobards, which afterwards ruled prosperously in Italy, deducing its origin from the German peoples, came from the island which is called Scadinavia, [2] although other causes of their emigration [3] are also alleged. [4]

CHAPTER II.

Pliny the Second also makes mention of this island in the books which he composed concerning the nature of things. This island then, as those who have examined it have related to us, is not so much placed in the sea as it is washed about by the sea waves which encompass the land on account of the flatness of the shores. [5] Since, therefore, the peoples established

[1] The word means "eager for battle" according to Bruckner (322). According to Schmidt (37) it is related to the Gothic *vinja*, "pasture."

[2] That Paul wrote Scadinavia and not Scandinavia see Mommsen, 62, note 1. In the Langobard Origo (see Appendix, II) the name is given as Scadan, Scandanan or Scadanan; in the Chronicon Gothanum, it is Scatenauge (Mon. Germ. Hist. Leges IV, p. 642). Paul appears to have transformed this into Scadinavia from Pliny's Natural History (Book IV, ch. 27, p. 823, Delphin ed.).

[3] Than over population (Jacobi, 12).

[4] The other causes of the emigration of the Winnili may be those suggested in the Chronicon Gothanum where the prophetess or sibyl Gambara "declared to them their migration." "Moved therefore not by necessity, nor hardness of heart, nor oppression of the poor, but that they should attain salvation from on high, she says that they are to go forth." (Monument, Germ. Hist. Leges, IV, 641.).

[5] What Paul meant by this island is hard to decide (Jacobi, 11).

within the island had grown to so great a multitude that they could not now dwell together, they divided their whole troop into three parts, as is said, and determined by lot which part of them had to forsake their country and seek new abodes. [1]

Hammerstein (Bardengau, 51) has pointed out that in the Middle Ages the territory in the north of Germany, between the North and the Baltic seas, was included under the name of Scandinavia, and claims that Paul referred to the so-called Bardengau, a tract in Northern Germany, southeast of Hamburg. But the fact that Paul calls upon Pliny is a proof that he had no definite idea of Scadinavia, and notwithstanding the extensive movement of the tide upon the Elbe and the important changes on the coast, it can hardly be said of Bardengau that it was "surrounded" by sea waves. Bluhme (Die Gens Langobardonum und ihre Herkunft), without sufficient reason, identifies the northernmost part of the Cimbrian peninsula, the so-called Wendsyssel, with Scadinavia. (See Schmidt, 36).

Schmidt (38 to 42) reviews the classical authorities, Mela, Pliny and Ptolemy, as well as Jordanes, the Geographer of Ravenna, and the Song of Beowulf, and concludes that the word refers to the Scandinavian peninsula which was then considered an island; but he rejects the tradition that the Langobards actually migrated from Sweden to Germany, since he considers that they belonged to the West-German stock, which in all probability came from the south-east, while only North-Germans (that is, those races which were found settled in Scandinavia in historical times) appear to have come from that peninsula. It is probable, however, that the Langobards came from North-German stock (Bruckner, 25–32), and while there can be no certainty whatever as to the place of their origin, it may well have been Scandinavia.

[1] The choosing by lot of a part of the people for emigration in the case of a famine is a characteristic peculiar to German folk-tales (Schmidt, 42).

Chapter III.

Therefore that section to which fate had assigned the abandonment of their native soil and the search for foreign fields, after two leaders had been appointed over them, to wit: Ibor and Aio,[1] who were brothers, in the bloom of youthful vigor and more eminent than the rest, said farewell to their own people, as well as their country, and set out upon their way to seek for lands where they might dwell and establish their abodes. The mother of these leaders, Gambara by name,[2] was a woman of the keenest ability and most prudent in counsel among her people, and they trusted not a little to her shrewdness in doubtful matters.

Chapter IV.

I do not think it is without advantage to put off for a little while the order of my narrative, and because my pen up to this time deals with Germany, to relate briefly a miracle which is there considered notable among all, as well as certain other matters. In the farthest boundaries of Germany toward the west-north-west, on the shore of the ocean itself, a cave is seen under a projecting rock, where for an unknown time seven men repose

---

[1] Ibor and Aio were called by Prosper of Aquitaine, Iborea and Agio ; Saxo-Grammaticus calls them Ebbo and Aggo ; the popular song of Gothland (Bethmann, 342), Ebbe and Aaghe (Wiese, 14).

[2] The word *gambar*, according to Grimm (Deutsche Mythologie, I, 336), is the equivalent of *strenuus*.

wrapped in a long sleep,[1] not only their bodies, but also
their clothes being so uninjured, that from this fact
alone, that they last without decay through the course
of so many years, they are held in veneration among
those ignorant and barbarous peoples.   These then, so
far as regards their dress, are perceived to be Romans.
When a certain man, stirred by cupidity, wanted to strip
one of them, straightway his arms withered, as is said,
and his punishment so frightened the others that no one
dared touch them further.   The future will show for
what useful purpose Divine Providence keeps them

[1] This is the version by Paul of the story of the Seven Sleepers
of Ephesus.   The earliest version is that of Jacobus Sarugiensis,
a bishop of Mesopotamia in the fifth or sixth century.   Gregory of
Tours was perhaps the first to introduce the legend into Europe.
Mohammed put it into the Koran ; he made the sleepers
prophesy his own coming and he gave them the dog Kratin also
endowed with the gift of prophecy.   The commonly accepted
legend was, however, that the Seven Sleepers were natives of
Ephesus, that the emperor Decius (A. D. 250), having come to
that city, commanded that the Christians should be sought out and
given their choice, either to worship the Roman deities or die ;
that these seven men took refuge in a cave near the city; that the
entrance to the cave was, by command of Decius, blocked up
with stone; that they fell into a preternatural sleep, and that two
hundred years later, under Theodosius II (A. D. 408–450), the cave
was opened and the sleepers awoke.   When one of them went to
the city stealthily to buy provisions for the rest he found that the
place was much changed, that his coins were no longer current, and that Christianity had been accepted by the rulers and
the people.   The original legend relates, however, that after awakening they died (Curious Myths of the Middle Ages, S. Baring-
Gould, p. 93).   It is not known from what source Paul derived
his version of the story.

through so long a period. Perhaps those nations are to be saved some time by the preaching of these men, since they cannot be deemed to be other than Christians.

CHAPTER V.

The Scritobini, for thus that nation is called, are neighbors to this place. They are not without snow even in the summer time, and since they do not differ in nature from wild beasts themselves, they feed only upon the raw flesh of wild animals from whose shaggy skins also they fit garments for themselves.[1] They deduce the etymology of their name[2] according to their barbarous language from jumping. For by making use of leaps and bounds they pursue wild beasts very skillfully with a piece of wood bent in the likeness of a bow. Among them there is an animal not very unlike a stag,[3] from whose hide, while it was rough with hairs, I saw a coat fitted in the manner of a tunic down to the knees, such as the aforesaid Scritobini use, as has been related. In these places about the summer solstice, a very bright light is seen for some days, even in the night time, and the days are much longer there than elsewhere, just as, on the other hand, about the winter solstice, although the light of day is present, yet the sun is not seen there and the days are

[1] What is said about the Scritobini (or Scridefinni) can be traced to one and the same source as the account of Thule given in Procopius' Gothic War, II, 15, or of Scandza in Jordanes' Gothic History, 3; see Zeuss, 684.

[2] Perhaps from *schreiten*, "to stride," or some kindred word.

[3] A reindeer (Waitz).

shorter than anywhere else and the nights too are longer, and this is because the further we turn from the sun the nearer the sun itself appears to the earth and the longer the shadows grow.   In short, in Italy (as the ancients also have written) about the day of the birth of our Lord, human statures at twelve o'clock measure in shadow nine feet.   But when I was stationed in Belgic Gaul in a place which is called Villa Totonis (Dieten-hofen, Thionville[1]) and measured the shadow of my stature, I found it nineteen and a half feet.   Thus also on the contrary the nearer we come to the sun toward midday the shorter always appear the shadows, so much so that at the summer solstice when the sun looks down from the midst of heaven in Egypt and Jerusalem and the places situated in their neighborhood, no shadows may be seen.   But in Arabia at this same time the sun at its highest point is seen on the northern side and the shadows on the other hand appear towards the south.

CHAPTER VI.

Not very far from this shore of which we have spoken, toward the western side, on which the ocean main lies open without end, is that very deep whirl-pool of waters which we call by its familiar name " the navel of the sea."   This is said to suck in the waves and spew them forth again twice every day, as is proved to be done by the excessive swiftness with which the waves advance and recede along all those shores.   A whirl-pool or maelstrom of this kind is called by the poet

[1] On the Moselle, where Charlemagne held his court.

Virgil "Charybdis," which he says in his poem [1] is in the Sicilian strait, speaking of it in this way:

> Scylla the right hand besets, and the left, the relentless Charybdis;
> Thrice in the whirl of the deepest abyss it swallows the vast waves
> Headlong, and lifts them again in turn one after another
> Forth to the upper air, and lashes the stars with the billows.

Ships are alleged to be often violently and swiftly dragged in by this whirlpool (of which indeed we have spoken) with such speed that they seem to imitate the fall of arrows through the air, and sometimes they perish by a very dreadful end in that abyss. But often when they are upon the very point of being overwhelmed they are hurled back by the sudden masses of waves and driven away again with as great speed as they were at first drawn in. They say there is another whirlpool of this kind between the island of Britain and the province of Galicia,[2] and with this fact the coasts of the Seine region and of Aquitaine agree, for they are filled twice a day with such sudden inundations that any one who may by chance be found only a little inward from the shore can hardly get away. You may see the rivers of these regions falling back with a very swift current toward their source, and the fresh waters of the streams turning salt through the spaces of many miles. The

[1] Æneid, VII, 420.

[2] In the northwestern part of Spain. Many manuscripts read "the province of Gaul." Evidently Paul's knowledge of the geography of these parts is most obscure.

island of Evodia (Alderney) is almost thirty miles distant from the coast of the Seine region, and in this
island, as its inhabitants declare, is heard the noise of
the waters as they sweep into this Charybdis. I have
heard a certain high nobleman of the Gauls relating that
a number of ships, shattered at first by a tempest, were
afterwards devoured by this same Charybdis. And
when one only out of all the men who had been in these
ships, still breathing, swam over the waves, while the
rest were dying, he came, swept by the force of the
receding waters, up to the edge of that most frightful
abyss. And when now he beheld yawning before him
the deep chaos whose end he could not see, and half
dead from very fear, expected to be hurled into it, suddenly in a way that he could not have hoped he was
cast upon a certain rock and sat him down. And now
when all the waters that were to be swallowed had run
down, the margins of that edge (of the abyss) had been
left bare, and while he sat there with difficulty, trem-
bling with fear and filled with foreboding amid so many
distresses, nor could he hide at all from his sight the death
that was a little while deferred, behold he suddenly sees,
as it were, great mountains of water leaping up from the
deep and the first ships which had been sucked in coming forth again! And when one of these came near
him he grasped it with what effort he could, and without
delay, he was carried in swift flight toward the shore
and escaped the fate of death, living afterwards to tell
the story of his peril. Our own sea also, that is, the
Adriatic, which spreads in like manner, though less violently, through the coasts of Venetia and Istria, is be-

lieved to have little secret currents of this kind by which the receding waters are sucked in and vomited out again to dash upon the shores. These things having been thus examined, let us go back to the order of our narrative already begun.

CHAPTER VII.

The Winnili then, having departed from Scadinavia with their leaders Ibor and Aio, and coming into the region which is called Scoringa,[1] settled there for some

[1] Scoringa, according to Müllenhoff's explanation in which Bluhme concurs, is "Shoreland" (see Schmidt, 43). Bluhme considers it identical with the later Bardengau, on the left bank of the lower Elbe where the town of Bardowick, twenty-four miles southeast of Hamburg, perpetuates the name of the Langobards even down to the present time. Hammerstein (Bardengau, 56) explains Scoringa as Schieringen near Bleckede in the same region. Schmidt (43) believes that the settlement in Scoringa has a historical basis and certainly, if the name indicates the territory in question, it is the place where the Langobards are first found in authentic history. They are mentioned in connection with the campaigns undertaken by Tiberius against various German tribes during the reign of Augustus in the fifth and sixth year of the Christian era, in the effort to extend the frontiers of the Roman empire from the Rhine to the Elbe (Mommsen, Römische Geschichte, V, 33). The Langobards then dwelt in that region which lies between the Weser and the lower Elbe. They were described by the court historian Velleius Paterculus (II, 106), who accompanied one of the expeditions as prefect of cavalry (Schmidt, 5), as "more fierce than ordinary German savagery," and he tells us that their power was broken by the legions of Tiberius. It would appear also from the combined testimony of Strabo (A. D. 20) and Tacitus (A, D. 117) that the

years.   At that time Ambri and Assi, leaders of the

Langobards dwelt near the mouth of the Elbe shortly after the beginning of the Christian era, and were in frequent and close relations with the Hermunduri and Semnones, two great Suevic
tribes dwelling higher up the stream.   Strabo (see Hodgkin,
V, 81) evidently means to assert that in his time the Hermunduri
and Langobards had been driven from the left to the right bank.
Ptolemy who wrote later (100–161) places them upon the left
bank.   Possibly both authors were right for different periods in
their history (Hodgkin, V, 82).

The expedition of Tiberius was the high-water mark of Roman
invasion on Teutonic soil, and when a Roman fleet, sailing up the
Elbe, established communication with a Roman army upon the
bank of that river, it might well be thought that the designs of
Augustus were upon the point of accomplishment, and that the
boundary of the empire was to be traced by connecting the Danube with the Elbe.   The dominions of Marobod, king of the Marcomanni, who was then established in Bohemia, would break the
continuity of this boundary, so the Romans proceeded to invade
his territories.   An insurrection, however, suddenly broke out in
Illyricum and the presence of the Roman army was required in
that region.   So a hasty peace was concluded with Marobod, leaving him the possessions he already held.   It required four successive campaigns and an enormous number of troops (Mommsen,
Rom. Gesch., Vol. V, pp. 35–38) to suppress the revolt.   While
the Roman veterans were engaged in the Illyrian war, great numbers of Germans led by Arminius, or Hermann, of the Cheruscan
tribe rose in rebellion.   In the ninth year of our era, Varus
marched against them at the head of a force composed largely of
new recruits.   He was surprised and surrounded in the pathless
recesses of the Teutoburg forest and his army of some twenty
thousand men was annihilated (id., pp. 38–44).   It is not known
whether the Langobards were among the confederates who thus
arrested the conquest of their country by the Roman army,
although they dwelt not far from the scene of this historic battle.

Wandals, were coercing all the neighboring provinces by

They were then considered, however, to belong to the Suevian stock and were subject, not far from this time, to the king of the Marcomanni, a Suevian race (id., p. 34; Tacitus Germania, 38–40; Annals, II, 45), and king Marobod took no part in this war on either side as he had made peace with the Romans.

The defeat of Varus was due largely to his own incompetency and it would not appear to have been irretrievable when the immense resources of the Roman empire are considered. Still no active offensive operations against the barbarians were undertaken until after the death of Augustus and the succession of Tiberius, A. D. 14, when in three campaigns, the great Germanicus thrice invaded Germany, took captive the wife and child of Arminius, defeated the barbarians in a sanguinary battle, and announced to Rome that in the next campaign the subjugation of Germany would be complete (Mommsen, id., pp. 44–50). But Tiberius permitted no further campaign to be undertaken. The losses suffered by the Romans on the sea as well as on land had been very severe, and whether he was influenced by this fact and by the difficulty of keeping both Gaul and Germany in subjection if the legions were transferred from the Rhine to the Elbe, or whether he was actuated by jealousy of Germanicus, and feared the popularity the latter would acquire by the subjugation of all Germany, cannot now be decided, but he removed that distinguished commander from the scene of his past triumphs and his future hopes, sent him to the East on a new mission, left the army on the Rhine divided and without a general-in-chief, and adopted the policy of keeping that river as the permanent boundary of the empire (id., p. 50–54).

Thus the battle in the Teutoburg forest resulted in the maintenance of German independence and ultimately perhaps in the overthrow of the Roman empire itself by German barbarians. It marked the beginning of the turn of the tide in Roman conquest and Roman dominion, for although the empire afterwards grew in other directions yet behind the dike here erected, the forces grad-

war.   Already elated by many victories they sent mes-

ually collected which were finally to overwhelm it when it became corrupted with decay.

When the legions of Varus were destroyed, the head of the Roman commander was sent to Marobod and his coöperation solicited.   He refused however to join the confederated German tribes, he sent the head to Rome for funeral honors, and continued to maintain between the empire and the barbarians, the neutrality he had observed in former wars.   This refusal to unite in the national aspirations for German independence, cost him his throne.   " Not only the Cheruscans and their confederates " says Tacitus (Ann. II, 45) "who had been the ancient soldiery of Arminius, took arms, but the Semnones and Langobards, both Suevian nations, revolted to him from the sovereignty of Marobod . . . . The armies (Ch. 46) . . . . were stimulated by reasons of their own, the Cheruscans and the Langobards fought for their ancient honor or their newly acquired independence, and the others for increasing their dominion."   This occurred in the seventeenth year of our era.   Marobod was finally overthrown, and took refuge in exile with the Romans, and it was not long until Arminius, accused of aspiring to despotic power, was assassinated by a noble of his own race (Mommsen, id. 54–56).   After his death the internal dissensions among the Cheruscans became so violent that the reigning family was swept away, and in the year 47 they asked the Romans to send them as their king the one surviving member of that family, Italicus, the nephew of Arminius, who was born at Rome where he had been educated as a Roman citizen.   Accordingly Italicus, with the approval of the emperor Claudius, assumed the sovereignty of the Cheruscans.   At first he was received with joy, but soon the cry was raised that with his advent the old liberties of Germany were departing and Roman power was becoming predominant.   A struggle ensued, and he was expelled from the country.   Again, the Langobards appear upon the scene, with sufficient power as it seems to control the destiny of the tribe which, thirty-eight years before, had been the leader in

sengers to the Winnili to tell them that they should
either pay tribute to the Wandals[1] or make ready for
the struggles of war. Then Ibor and Aio, with the
approval of their mother Gambara, determine that it is
better to maintain liberty by arms than to stain it by the
payment of tribute. They send word to the Wandals
by messengers that they will rather fight than be
slaves. The Winnili were then all in the flower of their
youth, but were very few in number since they had
been only the third part of one island of no great size.[2]

the struggle for independence, for they restored him to the
sovereignty of which he had been despoiled by his inconstant subjects (Tacitus Annals, XI, 16, 17). These events and other
internal disturbances injured the Cheruscans so greatly that they
soon disappeared from the field of political activity (Mommsen,
id., 132).

During the generations that followed there was doubtless many
a change in the power, the territories and even the names of the
various tribes which inhabited Germania Magna, but for a long
time peace was preserved along the frontiers which separated
them from the Roman world (id., p. 133). It is somewhat remarkable that none of those events appear in the Langobard
tradition as contained in the pages of Paul.

[1] Hammerstein (Bardengau, 71) considers the Wends who were
the eastern neighbors of the Langobards, to be the Wandals.
Jacobi (13, n. 1) thinks Paul is misled by the account of Jordanes
of the struggles of the Vandals and the Goths.

[2] Although it belongs to the legendary period of the Langobards,
there may well be some truth in this statement of the refusal to
pay tribute. Tacitus (Germania, 40) speaks of the slender number of the Langobards and declares that they are renowned because they are so few and, being surrounded by many powerful
nations, protect themselves, not by submission but by the peril of
battles.

CHAPTER VIII.

At this point, the men of old tell a silly story that the Wandals coming to Godan (Wotan) besought him for victory over the Winnili and that he answered that he would give the victory to those whom he saw first at sunrise; that then Gambara went to Frea (Freja) wife of Godan and asked for victory for the Winnili, and that Frea gave her counsel that the women of the Winnili should take down their hair and arrange it upon the face like a beard, and that in the early morning they should be present with their husbands and in like manner station themselves to be seen by Godan from the quarter in which he had been wont to look through his window toward the east. And so it was done. And when Godan saw them at sunrise he said: "Who are these long-beards?" And then Frea induced him to give the victory to those to whom he had given the name.[1] And thus Godan gave the victory to the Win-

---

[1] A still livelier description of this scene is given in the "Origo Gentis Langobardorum" (see Appendix II) from which Paul took the story. "When it became bright and the sun was rising, Frea, Godan's wife, turned the bed around where her husband was lying and put his face toward the east, and awakened him, and as he looked he saw the Winnili and their wives, how their hair hung about their faces. And he said: "Who are these long-beards?" Then spoke Frea to Godan: "My lord, thou hast given them the name, now give them also the victory." Mommsen remarks (pp. 65, 66) that Paul has spoiled the instructive story why one does better to put his business in the hands of the wife than of the husband, or rather that he has misunderstood the account. The fable rests upon this, that Godan, according to the position of his bed, looked toward the west upon awakening,

nili.   These things are worthy of laughter and are to be
held of no account.[1]   For victory is due, not to the
power of men, but it is rather furnished from heaven.

CHAPTER IX.

It is certain, however, that the Langobards were afterwards so called on account of the length of their beards

and that the Wandals camped on the west side and the Winnili
upon the east.   The true-hearted god could then appropriately
promise victory to his Wandal worshippers in the enigmatical
sentence, that he would take the part of those upon whom his
eyes should first fall on the morning of the day of the battle; but
as his cunning wife turned his bed around, he and his favorites
were entrapped thereby.   This can be easily inferred from the
Origo.   It may be asked what the women's hair arranged like a
beard has to do with Godan's promise.   Evidently, the affair was
so planned that the astonishment of the god should be noted when
he looked upon these extraordinary long-beards in place of the
Wandals he had supposed would be there; perhaps indeed his
cunning wife thus drew from her husband an expression which
put it beyond doubt that he actually let his glance fall in the
morning upon the Winnili.

That the account in the Origo was a Latin translation of a German alliterative epic poem—see Appendix II.

[1] Paul's narrative of the origin of the name of Langobards gives
the best example of the manner in which he has treated the
legends which have come down to him.   The transposition of the
direct speech into the indirect, the introduction of the phrase "to
preserve their liberty by arms," and similar classical phrases, the
new style and historical character given to the story, speak for
themselves ; but still the Langobard, in treating of the origin of
the proud name could not disown his national character and even
where "the ridiculous story told by the ancients" sets historical
treatment at defiance, he still does not suppress it (Mommsen, 65).

untouched by the knife, whereas at first they had been
called Winnili; for according to their language "lang"
means "long" and "bart" "beard."[1]   Wotan indeed,
whom by adding a letter they called Godan[2] is he who

[1] This derivation comes from Isidore of Seville.   He says, "The
Langobards were commonly so-called from their flowing and never
shaven beards" (Etym., IX, 2, 94, Zeuss, 109).   Schmidt, although he believes (p. 43) that the change of name was a historical fact, rejects (44, note i) this definition, since he considers that
the earlier name of the people was simply "Bards," to which
"lang" was afterwards prefixed.   Another proposed derivation
is from the Old High German word *barta*, an axe, the root which
appears in "halbert" and "partizan" (Hodgkin, V, 84).   Another authority, Dr. Leonhard Schmitz (see *Langobardi* in Smith's
Dictionary of Greek and Roman Geography) argues for its derivation from the root *bord*, which we have preserved in the word
"sea-board," and he contends that the Langobards received their
name from the long, flat meadows of the Elbe where they had
their dwelling.   As we adopt one or the other of these sugges-
tions, the Langobards will have been the long-bearded men, the
long-halbert-bearing men, or the long-shore-men.   Hodgkin (V,
85) as well as Bruckner (p. 33) prefers the interpretation given in
the text, "Long-beards."   Bruckner remarks that the name of
the people stands in close relation to the worship of Wotan who
bore the name of the "long-bearded" or "gray-bearded," and
that the Langobard name *Ansegranus*, "He with the Beard of the
Gods," showed that the Langobards had this idea of their chief
deity.   He further shows that the long halbert or spear was not a
characteristic weapon of the Langobards.   He also (p. 30) considers Koegel's opinion (p. 109) that the Langobards adopted the
worship of Wotan from the surrounding peoples after their migration to the Danube is not admissible, since the neighboring Anglo-
Saxons worshiped Wotan long before their migration to Britain as
their highest God.

[2] Or Guodan according to other MSS.

among the Romans is called Mercury, and he is worshiped by all the peoples of Germany as a god, though he is deemed to have existed, not about these times, but long before, and not in Germany, but in Greece.

CHAPTER X.

The Winnili therefore, who are also Langobards, having joined battle with the Wandals, struggle fiercely, since it is for the glory of freedom, and win the victory. And afterwards, having suffered in this same province of Scoringa, great privation from hunger, their minds were filled with dismay.

CHAPTER XI.

Departing from this place, while they were arranging to pass over into Mauringa,[1] the Assipitti[2] block

---

[1] Mauringa is mentioned by the Cosmographer of Ravenna (I, 11) as the land east of the Elbe. Maurungani appears to be another name of the great country of the Elbe which lies "in front of the Danes, extends to Dacia and includes Baias, Baiohaim." Or perhaps Mauringa was merely the name of the maurland or moorland east of the Elbe (Zeuss, 472). In the Traveler's Song, which had its origin in the German home of the Angles about the end of the 6th century, a Suevian race in Holstein bears the name of Myrginge, and this song also mentions the Headhobards (perhaps identical with the Langobards) who fight with the Danes in Zealand (Schmidt, 34, 47). See also Waitz.

[2] Hodgkin (V, 92) conjectures that possibly the Assipitti are the Usipetes mentioned in Tacitus' Annals (I, 51). See Caesar B. G. IV, 1, 4. Bluhme (see Hodgkin, V, 141) places them in the neighborhood of Asse, a wooded height near Wolfenbüttel. Such identifications of locality are highly fanciful.

their way, denying to them by every means a passage
through their territories. The Langobards moreover,
when they beheld the great forces of their enemies, did
not dare engage them on account of the smallness of
their army, and while they were deciding what they
ought to do, necessity at length hit upon a plan. They
pretend that they have in their camps Cynocephali,
that is, men with dogs' heads. They spread the rumor
among the enemy that these men wage war obstinately,
drink human blood and quaff their own gore if they
cannot reach the foe. And to give faith to this assertion, the Langobards spread their tents wide and
kindle a great many fires in their camps. The enemy
being made credulous when these things are heard and
seen, dare not now attempt the war they threatened.

Chapter XII.

They had, however, among them a very powerful
man, to whose strength they trusted that they could
obtain without doubt what they wanted. They offered
him alone to fight for all. They charged the Langobards
to send any one of their own they might wish, to go forth
with him to single combat upon this condition, to wit;
that if their warrior should win the victory, the Langobards would depart the way they had come, but if he
should be overthrown by the other, then they would not
forbid the Langobards a passage through their own
territories. And when the Langobards were in doubt
what one of their own they should send against this
most warlike man, a certain person of servile rank

offered himself of his own will, and promised that he would engage the challenging enemy upon this condition: that if he took the victory from the enemy, they would take away the stain of slavery from him and from his offspring. Why say more? They joyfully promised to do what he had asked. Having engaged the enemy, he fought and conquered, and won for the Langobards the means of passage, and for himself and his descendants, as he had desired, the rights of liberty.

CHAPTER XIII.

Therefore the Langobards, coming at last into Mauringa, in order that they might increase the number of their warriors, confer liberty upon many whom they deliver from the yoke of bondage, and that the freedom of these may be regarded as established, they confirm it in their accustomed way by an arrow, uttering certain words of their country in confirmation of the fact.[1] Then the Langobards went forth

---

[1] Complete emancipation appears to have been granted only among the Franks and the Langobards (Schmidt, 47 note 3). This system of incorporating into the body of their warriors and freemen, the peoples whom they subjugated in their wanderings, made of the Langobards a composite race, and it may well be that their language as well as their institutions were greatly affected by this admixture of foreign stock (Hartmann, II, pp. 8, 9), and that their High-German characteristics are due to this fact. This system of emancipation also had an important effect in furthering the union of the two races, Langobard and Roman, after the Italian conquest (Hartmann, II, 2, 15).

from Mauringa and came to Golanda,[1] where, having remained some time, they are afterwards said to
have possessed for some years Anthaib[2] and Banthaib,[3] and in like manner Vurgundaib,[4] which we

[1] Schmidt thinks this was further east, perhaps on the right
bank of the Oder (p. 49). He considers (see Hodgkin, V, 143)
that the name is the equivalent of Gotland and means simply
"good land." Golanda is generally considered, however, to be
Gothland, and as the Langobards were found in Pannonia in the
year 166 at the time of the war with Marcus Aurelius, and as the
Goths emigrated to the Euxine probably about the middle of the
second century, Hodgkin (V, 101) considers it probable that the
Langobards at this time were hovering about the skirts of the
Carpathians rather than that they had returned to Bardengau.
The fact that when they were next heard from, they were occupy-
ing Rugiland east of Noricum, on the north shore of the Danube,
confirms this view. Zeuss takes an alternative reading for Golanda
not well supported by manuscript authority, "Rugulanda," and
suggests that it may be the coast opposite the isle of Rugen
(Hodgkin, 141).

[2] Anthaib, according to the improbable conjecture of Zeuss, is
the pagus or district of the Antae who, on the authority of Ptolemy
and Jordanes were placed somewhere in the Ukraine in the countries of the Dniester and Dnieper (Hodgkin, p. 141). Schmidt
(p. 49) connects Anthaib through the Aenenas of the "Traveler's
Song" with Bavaria. These are mere guesses.

[3] Schmidt connects Banthaib with the Boii and Bohemia (49, 50).

[4] Zeuss connects Vurgundaib or Burgundaib with the Urugundi
of Zosimus which he seems inclined to place in Red Russia
between the Vistula and Bug. These names, he thinks, lead us in
the direction of the Black Sea far into the eastern steppes and he
connects this eastward march of the Langobards with their alleged
combats with the Bulgarians (Hodgkin, V, p. 141). Bluhme in
his monograph (Gens Langobardorum Bonn, 1868) thinks that
Burgundaib was the territory evacuated by the Burgundians when

can consider are names of districts or of some kinds of places.[1]

they moved westward to the Middle Rhine (Hodgkin, V, p. 142), and instead of the eastern migration he makes the Langobards wander westward toward the Rhine, following a passage of Ptolemy which places them near the Sigambri. He believes that this is confirmed by the Chronicon Gothanum which says that they stayed long at Patespruna or Paderborn and contends for a general migration of the tribe to Westphalia, shows the resemblance in family names and legal customs between Westphalia and Bardengau. Schmidt opposes Bluhme's Westphalian theory which indeed appears to have slender support and he more plausibly connects Burgundaib (p. 49) with the remnant of the Burgundians that remained in the lands east of the Elbe. Luttmersen (Die Spuren der Langobarden, Hanover, 1889) thinks that Burgundaib means "the valley of forts," and was perhaps in the region of the Rauhes Alp in Würtemberg; he notes the fact that the Swiss in Thurgau and St. Gall called an old wall built by an unknown hand " Langobardenmauer " and he claims that the Langobards were members of the Alamannic confederacy which occupied Suabia. No historical evidence of this appears (Hodgkin, V, 145).

[1] Names which have a termination "aib" are derived from the Old-High-German *eiba* (canton), the division of a state or population (Schmidt, 49).

The Latin word *pagus* a district, canton, was here used by Paul to designate these subdivisions instead of the word *aldonus* or *aldones* of the Origo from which Paul took this statement. This word *aldonus* comes from *aldius* or *aldio* the "half-free," referring to the condition of serfdom or semi-slavery in which the people dwelt in these lands. Hodgkin thinks (V, 94) the Origo means that the Langobards were in a condition of dependence on some other nation, when they occupied these districts. It seems more probable that these districts were so called because their inhabitants were subjected by the Langobards to a condition of semi-servitude, tilling the land for the benefit of their masters as

CHAPTER XIV.

Meanwhile the leaders Ibor and Aio, who had conducted the Langobards from Scadinavia and had ruled them up to this time, being dead, the Langobards, now

was afterwards done with the Roman population of Italy (Schmidt, 50).

The migrations described by modern German scholars are mostly hypothetical. The fact is, it is idle to guess where were the different places mentioned by Paul or when the Langobards migrated from one to the other. That people however may well have taken part (Hodgkin, V, 88) in the movement of the German tribes southward which brought on the Marcommanic war under Marcus Aurelius, for in a history written by Peter the Patrician, Justinian's ambassador to Theodahad (Fragment, VI, p. 124 of the Bonn. ed.) we are informed that just before that war 6,000 Langobards and Obii having crossed the Danube to invade Pannonia were put to rout by the Roman cavalry under Vindex and the infantry under Candidus, whereupon the barbarians desisted from their invasion and sent as ambassadors to Aelius Bassus, who was then administering Pannonia, Vallomar, king of the Marcommani, and ten others, one for each tribe. Peace was made, and the barbarians returned home. These events occurred about A. D. 165. (Hodgkin, V, 88.) It is clear from this that the Langobards had left the Elbe for the Danube as allies or subjects of their old masters, the Marcommani. Where the home was to which they returned can hardly be determined. Hodgkin believes that they withdrew to some place not far distant from Pannonia, while Zeuss (p. 471), Wiese (p. 28) and Schmidt (35, 36) believe that they did not depart permanently from their original abodes on the Elbe until the second half of the fourth century so that according to this view they must have returned to these original abodes. It is evident that a considerable number of the Langobards must have lived a long time on the lower Elbe —the names and institutions which have survived in Bardengau

unwilling to remain longer under mere chiefs (dukes)
ordained a king for themselves like other nations.[1]
Therefore Agelmund,[2] the son of Aio first reigned over
them[3] tracing out of his pedigree the stock of the Gun-

bear evidence of this. It is, however, highly probable that when
the bulk of the nation migrated, a considerable part remained
behind and afterwards became absorbed by the Saxon tribes in
the neighborhood, while the emigrants alone retained the name of
Langobards (Hartmann, II, part 1, 5).

After the Marcommanic war, information from Greek or Roman
writers as to the fortunes of the Langobards is entirely lacking
and for a space of three hundred years their name disappears
from history.

[1] More likely the reason was that the unity of a single command
was found necessary. Schmidt believes (p. 76) that the people
like other German nations, were divided according to cantons,
that the government in the oldest times was managed by a general
assembly that selected the chiefs of the cantons who were probably, as a rule, taken from the nobility and chosen for life. In
peace they acted as judges in civil cases, and in war as leaders of
the troops of the cantons. As commander-in-chief of the whole
army, a leader or duke was chosen by the popular assembly, but
only for the time of the war. Often two colleagues are found
together, as Ibor and Aio. As a result of their long-continued
wars during their wanderings, the kingly power was developed
and the king became the representative of the nation in foreign
affairs, in the making of treaties, etc. (p. 77). But the influence
of the people upon the government did not fully disappear.

[2] This name is found in a Danish song, and is written Hagel-
mund (Wiese, 3).

[3] Mommsen observes (68) that even those who recognize a genuine germ of history in this legend must regard as fiction this
connection of the leaders Ibor and Aio with the subsequent line of
kings; that we have no indication regarding the duration of this

gingi which among them was esteemed particularly noble.   He held the sovereignty of the Langobards, as is reported by our ancestors, for thirty years.

CHAPTER XV.

At this time a certain prostitute had brought forth seven little boys at a birth, and the mother, more cruel than all wild beasts, threw them into a fish-pond to be drowned.   If this seems impossible to any, let him read over the histories of the ancients[1] and he will find that one woman brought forth not only seven infants but even nine at one time.   And it is sure that this occurred especially among the Egyptians.   It happened therefore that when King Agelmund had stopped his horse and looked at the wretched infants, and had turned them hither and thither with the spear he carried in his hand, one of them put his hand on the royal spear and clutched it.   The king moved by pity and marveling greatly at the act, pronounced that he would be a great man.   And straightway he ordered him to be lifted from the fish-pond and commanded him to be brought to a nurse to be nourished with every care, and because he took him from

early leadership, and that it may as well have lasted centuries as decades.   The events already described probably required at least a number of generations for their accomplishment.   The words in the text, "Ibor and Aio who had . . . ruled them up to this time," appears to have been inserted by Paul upon conjecture to make a continuous line of rulers and is plainly an error (Waitz).

[1] See Pliny's Natural History, Book VII, ch. 3, on monstrous births.

a fish-pond which in their language is called " lama " [1] he gave him the name Lamissio. [2] When he had grown up he became such a vigorous youth that he was also very fond of fighting, and after the death of Agelmund he directed the government of the kingdom. [3] They say that when the Langobards, pursuing their way with their king, came to a certain river and were forbidden by the Amazons [4] to cross to the other side, this man fought with the strongest of them, swimming in the river, and killed her and won for himself the glory of great praise and a passage also for the Langobards. For it had

[1] *Lama* is not a German but a Latin word, found in Festus and meaning a collection of water (Waitz). It lived on in the romance languages. DuCange introduces it from the statutes of Modena, and Dante used it (Inferno, Canto XX, line 79). It meant, however, in Italian at this later period " a low plain." If Paul or his earlier authorities took it for Langobard this was because it was unknown to the Latin learning of that time, though it was a current peasant word in Northern Italy with which a discoverer of ancient Langobard tales could appropriately connect the indigenous king's name (Mommsen, 68).

[2] This name is called Laiamicho or Lamicho in the Origo and the form used here by Paul seems to have been taken from the Edict of Rothari (Waitz).

[3] This story of the origin of Lamissio is inconsistent with the statement in the Prologue of the Edict of Rothari and with the Madrid and La Cava manuscripts of the " Origo Gentis Langobardorum " which say that he was " of the race of Gugingus " (see Waitz, also Appendix II ; Mommsen, p. 68 ; Waitz, Neues Archiv, V, 423).

[4] This appears to be a transformation into classical form of some ancient German legend of swan-maidens or water-sprites (Schmidt, 17, note).

been previously agreed between the two armies that if
that Amazon should overcome Lamissio, the Langobards
would withdraw from the river, but if she herself were
conquered by Lamissio, as actually occurred, then the
means of crossing the stream should be afforded to the
Langobards.[1]   It is clear, to be sure, that this kind of
an assertion is little supported by truth, for it is known
to all who are acquainted with ancient histories that the
race of Amazons was destroyed long before these things
could have occurred, unless perchance (because the
places where these things are said to have been done
were not well enough known to the writers of history
and are scarcely mentioned by any of them), it might
have been that a class of women of this kind dwelt there
at that time, for I have heard it related by some that the
race of these women exists up to the present day in the
innermost parts of Germany.[2]

CHAPTER XVI.

Therefore after passing the river of which we have
spoken, the Langobards, when they came to the lands
beyond, sojourned there for some time.   Meanwhile,
since they suspected nothing hostile and were the less
uneasy on account of their long repose, confidence,

[1] Schmidt (p. 50) believes that the story of Lamissio is a fabu-
lous expansion of the original myth of Skeaf.   The germ of the
myth is that a hero of unknown origin came from the water to the
help of the land in time of need.

[2] Perhaps the Cvenas whom fable placed by the Baltic sea
or gulf of Bothnia in "The Land of Women" (Zeuss, 686, 687).

which is always the mother of calamities, prepared for them a disaster of no mean sort. At night, in short, when all were resting, relaxed by negligence, suddenly the Bulgarians, rushing upon them, slew many, wounded many more and so raged[1] through their camp that they killed Agelmund, the king himself, and carried away in captivity his only daughter.

CHAPTER XVII.

Nevertheless the Langobards, having recovered their strength after these disasters, made Lamissio, of whom we have spoken above, their king. And he, as he was in the glow of youth and quite ready for the struggles of war, desiring to avenge the slaughter of Agelmund, his foster-father, turned his arms against the Bulgarians. And presently, when the first battle began, the Langobards, turning their backs to the enemy, fled to their camp. Then king Lamissio seeing these things, began in a loud voice to cry out to the whole army that they should remember the infamies they had suffered and recall to view their disgrace; how their enemies had murdered their king and had carried off in lamentation as a captive, his daughter whom they had desired for their queen.[2] Finally he urged them to defend themselves and theirs by arms, saying that it was better to lay down life in war than to submit as vile slaves to the taunts of their enemies. Crying aloud, he said

---

[1] Read for *dibachati*, *debacchati*.

[2] Abel (p. 251) infers from this the right of succession to the throne in the female line.

these things and the like and now by threats, now by promises, strengthened their minds to endure the struggles of war; moreover if he saw any one of servile condition fighting he endowed him with liberty, as well as rewards. At last inflamed by the urging and example of their chief who had been the first to spring to arms, they rush upon the foe, fight fiercely and overthrow their adversaries with great slaughter, and finally, taking victory from the victors, they avenge as well the death of their king as the insults to themselves. Then having taken possession of great booty from the spoils of their enemies, from that time on they become bolder in undertaking the toils of war.[1]

Chapter XVIII.

After these things Lamissio, the second who had reigned, died, and the third, Lethu, ascended the throne of the kingdom, and when he had reigned nearly forty years, he left Hildeoc his son, who was the fourth in number, as his successor in the kingly power. And when he also died, Gudeoc, as the fifth, received the royal authority.[2]

[1] Schmidt (50) regards this struggle with the Bulgarians as having no authentic basis in history since the name of the Bulgarians does not occur elsewhere before the end of the fifth century.

[2] Mommsen calls attention (p. 75) to the close relation of the Gothic and Langobard legends. The Goths wandered from the island of Scandza, where many nations dwell (Jordanes, Ch. 3), among them the Vinoviloth, who may be the Winnili. From there the Goths sailed upon three vessels under their king Berich

Chapter XIX.

In these times the fuel of great enmities was consumed between Odoacar who was ruling in Italy now for some years,[1] and Feletheus, who is also called Feva,[2]

to the mainland (Ch. 4, 17). The first people they encountered in battle were the Vandals (Ch. 4). Further on the Amazons were introduced, and Mommsen concludes (p. 76): "It may be that these Langobard and Gothic traditions are both fragments of a great legend of the origin of the whole German people or that the Gothic story-teller has stirred the Langobard to the making of similar fables. The stories of the Amazons are more favorable to the latter idea."

Hodgkin (V, 98) also notices the similarity of Langobard history to that of the Goths, as told by Jordanes. But Jordanes exhibits a pedigree showing fourteen generations before Theodoric, and thus reaching back very nearly to the Christian era, while Paul gives only five links of the chain before the time of Odoacar, the contemporary of Theodoric, and thus reaches back, at furthest, only to the era of Constantine. This seems to show that the Langobards had preserved fewer records of the deeds of their fathers. Hodgkin (V, 99) adds that it is hopeless to get any possible scheme of Lombard chronology out of these early chapters of Paul; that his narrative would place the migration from Scandinavia about A. D. 320, whereas the Langobards were dwelling south of the Baltic at the birth of Christ; that he represents Agelmund, whose place in the narrative makes it impossible to fix his date later than 350, as slain in battle by the Bulgarians, who first appeared in Europe about 479.

[1] Here the tradition of the Langobards, as stated by Paul, begins again to correspond, at least in part, with known or probable historical facts.

[2] The manuscripts of the "Origo Gentis Langobardorum" spell this Theuvane (M. G., Script. Rer. Langob., p. 3) which is required by the meter if the word comes from an epic song (Bruckner, Zeitschrift für Deutches Alterthum, Vol. 43, p. 56).

king of the Rugii. This Feletheus dwelt in those days
on the further shore of the Danube, which the Danube
itself separates from the territories of Noricum. In
these territories of the Noricans at that time was the
monastery of the blessed Severinus,[1] who, endowed with
the sanctity of every abstinence, was already renowned
for his many virtues, and though he dwelt in these
places up to the end of his life, now however, Neapolis
(Naples) keeps his remains.[2] He often admonished
this Feletheus of whom we have spoken and his wife,
whose name was Gisa, in saintly language that they
should desist from iniquity, and when they spurned his
pious words, he predicted a long while beforehand that
that would occur which afterwards befel them. Odoacar then, having collected together the nations which
were subject to his sovereignty, that is the Turcilingi
and the Heroli and the portion of the Rugii he already
possessed [3] and also the peoples of Italy, came into
Rugiland and fought with the Rugii, and sweeping them
away in final defeat he destroyed also Feletheus their
king, and after the whole province was devastated, he re-

[1] At Eiferingen, at the foot of Mount Kalenberg, not far from
Vienna (Waitz).

[2] St. Severinus was the apostle of Noricum. He was born either
in Southern Italy or in Africa. After the death of Attila he trav-
eled through the territory along the Danube preaching Christianity
and converting many. He died A. D. 482, and his body was
taken to Italy and finally buried at Naples (Waitz).

[3] The statement that Rugians fought upon both sides was the
result of Paul's effort to reconcile the accounts of two contradictory
authorities (Mommsen, 103).

turned to Italy and carried off with him an abundant multitude of captives. Then the Langobards, having moved out of their own territories,[1] came into Rugiland,[2] which is called in the Latin tongue the country of the Rugii, and because it was fertile in soil they remained in it a number of years.

CHAPTER XX.

Meanwhile, Gudeoc died, and Claffo, his son, succeeded him. Claffo also having died, Tato, his son, rose as the seventh to the kingly power. The Langobards also departed from Rugiland, and dwelt in open fields, which are called "feld" in the barbarian tongue.[3] While they sojourned there for the space of three years, a war sprang up between Tato and Rodolf, king of the Heroli.[4] Treaties formerly bound them together, and

[1] Wiese (p. 33) believes that they were then dwelling in upper Silesia not far from the head waters of the Vistula.

[2] Bluhme considers this to be Moravia (Hodgkin, V, 142). It is more probably the region on the left bank of the Danube between Linz and Vienna (Schmidt, 51).

[3] The country between the Theiss and the Danube in Hungary as Schmidt (52) believes, quoting a passage from the Annals of Eginhard for the year 796: "Pippin having driven the Huns beyond the Theiss, destroyed completely the royal residence which these people called the *Ring*, and the Langobards the *Feld*." Since Procopius, (B. G. II, 14) says that the Langobards were then tributary to the Heroli, Wiese believes (p. 35, 36) that they were compelled by the Heroli to give up their fertile Rugiland. The Langobards became Christianized, at least in part, about this time (Abel, 241; Schmidt, 51, 52).

[4] The Heroli were, says Zeuss (p. 476), the most migratory

the cause of the discord between them was this: the
brother of king Rodolf had come to Tato for the purpose of concluding peace, and when, upon the comple-
tion of his mission, he sought again his native country,
it happened that his way passed in front of the house
of the king's daughter, who was called Rumetruda.
Looking upon the company of men and the noble escort,
she asked who this might be who had such a mag-
nificent train.   And it was said to her that the brother
of king Rodolf was returning to his native country, having accomplished his mission.   The girl sent to invite
him to deign to take a cup of wine.   He with simple
heart came as he had been invited, and because he was
small in stature, the girl looked down upon him in con-
temptuous pride and uttered against him mocking words.
But he, overcome equally with shame and rage, answered
back such words as brought still greater confusion upon
the girl.   Then she, inflamed by a woman's fury and
unable to restrain the rage of her heart, sought to accomplish a wicked deed she had conceived in her mind.

among all the German tribes and have wandered over nearly the
whole of Europe. They appeared on the Dneister and Rhine ; they
plundered in Greece and in Spain, and were found in Italy and
in Scandinavia.   Hodgkin believes that the tribe was split up into
two divisions, one of which moved from the Baltic to the Black
Sea, and the other eventually made its appearance on the Rhine.
It was the eastern branch, which at the close of the 5th century
was in Hungary on the eastern shore of the Danube, with which
the Langobards had their struggle (Hodgkin, V, 104).   The customs of the tribe were barbarous.   They engaged in human sac-
rifices, put the sick and the aged to death, and it was the duty of
a warrior's widow to die upon her husband's tomb (Hodgkin, 105).

She feigned patience, put on a lively countenance, and stroking him down with merry words, she invited him to take a seat, and arranged that he should sit in such a place that he would have the window in the wall at his shoulders. She had covered this window with costly drapery as if in honor of her guest, but really, lest any suspicion should strike him, and the atrocious monster directed her own servants that when she should say, as if speaking to the cup-bearer, " Prepare the drink," they should stab him from behind with their lances. And it was done; presently the cruel woman gave the sign, her wicked orders were accomplished, and he, pierced with wounds and falling to the earth, expired. When these things were announced to king Rodolf he bewailed his brother's cruel murder, and impatient in his rage, burned to avenge that brother's death. Breaking the treaty he had negotiated with Tato, he declared war against him.[1] Why say more? The lines of battle on both sides come together in the open fields.

[1] Procopius (B. G., II, 14 *et seq.*) gives a different account of the origin of this war. He states (Hodgkin, V, 106) that the warriors of the tribe having lived in peace for three years, chafed at this inaction and taunted Rodolf, calling him womanish and soft-hearted, until he determined to make war upon the Langobards, but gave no pretext for his attack. Three times the Langobards sent ambassadors to placate him, who offered to increase the tribute paid by their nation, but Rodolf drove them from his presence. Procopius' reason for the war is more favorable to the Langobards than that given by Paul. But it is quite possible that a rude people such as they were, might consider it more disgraceful to admit that they had paid tribute and humbly besought justice than that they had themselves given just cause for war.

Rodolf sends his men into the fight, but staying himself
in camp, he plays at draughts, not at all wavering in his
hope of victory. The Heroli were indeed at that time
well trained in martial exercises, and already very
famous from their many victories. And either to fight
more freely or to show their contempt for a wound inflicted by the enemy, they fought naked, covering only
the shameful things of the body.[1]   Therefore, while the
king himself in undoubting reliance on the power of
these men, was safely playing at draughts, he ordered
one of his followers to climb into a tree which happened
to be by, that he might tell him more quickly of the
victory of his troops, and he threatened to cut off the
man's head if he announced that the ranks of the Heroli
were fleeing. The man, when he saw that the line of the
Heroli was bent, and that they were hard pressed by the
Langobards, being often asked by the king what the
Heroli were doing, answered that they were fighting
excellently. And not daring to speak, he did not reveal
the calamity he saw until all the troops had turned their
backs upon the foe.   At last, though late, breaking into
voice he cried: "Woe to thee wretched Herolia who
art punished by the anger of the Lord of Heaven."
Moved by these words the king said: "Are my Heroli
fleeing?" And he replied: "Not I, but thou, king,
thyself hast said this." Then, as is wont to happen in
such circumstances, while the king and all, greatly
alarmed, hesitated what to do, the Langobards came

[1] Jordanis (ch. 49) says they fought light-armed.   Procopius
(Persian war, II, 25) speaks of their lack of defensive armor.

upon them and they were violently cut to pieces. The
king himself, acting bravely to no purpose, was also
slain. While the army of the Heroli indeed was scattering hither and thither, so great was the anger of
heaven upon them, that when they saw the green-
growing flax of the fields, they thought it was water fit
for swimming, and while they stretched out their arms
as if to swim, they were cruelly smitten by the swords
of the enemy.[1] Then the Langobards, when the victory
was won, divide among themselves the huge booty they
had found in the camp. Tato indeed carried off the
banner of Rodolf which they call Bandum, and his
helmet which he had been accustomed to wear in war.[2]
And now from that time all the courage of the Heroli
so decayed that thereafter they had no king over them

[1] Procopius (B. G., II, 14) gives another account of the battle.
He says the sky above the Langobards was covered with black
clouds, while above the Heroli it was clear, an omen which portended ruin to the Heroli, since the war god was in the storm
cloud (Wiese, 39). They disregarded it, however, and pressed
on hoping to win by their superior numbers, but when they fought
hand to hand, many of the Heroli were slain, including Rodolf
himself, whereupon his forces fled in headlong haste and most of
them were killed by the pursuing Langobards. The account of
Procopius, a contemporary (490–565), is in the main more reliable
than that of Paul, whose story is clearly of a legendary character.
The place of the battle is uncertain. The date, too, is doubtful.
Procopius places it at 494, but after a careful argument, Schmidt
(53, 54) places it about 508.

[2] Bruckner sees in the superfluous phrase "which he had been
accustomed to wear in war," the marks of the translation of a
German composite word used probably in some early Langobard
song (Zeitschrift für Deutsches Alterthum, vol. 43, part I, p. 55).

in any way.¹ From this time on the Langobards, having become richer, and their army having been aug-
mented from the various nations they had conquered,
began to aspire to further wars, and to push forward
upon every side the glory of their courage.

CHAPTER XXI.

But after these things Tato indeed did not long rejoice in the triumph of war, for Waccho, the son of his
brother Zuchilo,² attacked him and deprived him of his

¹ It is not true that the Heroli never afterwards had a king
(see next chapter).   As to their subsequent history, Procopius says
(B. G., II, 14) they first went to Rugiland, and driven thence by
hunger, they entered Pannonia and became tributaries of the
Gepidae, then they crossed the Danube, probably into upper
Moesia and obtained permission of the Greek emperor to dwell
there as his allies.   This took place in the year 512 (Hodgkin,
V, 112).   They soon quarreled with the Romans and although
under Justinian they came to profess Christianity they were
guilty of many outrages.   They killed their king Ochon, but
finding the anarchy which followed unendurable, they sent to
Thule (Scandinavia) for a royal prince to rule them (Hodgkin,
113), and Todasius set forth for that purpose with two hundred
young men to the country where the Heroli were living.   That
fickle people had now obtained a king, Suartuas, from the emperor Justinian, but they changed their minds again and deserted
to Todasius, whereupon Suartuas escaped to Constantinople, and
when Justinian determined to support him by force of arms, the
Heroli joined the confederacy of the Gepidae (p. 116).

² This is a misunderstanding by Paul of the words of the Origo
from which his account is taken, which says : "And Waccho the
son of Unichis killed king Tato, his uncle, together with Zuchilo."
(M. G. H. Script. Rer. Langob., p. 3.) See Appendix II.

life. Tato's son Hildechis also fought[1] against Waccho,
but when Waccho prevailed and he was overcome, he
fled to the Gepidae and remained there an exile up to
the end of his life. For this reason the Gepidae from
that time incurred enmities with the Langobards. At
the same time Waccho fell upon the Suavi and subjected
them to his authority.[2] If any one may think that this
is a lie and not the truth of the matter, let him read
over the prologue of the edict which King Rothari composed[3] of the laws of the Langobards and he will find

[1] Procopius (III, 35) makes Hildechis the son of Risulf, a cousin
of Waccho (Hodgkin, V, 117, note 2). He states that Risulf would
have been entitled to the throne upon Waccho's death, but in
order to get the crown for his own son, Waccho drove Risulf by
means of a false accusation from the country; that Risulf fled
with his two sons, one of whom was called Hildechis, to the
Warni, by whom, at the instigation of Waccho, he was murdered;
that Hildechis' brother died there of sickness and Hildechis
escaped and was first received by a Slav people and afterwards
by the Gepidae (Schmidt, 59).

[2] It is hard to see what people are designated by this name. The
Suavi who dwelt in the southwestern part of Germany, now Suabia,
are too far off. Hodgkin (p. 119) suggests a confusion between
Suavia and Savia, the region of the Save. Schmidt (55) says,
"There is ground to believe that this people is identical with the
Suevi of Vannius who possessed the mountain land between the
March and the Theiss." Other events in Waccho's reign are
mentioned by Procopius (II, 22), but omitted by Paul. For instance, in the year 539, Vitiges, the Ostrogoth, being hard pressed
by Belisarius, sent ambassadors to Waccho offering large sums of
money to become his ally, but Waccho refused because a treaty
had been concluded between the Langobards and Byzantines.

[3] Paul here refers to the famous " Origo Gentis Langobardorum "
from which, or from a common original, Paul has taken much of

this written in almost all the manuscripts as we have
inserted it in this little history.   And Waccho had three
wives, that is, the first, Ranicunda, daughter of the king
of the Turingi (Thuringians) ; then he married Aus-
trigusa, the daughter of the king of the Gepidae, from
whom he had two daughters ; the name of one was
Wisegarda, whom he bestowed in marriage upon Theudepert, king of the Franks, and the second was called
Walderada, who was united with Cusupald, another king
of the Franks, and he, having her in hatred,[1] gave her
over in marriage to one of his followers called Garipald.[2]
And Waccho had for his third wife the daughter of the
king of the Heroli,[3] by name Salinga.   From her a son
was born to him, whom he called Waltari, and who
upon the death of Waccho reigned as the eighth[4] king

his early Langobard history.   See Appendix II.   Paul appears
to have considered the Origo as the Prologue to Rothari's Edict.
The two were, however, different, though both were prefixed to
the Edict in at least some of the MSS.   Mommsen (58, note)
thinks it probable that the Origo was not an official but a private
work, prefixed to the Edict for the first time in the year 668.
Rothari composed the Edict and not the Origo, though Paul
seems to have considered him the author of the latter (Jacobi 5).

[1] Gregory of Tours relates (IV, 9) that he repudiated her because
he was accused by the clergy, probably on account of some
ecclesiastical impediment.

[2] Garipald was duke of the Bavarians (Greg. Tours, IV, 9 ;
Waitz ; see *infra* III, 10, 30).

[3] And yet Paul has just told us in the preceding chapter that
at this time the Heroli had no king.

[4] An error in enumeration, Tato being mentioned as seventh and
Waccho omitted (Waitz).

over the Langobards. All these were Lithingi; for
thus among them a certain noble stock was called.

Chapter XXII.

Waltari, therefore, when he had held the sovereignty
for seven years,[1] departed from this life,[2] and after him
Audoin[3] was the ninth[4] who attained the kingly power
(546–565), and he, not long afterwards, led the Langobards into Pannonia.[5]

Chapter XXIII.

THEN the Gepidae and the Langobards at last give
birth to the strife which had been long since conceived
and the two parties make ready for war.[6]   When battle

[1] Probably 539 to 546 or thereabouts. (Hartmann, II, 1, 30.)

[2] Procopius says by disease (B. G., III, 35).

[3] The same, probably, as the Anglo-Saxon and English "Edwin"
(Hodgkin, V, 122, note 1).

[4] The race of Lethingi became extinct with Waltari.   Audoin
came from the race of Gausus (see Chronicon Gothanum, M. G.,
H. LL., IV, p. 644).

[5] Justinian, says Procopius (B. G., III, 33), had given this
and other lands to the Langobards together with great sums of
money (Schmidt, 58).   They appear to have been in fact subsi-
dized as allies and confederates of the Roman Empire (Hartmann,
II, 1, 12), and it seems to have been at Justinian's instigation that
Audoin married a Thuringian princess, the great-niece of Theoderic, who after the overthrow of the Thuringians had fled to Italy,
and later had been brought by Belisarius to the court of Constantinople (Hartmann, II, 1, 14).   The invasion of Pannonia probably
occurred not far from 546 (id., p. 30).

[6] Paul does not state the cause of this war.   Schmidt believes (p.
58) that it was probably begun at the instigation of Justinian whose

was joined, while both lines fought bravely and neither
yielded to the other, it happened that in the midst of
struggle, Alboin, the son of Audoin, and Turismod, the
son of Turisind encountered each other. And Alboin,
striking the other with his sword, hurled him headlong
from his horse to destruction. The Gepidae, seeing that
the king's son was killed, through whom in great part
the war had been set on foot, at once, in their discour-
agement, start to flee. The Langobards, sharply following them up, overthrow them and when a great number had been killed they turn back to take off the spoils
of the dead. When, after the victory had been won,

interest it was to break up the friendship of two peoples who threatened to become dangerous to his empire and that in addition to
this, the desire of the Langobards to get the important city of Sirmium, then held by the Gepidae coöperated, and above all, the
hostile feeling which had been called out by contests for the throne.
It must be remembered that the Heroli, enemies to the Langobards, had been received in the confederacy of the Gepidae and
that Hildechis, the descendant of Tato, was harbored by the Gepid
king Turisind, just as Ustrigotthus, Turisind's rival for the Gepid
throne, and son of his predecessor, Elemund, had found refuge at
the court of Audoin. Prior to this, both nations had sought the
alliance of the emperor (Hodgkin, V, 122–126). Justinian decided
to help the Langobards since they were weaker and less dangerous
to him than the Gepidae, so a Roman army of about 10,000 cavalry and 1500 Heroli marched against the Gepidae. Upon the
way they annihilated a division of 3,000 Heroli who were allied to
the Gepidae, and the Gepidae made a separate peace with the
Langobards (p. 129). Audoin demanded of Turisind, king of
the Gepidae, the delivery of Hildechis, but the latter escaped and
wandered about in different countries (Schmidt, 60).

A second war between the Langobards and Gepidae occurred

the Langobards returned to their own abodes, they suggested to their king Audoin that Alboin, by whose valor they had won the victory in the fight, should become his table companion so that he who had been a comrade to his father in danger should also be a comrade at the feast. Audoin answered them that he could by no means do this lest he should break the usage of the nation. " You know," he said, " that it is not the custom among us that the son of the king should eat with his father unless he first receives his arms from the king of a foreign nation."

about 549 (Procopius, IV, 18), when a desperate panic seized both armies at the beginning of a battle, whereupon the two kings concluded a two years' truce. At the end of this time hostilities began anew. Justinian took the side of the Langobards and sent troops into the field, one division of which, under command of Amalafrid, joined the Langobards, while the rest of the troops remained by command of the emperor in Ulpiana to quell certain disturbances (Schmidt, 60, 61). The Langobards pushed into the territory of the Gepidae and defeated their adversaries. The field of battle was probably near Sirmium. Procopius (B. G., IV, 25) puts this battle in the seventeenth year of the war (March, 551, to March, 552). Probably this is the same battle which Paul relates. The Gepidae now begged for peace which was accorded to them through the intervention of Justinian. As a condition the Langobards and the emperor demanded the delivery of Hildechis. But as the Gepidae were resolved not to violate the sanctity of a guest, and as the Langobards refused to deliver Ustrigotthus, neither of these were surrendered, but both perished by assassination, not without the knowledge of the two kings (Schmidt, 62 ; Hodgkin, V, 134).

CHAPTER XXIV.

When he heard these things from his father, Alboin, taking only forty young men with him, journeyed to Turisind, king of the Gepidae with whom he had before waged war, and intimated the cause in which he had come.   And the king, receiving him kindly, invited him to his table and placed him on his right hand where Turismod, his former son had been wont to sit.   In the meantime, while the various dishes were made ready, Turisind, reflecting that his son had sat there only a little while before, and recalling to mind the death of his child and beholding his slayer present and sitting in his place, drawing deep sighs, could not contain himself, but at last his grief broke forth in utterance. " This place," he says, " is dear to me, but the person who sits in it is grievous enough to my sight."   Then another son of the king who was present, aroused by his father's speech, began to provoke the Langobards with insults declaring (because they wore white bandages from their calves down) that they were like mares with white feet up to the legs, saying: " The mares that you take after have white fetlocks." [1]   Then one of the Langobards thus answered these things: " Go to the field of Asfeld and there you can find by experience beyond a doubt how stoutly those you call mares succeed in kicking; there the bones of your brother are scattered in the midst of the meadows like those of a vile beast."   When they

[1] Or hoofs.   *Fetilus* for *petilus*.   The white hoof of a horse was so called.   Others make it *foetidae*, " evil smelling."   See Gibbon, ch. 45.   Hodgkin, V, 136.

heard these things, the Gepidae, unable to bear the tumult of their passions, are violently stirred in anger and strive to avenge the open insult. The Langobards on the other side, ready for the fray, all lay their hands on the hilts of their swords. The king leaping forth from the table thrust himself into their midst and restrained his people from anger and strife, threatening first to punish him who first engaged in fight, saying that it is a victory not pleasing to God when any one kills his guest in his own house. Thus at last the quarrel having been allayed, they now finished the banquet with joyful spirits. And Turisind, taking up the arms of Turismod his son, delivered them to Alboin and sent him back in peace and safety to his father's kingdom. Alboin having returned to his father, was made from that time his table companion. And when he joyfully partook with his father of the royal delicacies, he related in order all the things which had happened to him among the Gepidae in the palace of Turisind.[2] Those who were present were astonished and applauded the boldness of Alboin nor did they less extol in their praises the most honorable behavior of Turisind.

CHAPTER XXV.

At this period the emperor Justinian was governing the Roman empire with good fortune. He was both prosperous in waging wars and admirable in civil matters. For by Belisarius, the patrician, he vigorously subdued the Persians and by this same Belisarius he

---

[1] Read *Turisindi* with many MSS. instead of *Turismodi.*

reduced to utter destruction the nation of the Wandals, captured their king Gelismer and restored all Africa to the Roman empire after ninety-six years. Again by the power of Belisarius he overcame the nation of the Goths in Italy and took captive Witichis their king. He subdued also the Moors who afterwards infested Africa together with their king Amtalas, by John the ex-consul, a man of wonderful courage. In like manner too, he subjugated other nations by right of war. For this reason, on account of his victories over them all, he deserved to have his surnames and to be called Alamannicus, Gothicus, Francicus, Germanicus, Anticus, Alanicus, Wandalicus, and Africanus. He also arranged in wonderful brevity the laws of the Romans whose prolixity was very great and whose lack of harmony was injurious. For all the laws of the emperors which were certainly contained in many volumes he abridged into twelve books, and he ordered this volume called the Justinian Code. On the other hand, the laws of special magistrates or judges which were spread over almost two thousand books, he reduced to the number of fifty and called that work by the name of "Digests" or "Pandects." He also composed anew four books of "Institutes" in which the texture of all laws is briefly described; he also ordered that the new laws which he himself had ordained, when reduced to one volume, should be called in the same way the "New Code" (Novels). The same emperor also built within the city of Constantinople to Christ our Lord, who is the wisdom of God the Father, a church which he called by the Greek name "Hagia Sophia," that is, "Divine Wisdom."

The workmanship of this so far excels that of all other
buildings that in all the regions of the earth its like
cannot be found.   This emperor in fact was Catholic in
his faith, upright in his deeds, just in his judgments,
and therefore, to him all things came together for
good.   In his time Cassiodorus was renowned in the
city of Rome [1] for knowledge both human and divine.
Among other things which he nobly wrote, he ex-
pounded particularly in a most powerful way the obscure parts of the Psalms.   He was in the first place a
consul, then a senator, and at last a monk.   At this
time also Dionisius, an abbott established in the city of
Rome, computed a reckoning of Easter time by a wonderful argumentation.[2]   Then also, at Constantinople,
Priscian of Cæsarea explored the depths of the grammatical art, as I might say, and then also, Arator, a
subdeacon of the Roman church, a wonderful poet,
wrote the acts of the apostles in hexameter verses.

Chapter XXVI.

In these days also the most blessed father Benedict,
first in a place called Sublacus (Subiaco), which is distant forty miles [3] from the city of Rome, and afterwards

---

[1] His work was done mostly at Ravenna and Viviers in Bruttium (where he retired to a monastery).   His fame was not confined to Rome but extended throughout Italy, and the entire
Roman world.

[2] In his Cyclus Paschalis he also introduced the annunciation of
the birth of Christ as the starting-point of chronology.

[3] A Roman mile is 142 yards less than the English statute mile.

in the stronghold of Cassinum (Monte Cassino [1]), which is called Arx, was renowned for his great life and his apostolic virtues. His biography, as is known, the blessed Pope Gregory composed in delightful language in his Dialogues. I also, according to my meager talent, have braided together in the following manner in honor of so great a father, each of his miracles by means of corresponding distichs in elegiac meter.[2] . . . We have woven also in this manner a hymn in iambic Archilochian meter, containing each of the miracles of the same father.[3] . . .

I may here briefly relate a thing that the blessed pope Gregory did not at all describe in his life of this most holy father. When, by divine admonition, he had come almost fifty miles from Sublacus to this place where his body reposes, three ravens, whom he was accustomed to feed, followed him, flying around him. And at every crossway, while he came hither, two angels appearing in the form of young men, showed him which way he ought to take. And in this place [Cassinum] a certain servant of God then had a dwelling, to whom a voice from heaven said:

Leave these sacred spots, another friend is at hand.

[1] A famous monastery, 45 miles N. W. of Naples, the cradle of the Benedictine order.

[2] The sixty-four distichs which follow are found in Appendix III, as they have no proper connection with the history. They had been written by Paul previously, and certain additions to them contained in other MSS. are published by Bethmann (331).

[3] These verses are also contained in Appendix III.

And when he had come here, that is to the citadel of Cassinum he always restrained himself in great abstinence, but especially at the time of Lent he remained shut up and removed from the noise of the world. I have taken all these things from the song of the poet Marcus, who coming hither to this same father, composed some verses in his praise, but to guard against too great prolixity, I have not described them in these books. It is certain, however, that this illustrious father came to this fertile place overlooking a rich valley, being called by heaven for this purpose, that there should be here a community of many monks, as has actually occurred under God's guidance. These things, which were not to be omitted, having been briefly told, let us return to the regular order of our history.

CHAPTER XXVII.

Now Audoin, king of the Langobards, of whom we have spoken, had to wife Rodelinda, who bore him Alboin, a man fitted for wars and energetic in all things. Then Audoin died,[1] and afterwards Alboin, the tenth king, entered upon the government of his country according to the wishes of all, and since he had everywhere a name very illustrious and distinguished for power, Chlothar, the king of the Franks, joined to him in marriage his daughter Chlotsuinda. From her he begot one daughter only, Alpsuinda by name. Meanwhile Turisind, king of the Gepidæ, died, and Cunimund succeeded him in the sovereignty. And he,

---

[1] Probably about 565 (Hodgkin, V, 137).

desiring to avenge the old injuries of the Gepidæ, broke his treaty with the Langobards and chose war rather than peace.[1]   But Alboin entered into a perpetual treaty with the Avars, who were first called Huns, and afterwards Avars, from the name of their own king.[2] Then he set out for the war prepared by the Gepidæ. When the latter were hastening against him in a different direction, the Avars, as they had agreed with Alboin, invaded their country.   A sad messenger coming to Cunimund, announced to him that the Avars had entered his territories.   Although cast down in spirit, and put into sore straits on both sides, still he urged his people to fight first with the Langobards, and that, if they should be able to overcome these, they should then drive the army of the Huns from their country.   Therefore battle is joined and they fight with all their might. The Langobards become the victors, raging against the

[1] Paul apparently confounds two wars in one.   Alboin in the first overcomes Cunimund; then the emperor Justin prepares to aid the Gepidæ and Alboin offers to make peace and to marry Rosemund.   His offer is refused and in the second war Cunimund is killed (Waitz).

[2] These were a horde of Asiatics who had entered Europe in the closing years of the reign of Justinian, had extorted large subsidies from him and had penetrated westward as far as Thuringia (Hodgkin, V, 137).   Their chief bore the title of cagan or khan. The treaty made by Alboin with the khan Baian shows that the Avars drove a hard bargain with the Langobards.   Baian consented to the alliance only on condition that the Langobards should give the Avars a tenth part of their livestock and that in the event of victory the Avars should receive one-half of the spoils and the whole of the lands of the Gepidæ (Schmidt, 63–64).

Gepidæ in such wrath that they reduce them to utter
destruction, and out of an abundant multitude scarcely
the messenger survives.[1] In this battle Alboin killed
Cunimund, and made out of his head, which he carried
off, a drinking goblet. This kind of a goblet is called
among them " scala," [2] but in the Latin language
" patera." And he led away as a captive,[3] Cunimund's
daughter, Rosemund by name, together with a great
multitude of both sexes and every age, and because
Chlotsuinda had died he married her, to his own injury,
as afterwards appeared. Then the Langobards secured
such great booty that they now attained the most ample

[1] The destruction of the kingdom of the Gepidæ occurred in
566 or 567 (Hartmann, II, 1, 31).

[2] Compare the Norse word *skaal, skoal*, German *Schale*. Hodgkin, however, thinks it is related rather to the German *Schädel*,
our skull (V, 139).

[3] It appears he first saw Rosemund when he went to the court
of Turisind to get his arms (Schmidt, 62). On account of political
considerations he had to marry Chlotsuinda, daughter of the
Frankish king, Chlothar I, but when she died, he sued for the hand
of Rosemund, and when it was refused, he forcibly carried her
away into his kingdom (p. 63). Cunimund vainly demanded the
return of his daughter, and was unwilling that she should marry
the hated Langobard. War followed, in which at first the Langobards had the better, but finally they were defeated as the Gepidæ
had brought Justin II, who had succeeded Justinian, over to their
side. The result was that Rosemund was set free. Then Alboin
sought allies and found them in the Avars (id.). When Cunimund
heard of this he again sought the aid of Justin and promised to
cede Sirmium and other possessions to the empire in return for
assistance. Justin delayed and remained neutral, but finally took
Sirmium after the Gepidæ were defeated (Schmidt, 64).

riches, but the race of the Gepidae were so diminished that from that time on they had no king.   But all who were able to survive the war were either subjected to the Langobards or groan even up to the present time in bondage to a grievous mastery, since the Huns possess their country.   But the name of Alboin was spread abroad far and wide, so illustrious, that even up to this time his noble bearing and glory, the good fortune of his wars and his courage are celebrated, not only among the Bavarians and the Saxons, but also among other men of the same tongue in their songs. It is also related by many up to the present time that a special kind of arms was made under him.

BOOK II.

Chapter I.

Now when the frequent victories of the Langobards were noised about in every direction, Narses, keeper of the imperial archives, who was then ruling over Italy and preparing for war against Totila, king of the Goths, inasmuch as he long before had the Langobards for allies, directed messengers to Alboin, asking that he should furnish him assistance to fight with the Goths. Then Alboin sent a chosen band of his [1] to give support to the Romans against the Goths. They were transported into Italy by a bay [2] of the Adriatic sea, and having joined the Romans, began the struggle with the Goths, and when these were reduced to utter destruction, together with Totila, their king, the Langobards returned as victors, honored with many gifts, to their own country. [3] During all the time the Lango-

[1] This actually occurred under Audoin, not Alboin (Procopius, B. G., IV, 26). Twenty-five hundred Langobards were chosen and Audoin sent with them a retinue of three thousand other armed men (id.).

[2] The dwellers in the lagoons at the northern extremity of the Adriatic transported the army along the shores, crossing the mouths of the rivers in small boats (id.).

[3] They were sent to Italy A. D. 554, returned A. D. 552 (Waitz). Their disorderly conduct and the outrages they committed made them dangerous allies, and Narses took an early occasion to send them home (Procopius, B. G., IV, 33).

bards held Pannonia, they were the allies of the Roman state againt its rivals.

Chapter II.

In these times Narses also waged war against Duke Buccellinus, whom Theudepert,[1] king of the Franks, when he entered Italy and returned to Gaul, had left behind with Amingus, another duke, to conquer the country. This Buccellinus, after devastating nearly all Italy with rapine, and after bestowing upon Theude-

[1] Grandson of Clovis, the founder of the Frankish monarchy. Theudepert had invaded Italy in the year 539 (Muratori Ann., III, p. 388; Hodgkin, V, p. 11), but the dysentery swept away a third of his army, and the clamor of his own subjects, as well as the representations of Belisarius, the general of Justinian, induced him to return home (Gibbon, ch. 41). When he departed from Italy he did not relinquish all he had won. The larger part of Venetia, a good deal of Liguria and the provinces of the Cottian Alps were retained (Hodgkin, V, 11).

Theudepert died in 548, leaving as his successor his feeble child Theudebald (p. 13). Five years later (A. D. 533), when the Goths in Italy were overthrown by Narses, those who still held out in the north besought the Frankish king for aid, and Buccellinus (Butilin) and his brother Leutharius, leaders of the barbarous Alamanni, ravaged northern Italy (pp. 16–17), and then swept down toward the south. The armies of the two brothers kept together as far as Samnium, then they divided. Buccellinus ravaged the west coast and Leutharius the east, down to the end of the peninsula (A. D. 554). Finally Leutharius determined to return with his booty, but when he was about to cross the Alps a pestilence broke out in his army and he perished (pp. 33–36). Buccellinus was attacked by Narses near Capua, his army was destroyed and he was slain. This expedition of Buccellinus, therefore, occurred not under Theudepert but after his death.

pert, his king, abundant gifts from the booty of the country, was arranging to winter in Campania, but was overcome at length in disastrous war by Narses at a place whose name is Tannetum,[1] and was slain. And when Amingus attempted to bring aid to Widin, a count of the Goths rebelling against Narses, both were overcome by Narses. Widin being captured, was banished to Constantinople, but Amingus, who had offered him assistance, perished by the sword of Narses. Also a third duke of the Franks, by name Leutharius, the brother of Buccellinus, when he desired to return to his country laden with great booty, died a natural death between Verona and Tridentum (Trent), near Lake Benacus (Lago di Garda).[2]

CHAPTER III.

Narses had also a struggle with Sinduald, king of the Brenti,[3] a surviving descendant of the stock of the Heroli whom Odoacar, when he formerly came into Italy, had brought with him. Upon this man, who at first adhered to him faithfully, Narses conferred many benefits, but defeated him in war, captured him and

[1] This battle occurred near Capua, on the banks of the river Casilinum, another name for the Vulturnus (Volturno) (Waitz ; Hodgkin, V, 36–44.) The name Tannetum cannot be positively identified.

[2] He died of the pestilence which had broken out in his army. See previous note.

[3] Perhaps the same as those called Breones or Briones, dwelling in the Alps of Noricum or in the neighborhood of the Brenner in Tyrol (Waitz; Abel; see Zeuss, 484).

hung him from a lofty beam, when at last he insolently rebelled and sought to obtain the sovereignty.[1]　At this time also Narses, the patrician, by means of Dagisteus, the Master of Soldiers, a powerful and warlike man, got possession of all the territories of Italy.[2]　This Narses indeed was formerly keeper of the archives,[3] and afterwards on account of the value of his high qualities, he earned the honor of the patriciate.　For he was a very pious man, a Catholic in religion, generous to the poor, very zealous in restoring churches,[4] and so much devoted to vigils and prayers that he obtained victory more by the supplications which he poured forth to God, than by the arms of war.

CHAPTER IV.

In the times of this man a very great pestilence broke out, particularly in the province of Liguria.[5]　For sud-

[1] A. D. 565 (Hodgkin, V, 56).

[2] Narses took the city of Rome largely through the agency of Dagisteus (Procopius, IV, 33), who thus became the means of the recovery of Italy (Waitz).　The title "Master of Soldiers," (*magister militum*,) was given at the time of Constantine to important ministers of state, and there were then only eight of these in the whole empire (Hodgkin, VI, 539); in the time of Theoderic, the king alone (Hartmann, I, 99), and later, Belisarius, the general-in-chief of Justinian, held this important military office (id., p. 258).　Afterwards however, the title became cheapened, the number of *magistri militum* increased, and at last the rank became much the same as that of *dux* or duke (Hodgkin, VI, 540).

[3] *Chartularius*, see DuCange.

[4] After their desecration by the Arian Goths.

[5] Probably A. D. 566 (Hodg., V, 166, note 2).

denly there appeared certain marks among the dwellings, doors, utensils, and clothes, which, if any one wished to wash away, became more and more apparent. After the lapse of a year indeed there began to appear in the groins of men and in other rather delicate[1] places, a swelling of the glands, after the manner of a nut or a date, presently followed by an unbearable fever, so that upon the third day the man died. But if any one should pass over the third day he had a hope of living. Everywhere there was grief and everywhere tears. For as common report had it that those who fled would avoid the plague, the dwellings were left deserted by their inhabitants, and the dogs only kept house. The flocks remained alone in the pastures with no shepherd at hand. You might see villas or fortified places lately filled with crowds of men, and on the next day, all had departed and everything was in utter silence. Sons fled, leaving the corpses of their parents unburied; parents forgetful of their duty abandoned their children in raging fever. If by chance long-standing affection constrained any one to bury his near relative, he remained himself unburied, and while he was performing the funeral rites he perished; while he offered obsequies to the dead, his own corpse remained without obsequies. You might see the world brought back to its ancient silence: no voice in the field; no whistling of shepherds; no lying in wait of wild beasts among the cattle; no harm to domestic fowls. The crops, outliving the time of the harvest, awaited the reaper un-

[1] Read *delicatioribus* in place of *deligatioribus*.

touched; the vineyard with its fallen leaves and its shining grapes remained undisturbed while winter came on; a trumpet as of warriors resounded through the hours of the night and day; something like the murmur of an army was heard by many; there were no footsteps of passers by, no murderer was seen, yet the corpses of the dead were more than the eyes could discern; pastoral places had been turned into a sepulchre for men, and human habitations had become places of refuge for wild beasts. And these evils happened to the Romans only and within Italy alone, up to the boundaries of the nations of the Alamanni and the Bavarians. Meanwhile, the emperor Justinian departed from life and Justin the younger undertook the rule of the state at Constantinople. In these times also Narses the patrician, whose care was watching everything, at length seized Vitalis, bishop of the city of Altinum (Altino), who had fled many years before to the kingdom of the Franks—that is, to the city of Aguntum (Innichen)[1]—and condemned him to exile in Sicily.

CHAPTER V.

Now the whole nation of the Goths having been destroyed or overthrown, as has been said, and those also of whom we have spoken [2] having been in like manner conquered, Narses, after he had acquired much gold and silver and riches of other kinds, incurred the great envy of the Romans although he had labored much

[1] At the headwaters of the Drave in Tyrol (Waitz).

[2] In ch. 2 and 3 supra.

for them against their enemies, and they made insinuations against him to the emperor Justin[1] and his wife Sophia, in these words, saying, "It would be advantageous for the Romans to serve the Goths rather than the Greeks wherever the eunuch Narses rules and oppresses us with bondage, and of these things our most devout emperor is ignorant: Either free us from his hand or surely we will betray the city of Rome and ourselves to the heathens."[2] When Narses heard this he answered briefly these words: " If I have acted badly with the Romans it will go hard with me." Then the emperor was so greatly moved with anger against Narses that he straightway sent the prefect Longinus into Italy to take Narses' place. But Narses, when he knew these things, feared greatly, and so much was he alarmed, especially by the same empress Sophia, that he did not dare to return again to Constantinople. Among other things, because he was a eunuch, she is said to have sent him this message, that she would make him portion out to the girls in the women's chamber the daily tasks of wool.[3] To these words Narses is said to have given this answer, that he would begin to weave her such a web as she could not lay down as long as she lived.[4]

[1] Read *Justino* for *Justiniano*. It was Justin II who was the husband of Sophia and to whom this complaint was made.

[2] The Arian Goths were so considered.

[3] In Fredegarius (Epitome, iii, 65) it is said that the empress sent him a golden instrument used by women with which he might spin and told him that henceforth he might rule over wool-workers, not over nations.

[4] Or, as Fredegarius has it (id.): " I will spin a thread of which

Therefore, greatly racked by hate and fear, he withdrew
to Neapolis (Naples), a city of Campania, and soon
sent messengers to the nation of the Langobards, urging
them to abandon the barren fields of Pannonia and come
and take possession of Italy, teeming with every sort of
riches.   At the same time he sends many kinds of fruits
and samples of other things with which Italy is well supplied, whereby to attract their minds to come.[1]   The

neither the emperor Justin nor the empress shall be able to find
the end '' (Hodgkin, V, 62).

[1] The charge that Narses in revenge for his recall (A. D. 566 or
567) invited the Langobards into Italy is subject to grave doubt.
Paul's statement that he sent them the fruits and products of that
country contains an obvious improbability, since their troops had
served in Italy fifteen years before and they needed no information on that subject (Hodgkin, V, 62).   Paul followed the popular tradition, and tracing this back, we find that the account
occurs in the so-called Fredegarius (A. D. 642 to 658), but without the statement concerning the fruits and other products of Italy.
Bishop Isidore of Seville, whose chronicle came down to 615, tells
us that Narses, terrified by the threats of Sophia, invited the
Langobards from Pannonia and introduced them into Italy.   The
Copenhagen continuer of Prosper (about 625) copies from Isidore.
The Liber Pontificalis (Life of John III, A. D. 579–590) says
that Narses went to Campania and wrote to the Langobards to
come and take possession of Italy (Hodgkin, V, 60, 61).   This
book was nearly contemporary and shows a popular belief that
Narses was disloyal to the empire.   Neither of the two best contemporary authors, Marius of Avenches or Gregory of Tours, who
died about 594, speak of Narses' invitation to the Langobards,
though the former mentions his recall and both speak of the invasion of Alboin.   The Annals of Ravenna are equally silent.
While Narses' recall was probably due to the empress and furnished the Langobards with their opportunity, the statement that

Langobards receive joyfully the glad tidings which they themselves had also been desiring, and they form high expectations of future advantages. In Italy terrible signs were continually seen at night, that is, fiery swords appeared in heaven gleaming with that blood which was afterwards shed.

CHAPTER VI.

But Alboin, being about to set out for Italy with the Langobards, asked aid from his old friends, the Saxons, that he might enter and take possession of so spacious a land with a larger number of followers. The Saxons came to him, more than 20,000 men, together with their wives and children, to proceed with him to Italy according to his desire. Hearing these things, Chlothar and Sigisbert, kings of the Franks, put the Suavi and other nations into the places from which these Saxons had come.[1]

he invited them is hardly sustained by sufficient evidence to establish the treason of that eminent commander, though it shows that after the invasion his agency was suspected (Hodgkin, V, 64, 65). Certain it is that when his body was brought to Constantinople, the emperor whom he is said to have betrayed, carried his bier and paid the last honors to his memory (Hartmann II, 1, 24).

[1] Hodgkin believes (V, 156 note) that the fact that the Suavi, whom he considers the same as the Alamanni, occupied the homes of these Saxons, indicates that they were located in southern Germany.

Chapter VII.

Then Alboin bestowed his own abode, that is, Pannonia, upon his friends the Huns[1] on this condition: that if at any time it should be necessary for the Langobards to return[2] they should take back their own fields. Then the Langobards, having left Pannonia, hastened to take possession of Italy with their wives and children and all their goods. They dwelt in Pannonia forty-two years.[3] They came out of it in the month of April in the first indiction[4] on the day after holy Easter,

[1] That is the Avars (Waitz). See *supra* I, 27.

[2] " At any time within two hundred years," adds the Chronicon Gothanum (M. G. Leges IV, 644), and it was also provided in the agreement that the Avars should aid the Langobards in Italy.

[3] This period is impossible since the Langobards entered Pannonia not far from 546, and left it in 568. Probably 22 should be substituted for 42 (Hartmann, II, 1, 30).

[4] The word " indiction " originally meant the declaration of the imposition of a tax. When Constantine the Great reorganized the Roman Empire he established a fiscal period of fifteen years for this imposition, beginning A. D. 313. Hence the word in chronology means the number attached to the year showing its place in a cycle of fifteen years, beginning A. D. 313. There were three kinds of indiction. The original Greek or Constantinopolitan indiction (here referred to) is reckoned from September 1st of what we consider the previous year. To find the indiction, add three to the number of the year in the vulgar era and divide it by 15, the remainder is the indiction. If nothing is left over, it is the 15th indiction. The year when Alboin left Pannonia was A. D. 568. Adding 3 and dividing by 15 we have 1 remaining, and as the indiction began in September, 567, April of the year 568 was in the 1st indiction, and the 2d indiction began in September of that year.

It will be observed that this date is given by Paul for Alboin's

whose festival that year, according to the method of

departure from Pannonia, not for his actual entrance into Italy. Paul apparently takes this from the Origo (see Appendix II): "And Alboin, king of the Langobards, moved out of Pannonia in the month of April after Easter, in the first indiction. In the second indiction indeed (September, 568, to September, 569), they began to plunder in Italy, but in the third indiction he became master of Italy." A question has arisen whether the actual invasion of Italy occurred in 568 or 569. The edict of Rothari, of Nov., 643, states that it was published (M. G., LL., IV, p. 1) in the 76th year after the arrival of the Langobards in the province of Italy. This indicates that the invasion must have occurred before Nov., 568. But a fragment of Secundus of June, 580, speaks of the Langobards as "remaining in Italy 12 years since they entered it in the month of May in the second indiction." In these 12 years, according to a common method of computation at that time, the 12th year may not have been completed and Secundus' date for the invasion is clearly May, 569 (see M. G., Script. Rerum Lang. et Ital., p. 25, n. 3 a). Marius of Avenches says that in 569 Alboin "occupied" Italy, which Muratori thinks (Annals, A. D. 568) must have been a mistake in the copyist. The Annals of Ravenna (Agnello, a. c. 94) says that in the 2d indiction (Sept. 1, 568, to Sept. 1, 569) Venetia was invaded and occupied by the Langobards. Pope Gregory I wrote June, 595 (Indic. 13, lib. V, 21) that the Romans had been threatened by the Langobards for 27 years, and in July, 603 (Indic. 6, lib. XIII, 38), for 35 years, but in computing this time the final year is not complete, so that the probable date of the invasion would be 569 (see Roviglio, *infra*, p. 12). Cipolla (Atti del R. Istituto Veneto, x, 1889–90, series 7, t. 1, pp. 686–688) and Roviglio (Sopra Alcuni Dati Cronologici, Reggio-Emilia, 1899 contend for 569; Crivellucci (Studii Storici, I, 478–497) and Hodgkin (V, 158) for 568. The authorities are very equally divided. Secundus, a contemporary and considered reliable, would perhaps be entitled to the greatest weight, were it not that the official statement in the Edict supports the year given by Paul.

calculation, fell upon the calends (the first) of April, when five hundred and sixty-eight years had already elapsed from the incarnation of our Lord.

Chapter VIII.

Therefore, when king Alboin with his whole army and a multitude of people of all kinds [1] had come to the limits of Italy, he ascended a mountain which stands forth in those places, and from there as far as he could see, he gazed upon a portion of Italy. Therefore this mountain it is said, was called from that time on " King's Mountain." [2] They say wild oxen graze upon it, and no wonder, since at this point it touches Pannonia, which is productive of these animals. In fine, a certain very truthful old man related to me that he had seen the hide of a wild ox killed on this mountain of such size that in it fifteen men, as he said, could lie one against the other.

Chapter IX.

When Alboin without any hindrance had thence

[1] Including no doubt inhabitants of Noricum and Pannonia, Slavs from the East a strong contingent of Saxons, and many others belonging to different German races (Hartmann, II, 1, p. 19).

[2] Rudolf Virchow said at the meeting of the German Anthropological Society, Sept. 5, 1899 (see Correspondenz-blatt of that Society for 1898–99, p. 180) that he had taken a special journey to follow the course of the Langobards into Italy and was convinced that their irruption was by the road over the Predil pass, thence into the valley of the Isonzo, and that Monte Maggiore (north of Cividale) is the " King's Mountain " of Paul.

entered the territories of Venetia, which is the first
province of Italy—that is, the limits of the city or rather
of the fortress of Forum Julii (Cividale)[1]—he began
to consider to whom he should especially commit
the first of the provinces that he had taken. For
indeed all Italy (which extends toward the south, or
rather toward the southeast), is encompassed by the
waves of the Tyrrhenian and Adriatic seas, yet from
the west and north it is so shut in by the range of Alps
that there is no entrance to it except through narrow
passes and over the lofty summits of the mountains.
Yet from the eastern side by which it is joined to Pannonia it has an approach which lies open more broadly
and is quite level. When Albion therefore, as we have
said, reflected whom he ought to make duke[2] in these
places, he determined, as is related, to put over the city
of Forum Julii and over its whole district,[3] his nephew

[1] See, however, Waitz, who thinks Colonia Julia Carnia, north
of Osopus, is referred to.

[2] As to the meaning of the word "duke" at this time see note
to II, 32, *infra*.

The district or duchy of Friuli which Gisulf was to rule cannot be definitely bounded. It reached northward probably to
the Carnic Alps, eastward to the Julian Alps, and southward to a
line not far from the coast which was subject to the sea power of
the Eastern Empire. Concordia was not won from the empire
until about 615, and Opitergium in 642. To the west, Friuli was
bounded by other Langobard territory, especially by the duchy of
Ceneda from which it was separated by the Tagliamento or
Livenza (Hodg., VI, 43, 44). The Bavarians dwelt northwest of
the duchy, the Slavonians northeast, and behind them the Asiatic
Avars (Hodgkin, VI, 44). Cividale was made the capital instead

Gisulf,[1] who was his master of horse—whom they call in their own language "marpahis"[2]—a man suitable in every way. This Gisulf announced that he would not first undertake the government of this city and people unless Alboin would give him the " faras," that is, the families or stocks of the Langobards that he himself wished to choose. And this was done, and with the approval of the king he took to dwell with him the chief families of the Langobards he had desired.[3] And thus finally, he acquired the honor of a leader.[4] He asked also from the king for herds of high-bred mares, and in this also he was heeded by the liberality of his chief.

CHAPTER X.

In these days in which the Langobards invaded Italy, the kingdom of the Franks, divided into four parts upon the death of their king Chlotar, was ruled by his four sons. The first among these, Aripert (Charibert) had

of Aquileia which had been the chief city (Hodgkin, VI, 39). Friuli is the first mentioned of the four great dukedoms conspicuous by their size and power over all others during the period of the Langobards: Friuli, Trent, Spoleto, and Benevento. The two last were largely independent of the Langobard kingdom. Trent and Friuli never succeeded in achieving their independence although this was several times attempted (Hodg., VI, 23).

[1] Bethmann believes that it was Grasulf, Gisulf's father (Waitz).

[2] From *mar*, *märe* a horse and *paizan* to put on the bit, according to Grimm (Abel, Hodgkin, VI, 42; V, 161).

[3] Indeed it was by *faras* or clans that Italy in general was first occupied by the Langobards (Hartmann II, 1, 21).

[4] Read *ductor* instead of *doctor*.

the seat of his kingdom at Paris; [1] the second indeed, Gunthram held sway at the city of Aureliani (Orleans) ; the third, Hilperic (Chilperic) had his throne at Sessionae (Soissons), in the place of Chlotar, his father; the fourth, Sigisbert, ruled at the city of Mettis (Metz).[2] At this time, too, the most holy Benedict as pope governed the Roman Church.[3] Also the blessed patriarch Paul presided over the city of Aquileia and its people and, fearing the barbarity of the Langobards, fled from Aquileia to the island of Grado; [4] and he carried away with him all the treasure of his church.[5] In this year in the early winter as much snow fell in the plain as is wont to fall upon the summits of the Alps, and in the following summer there was such great fertility as no other age claims to remember. At this time too when they had learned of the death of king Chlotar, the Huns, who are also called Avars, attacked his son Sigisbert and the latter, coming up to meet them in Turingia, overcame them with great force near the river

[1] Charibert in fact had died in 567, just before the Langobards invaded Italy (Hodgkin, V, 199).

[2] See *infra*, III, 10, note. The name is there spelled Sigispert.

[3] This is erroneous. It was John III who was pope from 560 to 573 (Jacobi, 48). Benedict was pope 573-578. Paul was led into this error by a statement in the Liber Pontificalis from which he took the account, that at the time of Benedict, the Langobards invaded all Italy (Ed L. Duchesne, I, 308; Atti del Congresso in Cividale, 1899, p. 118, note.)

[4] An island near Aquileia and close to the mainland but inaccessible to the Langobards who had no boats.

[5] It was Paulinus, not Paul who thus fled to Grado (Waitz).

Albis (Elbe) and gave peace to them when they sought it. Brunicheldis,[1] coming from Spain, is joined in marriage to this Sigisbert, and from her he had a son by name Childepert. The Avars, fighting again with Sigisbert in the same places as before, crushed the army of the Franks and obtained the victory.

CHAPTER XI.

Narses indeed returned from Campania to Rome and there not long afterwards, departed from this life,[2] and his body, placed in a leaden casket, was carried with all his riches to Constantinople.

CHAPTER XII.

When Alboin then came to the river Plavis (Piave), Felix the bishop of the church of Tarvisium (Treviso) came forth there to meet him, and the king, since he was very generous,[3] granted to him at his request all the property of his church and confirmed the things asked for by a solemn document.[4]

CHAPTER XIII.

Because indeed, we have made mention of this Felix, we may also relate a few things concerning the vener-

---

[1] Or Brunichildis, Brunihilde, as Paul variously spells it.

[2] About 573 or perhaps a year or two earlier (Hodg., V, 65).

[3] His generosity is also extolled in the song of Widsith (Hodgkin, V, 176).

[4] This has been questioned since the Langobards were then ignorant of writing, but it is not impossible (Waitz).

able and very wise man Fortunatus, who had declared
that this Felix was his colleague. In short, this Fortunatus of whom we speak was born in a place which is
called Duplabilis, which place lies not far from the
fortress of Ceneta (Ceneda) and the city of Tarvisium
(Treviso). He was, however, brought up and instructed
at Ravenna and became very distinguished in the grammatical, the rhetorical and also the metrical art. And
since he suffered a very grievous disease of the eyes,
and this Felix also, his colleague, in like manner suffered in his eyes, they both proceeded to the church of
the blessed Paul and John, which is situated within that
city, and in which an altar, built in honor of St. Martin
the Confessor, has a window near by in which a lamp
was set to give light. With the oil of this, these men,
that is, Fortunatus and Felix, presently touched their
suffering eyes. Instantly the disease was driven away,
and they obtained the health they longed for. For this
reason Fortunatus adored the blessed Martin so much
that he abandoned his country a little before the Langobards invaded Italy, and set out for the sepulchre of
that blessed man at Turones (Tours), and he relates that
his way of proceeding thither, as he tells it himself in
his songs, was by the streams of Tiliamentum (Tagliamento) and Reuna (Ragogna), and by Osupus
(Osopo) and the Julian Alps,[1] and by the fortress of
Aguntum (Innichen) and the rivers Drave and Byrrus
(Rienz), and by Briones (the Brenner), and the city of

[1] This part of the range is to-day called the Carnic Alps (Studii
Storici, 1899, p. 405).

Augusta (Augsburg), which the Virdo (Wertach) and
Lecha (Lech) water.   And after he had come to Turones (Tours), according to his own vow, passing on
through Pictavi (Poitiers), he dwelt there and wrote at
that place of the doings of many saints, part in prose
and part in metrical fashion, and lastly in the same city
he was ordained, first as a presbyter and then as a
bishop, and in the same place he reposes buried with
befitting honor.   Here he wrote the life of St. Martin
in four books in heroic meter, and he composed many
other things, most of all hymns for particular festivals
and especially little verses to particular friends, being
second to none of the poets in soft and fluent speech.
At his grave, when I came thither for the purpose of
prayer,[1] upon the request of Aper the abbot of that
place I composed this epitaph to be inscribed there:

Here in this soil Fortunatus lies buried, the first among prophets,
    Born in Ausonian land, worthy of honor in deed,
Famous in talent, quick to perceive and in speech ever gentle.
    Many an eloquent page sings his melodious lay.
Fresh from his holy lips, to show us the way to salvation,
    Deeds of the saints we learn—fathers of primitive times.
Happy art thou, O land of Gaul, with such jewels emblazoned,
    Whose resplendent fire scatters the shadows of night !
Verses of commonplace song, in thy honor, O saint, have I written,
    Lest thy fame lie hid, lost in the depths of the crowd.
Render I pray a return, and ask through thy infinite merits
    That the Eternal Judge mercy show also to me.

In a few words we have touched upon these things

---

[1] Between the years 782–786 (Waitz).

concerning so great a man, that his fellow citizens might not be wholly ignorant of his life; now let us return to the thread of our history.

Chapter XIV.

Then Alboin took Vincentia (Vicenza) and Verona and the remaining cities of Venetia, except Patavium (Padua), Mons Silicis (Monselice) and Mantua.[1] For Venetia is composed not only of the few islands which we now call Venice, but its boundary stretches from the borders of Pannonia to the river Addua (Adda). This is proved in the books of annals in which Pergamus (Bergamo) is said to be a city of Venetia and in histories we thus read of lake Benacus (Lago di Garda): " Benacus, a lake of Venetia from which the river Mincius (Mincio) flows." The Eneti, indeed (though a letter is added among the Latins), are called in Greek the " praiseworthy." Histria is also joined to Venetia and both are considered one province. Histria is named from the river Hister which, according to Roman history, is said to have been broader than it is now. The city of Aquileia was the capital of this Venetia, in place of which is now Forum Julii (Cividale), so called because Julius Caesar had established there a market for business.

Chapter XV.

I do not think we are wandering from the subject if

[1] Paui is probably in error in saying that Mantua was not taken by Alboin. It was indeed later taken by Agilulf, but this was after it had been recaptured by the Greeks during the reign of Authari (Pabst, p. 409, note).

we also touch briefly upon other provinces of Italy.[1]
The second province is called Liguria from gathering,
that is, collecting leguminous plants with which it is well
supplied.   In this are Mediolanum (Milan) and Ticinum,
which is called by another name, Papia (Pavia).   It extends to the boundaries of the Gauls.   Between it and
Suavia (Suabia), that is, the country of the Alamanni,
which is situated toward the north, two provinces,
namely, the first Retia (Rhaetia) and the second Retia
are placed among the Alps in which, strictly speaking,
the Reti (Rhaetians) are known to dwell.

CHAPTER XVI.

The Cottian Alps are called the fifth province, which
were thus named from king Cottius, who lived at the
time of Nero.   This (province) extends from Liguria
toward the southeast[2] to the Tyrrhenian sea; on the
west indeed it is joined to the territories of the Gauls.
In it are contained the cities of Aquis[3] (Acqui) where
there are hot springs, Dertona (Tortona), the monastery of Bobium (Bobbio), Genua (Genoa), and Saona
(Savona).   The sixth province is Tuscia (Tuscany)
which is thus called from " tus " (frankincense) which
its people were wont to burn superstitiously in the sacri-
fices to their gods.   This includes Aurelia toward the
northwest and Umbria on the eastern side.   In this
province Rome was situated, which was formerly the

[1] A full account of these provinces is found near the end of
Appendix II.

[2] Read *eurum* in place of *eorum*.

[3] Or Aquae Statiellae.

capital of the whole world. In Umbria indeed, which is counted a portion of it, are Perusium (Perugia) and lake Clitorius (Lago di Bolsena) and Spoletium (Spoleto), and it is called Umbria because it remained above the furious rains (imbres) when long ago a watery scourge devastated the nations.

CHAPTER XVII.

Campania, the seventh province, stretches from the city of Rome to the Siler (Sele), a river of Lucania. In it the very rich cities of Capua, Neapolis (Naples) and Salernus (Salerno) are situated. It is called Campania on account of the very fertile plain (campus) of Capua, but it is for the most part mountainous. Next the eighth province, Lucania, which received its name from a certain grove (lucus), begins at the river Siler and extends with Brittia (Bruttium [1]), which was thus called from the name of its former queen, along the coast of the Tyrrhenian sea like the two last named provinces, as far as the Sicilian strait, and it embraces the right horn of Italy. In it are placed the cities of Pestus (Paestum), Lainus (Lao), Cassianum (Cassano), Consentia (Cosenza), and Regium (Reggio).

CHAPTER XVIII.

Then the ninth province is reckoned in the Apennine Alps [2] which take their origin from the place where

[1] Now Calabria.

[2] This province described by Paul is wholly imaginary. The others are substantially accurate. See Appendix II near the end.

the Cottian Alps terminate. These Apennine Alps, stretching through the middle of Italy, separate Tuscia (Tuscany) from Emilia and Umbria from Flamminia. Here are the cities of Ferronianus (Frignano) and Montembellium (Monteveglio), Bobium (Bobbio) and Urbinum (Urbino), and also the town which is called Verona.[1] The Apennine Alps were named from the Carthaginians (Poeni)—that is, from Hannibal and his army who had a passage through them when marching upon Rome.[2] There are some who say that the Cottian and Apennine Alps are one province, but the history of Victor[3] which called the Cottian Alps a province by itself refutes them. The tenth province Emilia, beginning from Liguria extends towards Ravenna between the Apennine Alps and the waters of the Padus (Po). It is adorned with wealthy cities, to wit, Placentia (Piacenza), Parma, Regium (Reggio),[4] Bononia (Bologna), and the Forum of Cornelius, the fortress of which is called Imolas (Imola). There were also some who called Emilia and Valeria and Nursia one province, but the opinion of these cannot stand because Tuscia and Umbria are situated between Emilia and Valeria and Nursia.

[1] Paul elsewhere shows that Frignano and Monteveglio were actually in Æmilia, Bobbio in the Cottian Alps and Verona in Venetia (Mommsen, 87).

[2] It will be observed that most of Paul's derivations, though taken from earlier authorities, are highly fanciful.

[3] Life of Nero by Sextus Aurelius Victor.

[4] This was the ancient Regium Lepidi now Reggio d'Emilia, to distinguish it from Reggio in Calabria.

Chapter XIX.

The eleventh of the provinces is Flamminia, which
lies between the Apennine Alps and the Adriatic
sea. In it are situated Ravenna, the most noble of
cities, and five other towns which are called by a Greek
name, the Pentapolis.[1] Now it is agreed that Aurelia,
Emilia and Flamminia are called by these names from
the paved roads which come from the city of Rome and
from the names of those by whom they were paved.
After Flamminia comes the twelfth province, Picenus,
having upon the south the Apennine mountains and on
the other side the Adriatic sea. It extends to the river
Piscaria.[2] In it are the cities of Firmus (Fermo), Asculus (Ascoli), Pinnis (Penne), and Hadria, already
fallen to ruin with old age, which has given its name to
the Adriatic sea. When the inhabitants of this district
hastened thither from the Sabines, a griffin (picus) sat
upon their banner and from this cause it took the name
Picenus.

Chapter XX.

Valeria, the thirteenth province, to which Nursia is
attached, is situated between Umbria and Campania and
Picenus, and it touches on the east the region of the
Samnites. Its western part, which takes its beginning
from the city of Rome, was formerly called Etruria
from the Etruscan people. It contains the cities of

[1] The five cities are Rimini, Ancona, Fano, Pesaro and Sinigaglia.

[2] Mommsen (92) considers that this boundary is incorrect.

Tibur (Tivoli), Carsioli and Reate (Rieti), Furcona
(Aquila), Amiternum (San Vettorino) and the region
of the Marsians and their lake which is called Fucinus
(Celano). I think that the territory of the Marsians
should be reckoned within the province of Valeria,
because it is not at all described by the ancients in the
catalogue of the provinces of Italy, but if any one
may prove by correct reasoning that this is a province by itself, his sensible opinion by all means should
be accepted. The fourteenth province, Samnium, beginning from the Piscaria, lies between Campania, the
Adriatic Sea and Apulia. In it are the cities of Theate
(Chieti), Aufidena, Hisernia and Samnium, fallen to
ruin by old age, from which the whole province is
named, and that most wealthy Beneventum (Benevento)
the capital of these provinces. Furthermore, the Samnites received their name formerly from the spears
which they were wont to carry and which the Greeks
called " saynia." [1]

Chapter XXI.

The fifteenth of the provinces is Apulia, and united
with it is Calabria.[2] In it is the Salentine territory.
This has Samnium and Lucania on the west and south-
west, but on the east it is bounded by the Adriatic Sea.
It contains the tolerably rich cities of Luceria (Lucera),
Sepontum (Siponto), Canusium (Canosa), Agerentia

[1] Σάννια, more properly a javelin.

[2] Not the present Calabria but the southeastern extremity of the
Adriatic shore of Italy.

(Acerenza?), Brundisium (Brindisi), Tarentum (Taranto) and in the left horn of Italy which extends fifty miles, Ydrontum (Otranto), well adapted to commerce.[1] Apulia is named from " destruction,"[2] for more quickly there (than elsewhere) does the herbage of the land perish in the heat of the sun.

CHAPTER XXII.

The island of Sicily is reckoned the sixteenth province. This is washed by the Tyrrhenian sea and by the Ionian, and is so called from the proper name of the leader Siculus. Corsica is put down as the seventeenth, Sardinia as the eighteenth province. Both of these are girt by the waves of the Tyrrhenian sea. Corsica is named from the leader Corsus; Sardinia from Sardis (Serdis?) the son of Hercules.

CHAPTER XXIII.

It is certain, moreover,[3] that the old writers of history called Liguria and part of Venetia, as well as Emilia and Flamminia, Cisalpine Gaul. Hence it is that Donatus, the grammarian, in his explanation of Virgil, says that Mantua is in Gaul. Hence it is that we read in Roman history that Ariminum (Rimini) is situated in Gaul. Indeed, in the most ancient period, Brennus, king of the Gauls, who reigned at the city of Senonae

[1] *Mercimoniis.* See DuCange.

[2] ᾿Απώλεια from ἀπόλλυμι to destroy.

[3] *Tamen*—but here used in a copulative and not an adversative sense. See Crivellucci Studii Storici, 1899, p. 259.

(Sens), came with 300,000 Senonian Gauls to Italy and occupied it as far as Senogallia (Sinigaglia), which is named from the Senonian Gauls. And the reason why the Gauls came to Italy is represented to have been this: When they tasted the wine brought from that country, they were enticed by greed for this wine and passed over into Italy. While a hundred thousand of these were hastening along not far from the island of Delphi, they were killed by the swords of the Greeks. Another hundred thousand, having entered Galatia,[1] were first called Gallogreci, but afterwards Galatians, and these are those to whom Paul, the teacher of the heathen, wrote his epistle. Also a hundred thousand of the Gauls who remained in Italy built Ticinum (Pavia), Mediolanum (Milan), Pergamus (Bergamo) and Brixia (Brescia), and gave to the region the name of Cisalpine Gaul, and they are the Senonian Gauls who formerly invaded the city of Romulus. For as we call what is beyond the Alps, Transalpine Gaul, so we name what is within the Alps on this side, Cisalpine Gaul.

Chapter XXIV.

Italy then, which contains these provinces received its name from Italus, the leader of the Siculi, who took possession of it in ancient times. Or it is denominated Italy on this account, because large oxen, that is, "itali," are found in it; and the name comes from this, that by abbreviation "vitulus" (a calf) is "italus," one letter being added and another changed. Italy is also called

---

[1] In Asia Minor.

Ausonia from Ausonus, son of Ulysses. Originally indeed, the region of Beneventum was called by this name but afterwards all Italy began to be called so. Italy is also called Latium on this account, because Saturn fleeing from Jupiter his son found a hiding place (latebra) within it. Since enough then has been said concerning the provinces and name of Italy, the events within which we are narrating, let us now return to the regular order of our history.

CHAPTER XXV.

Alboin then, came into Liguria at the beginning of the third indiction [1] on the third day before the nones [2] of September, and entered Mediolanum during the times of the archbishop Honoratus. Then he took all the cities of Liguria except those which were situated upon the shores of the sea. The archbishop Honoratus indeed, deserting Mediolanum, fled to the city of Genoa. The patriarch Paul [3] too, after administering his priestly office for twelve years, departed from this life and left the church to be managed by Probinus.

[1] A. D. 569, see Bk. II, ch. VII, note.

[2] The nones was the 9th day before the ides, both days being included, and the ides fell upon the 15th of March, May, July and October and upon the 13th of the remaining months. The nones therefore fell upon the 7th of March, May, July and October and upon the 5th of other months. The 3rd day before the nones of September, reckoned backward from the 5th and including both days, would therefore be the 3rd of September, and this is the day given by Muratori in his Annals, Vol. 3, p. 479.

[3] Of Aquileia.

Chapter XXVI.

The city of Ticinum (Pavia) at this time held out
bravely, withstanding a siege more than three years,
while the army of the Langobards remained close at
hand on the western side.   Meanwhile Alboin, after
driving out the soldiers, took possession of everything as far as Tuscany except Rome and Ravenna and
some other fortified places which were situated on the
shore of the sea.   The Romans had then no courage to
resist because the pestilence which occurred at the time
of Narses had destroyed very many in Liguria and
Venetia, and after the year of plenty of which we spoke,
a great famine attacked and devastated all Italy.   It is
certain that Alboin then brought with him to Italy many
men from various peoples which either other kings or
he himself had taken.   Whence, even until to-day, we
call the villages in which they dwell Gepidan, Bulgar-
ian, Sarmatian, Pannonian, Suabian, Norican, or by
other names of this kind.

Chapter XXVII.

The city of Ticinum indeed, after enduring the
siege for three years and some months, at length surrendered to Alboin and to the Langobards besieging it.
When Alboin entered it through the so-called gate of
St. John from the eastern side of the city, his horse fell
in the middle of the gateway, and could not be gotten
up, although urged by kicks and afterwards struck by
the blows of spears.   Then one of those Langobards
thus spoke to the king, saying: " Remember sir king,
what vow you have plighted.   Break so grievous a vow

and you will enter the city, for truly there is a Christian people in this city." Alboin had vowed indeed that he would put all the people to the sword because they had been unwilling to surrender. After he broke this vow and promised mercy to the citizens, his horse straightway rose and he entered the city and remained steadfast in his promise, inflicting injury upon no one. Then all the people, gathering around him in the palace which king Theoderic had formerly built, began to feel relieved in mind, and after so many miseries were already confident in hope for the future.

CHAPTER XXVIII.

After this king had ruled in Italy three years and six months, he was slain by the treachery of his wife,[1] and the cause of his murder was this: While he sat in merriment at a banquet at Verona longer than was proper, with the cup which he had made of the head of his father-in-law, king Cunimund, he ordered it to be given to the queen to drink wine, and he invited her to drink merrily with her father. Lest this should seem impossible to any one, I speak the truth in Christ. I saw king Ratchis holding this cup in his hand on a certain festal day to show it to his guests. Then Rosemund, when she heard the thing, conceived in her heart deep anguish she could not restrain, and straightway she burned to revenge the death of her father by the

[1] Probably May 25th or June 28th, A. D. 572, or possibly 573 (Hodg., V, 168, 181; Roviglio, Sopra Alcuni Dati Cronologici di Storia Langobardica. Reggio-Emilia, 1899, pp. 21 to 27).

murder of her husband, and presently she formed a plan
with Helmechis who was the king's squire (scilpor)—
that is, his armor-bearer—and his foster brother, to kill
the king, and he persuaded the queen that she ought to
admit to this plot Peredeo, who was a very strong man.
As Peredeo would not give his consent to the queen
when she advised so great a crime, she put herself at
night in the bed of her dressing-maid with whom
Peredeo was accustomed to have intercourse, and then
Peredeo, coming in ignorance, lay with the queen. And
when the wicked act was already accomplished and she
asked him whom he thought her to be, and he named
the name of his mistress that he thought she was, the
queen added : " It is in no way as you think, but I am
Rosemund," she says, " and surely now you have perpe-
trated such a deed, Peredeo, that either you must kill Alboin or he will slay you with his sword." Then he learned
the evil thing he had done, and he who had been unwilling of his own accord, assented, when forced in such
a way, to the murder of the king.   Then Rosemund,
while Alboin had given himself up to a noon-day sleep,
ordered that there should be a great silence in the
palace, and taking away all other arms, she bound his
sword tightly to the head of the bed so it could not be
taken away or unsheathed, and according to the advice
of Peredeo, she, more cruel than any beast, let in Helmechis the murderer.[1]   Alboin suddenly aroused from

[1] This reading of Paul seems to reverse the parts, making Peredeo the adviser and Helmechis the actual murderer, and seems to
indicate that Paul has misunderstood his authorities or confused
them.   The names are transposed in some of the manuscripts to

sleep perceived the evil which threatened and reached
his hand quickly for his sword, which, being tightly
tied, he could not draw, yet he seized a foot-stool and
defended himself with it for some time. But unfortun-
ately alas! this most warlike and very brave man being
helpless against his enemy, was slain as if he were one
of no account, and he who was most famous in war
through the overthrow of so many enemies, perished
by the scheme of one little woman. His body was
buried with the great grief and lamentations of the
Langobards under the steps of a certain flight of stairs
which was next to the palace. He was tall in stature
and well fitted in his whole body for waging wars. In
our own days Giselpert, who had been duke of Verona,
opened his grave and took away his sword and any
other of his ornaments found there. And for this
reason he boasted with his accustomed vanity among
ignorant men that he had seen Alboin.[1]

bring the sentence into harmony with what precedes. Agnellus
ignores Peredeo altogether and assigns the whole responsibility for
the murder to Helmechis, instigated by Rosemund (Hodgkin, V,
170). But after deducting what is undoubtedly legendary we have
statements from contemporary sources essentially harmonious.
The Annals of Ravenna (Exc. Sang. Agnell., ch. 96) says, "Alboin was killed by his followers in his palace by command of his
wife Rosemund." John Biclaro: "Alboin is killed at night at
Verona by his followers by the doing of his wife." Marius: "Alboin was killed by his followers, that is by Hilmaegis with the rest,
his wife agreeing to it." The Copenhagen Continuer of Prosper:
"Alboin was killed at Verona by the treachery of his wife Rosemund, the daughter of king Conimund, Elmigisilus aiding her"
(Schmidt, p. 72).

[1] Hodgkin (V, 175) notices a reference to Alboin in the so-called

Chapter XXIX.

Helmechis then, upon the death of Alboin, attempted to usurp his kingdom, but he could not at all do this, because the Langobards, grieving greatly for the king's death, strove to make way with him.   And straightway Rosemund sent word to Longinus, prefect of Ravenna, that he should quickly send a ship[1] to fetch them. Longinus, delighted by such a message, speedily sent a ship in which Helmechis with Rosemund his wife embarked, fleeing at night.   They took with them Albsuinda, the daughter of the king, and all the treasure of the Langobards, and came swiftly to Ravenna.[2]   Then

Traveler's song or Widsith which was composed probably about the middle of the sixth century.   Lines 139 to 147 say, "So was I in Eatule with Ealfwin, son of Eadwin, who of all mankind had to my thinking the lightest hand to win love, the most generous heart in the distribution of rings and bright bracelets."   It seems probable that Eatule means Italy ; Ealfwin, Alboin ; Eadwin, Audoin.

[1] Probably to some point on the Po not far from Verona (Hodg., V, 172, note 1).

[2] As to Rosemund's flight to Longinus, the Ravenna Annals (Agnello, ch. 96) show that Rosemund with a multitude of Gepidae and Langobards came to Ravenna in the month of August with all the royal treasure and was honorably received by Longinus the prefect.   Marius says that Helmegis, with his wife and all the treasure and a part of the army, surrendered to the republic at Ravenna.   John Biclaro says: that Alboin's treasure with the queen came into the power of the republic and the Langobards remained without king and treasure.   The Copenhagen Continuer of Prosper (p. 34) says she attempted to unite Helmigis to herself in marriage and in the kingdom, but when she perceived that her treacherous usurpation displeased the Langobards, she fled with the royal treasure and her husband to Ravenna (Schmidt, 73).

the prefect Longinus began to urge Rosemund to kill
Helmechis and to join him in wedlock. As she was
ready for every kind of wickedness and as she desired to become mistress of the people of Ravenna, she
gave her consent to the accomplishment of this great
crime, and while Helmechis was bathing himself, she
offered him, as he came out of the bath, a cup of poison
which she said was for his health. But when he felt
that he had drunk the cup of death, he compelled Rosemund, having drawn his sword upon her, to drink what
was left, and thus these most wicked murderers perished
at one moment by the judgment of God Almighty.

Chapter XXX.

When they had thus been killed, the prefect Longinus sent Albsuinda with the treasures of the Langobards
to Constantinople to the emperor. Some affirm that
Peredeo also came to Ravenna in like manner with
Helmechis and Rosemund, and was thence sent with
Albsuinda to Constantinople, and there in a public show
before the emperor killed a lion of astonishing size and,
as they say, by command of the emperor, his eyes were
torn out lest he should attempt anything in the imperial
city because he was a strong man. After some time he
prepared for himself two small knives, hid one in each
of his sleeves, went to the palace and promised to say
something serviceable to the emperor if he were admit-
ted to him. The emperor sent him two patricians,
familiars of the palace, to receive his words. When
they came to Peredeo, he approached them quite
closely as if about to tell them something unusually

secret, and he wounded both of them severely with the weapons he held concealed in each hand so that immediately they fell to the ground and expired. And thus in no way unlike the mighty Sampson, he avenged his injuries, and for the loss of his two eyes he killed two men most useful to the emperor.

CHAPTER XXXI.

All the Langobards in Italy by common consent installed as their king in the city of Ticinum, Cleph, a very noble man among them.[1] Of many powerful men of the Romans some he destroyed by the sword and others he drove from Italy. When he had held the sovereignty with Masane, his wife one year and six months, he was slain with the sword by a servant of his train.[2]

CHAPTER XXXII.

After his death the Langobards had no king for ten years[3] but were under dukes,[4] and each one of the

[1] "Of the race of Beleo" says the Origo. Marius of Avenches (Chron., 573, Roncalli, p. 413, see Pabst, 415, note 5) says he had been one of the dukes.

[2] The precise dates are uncertain. Marius of Avenches says he was elected in the sixth indiction and slain in the seventh, hence both events took place between Sept. 1st, 572, and Sept. 1st, 574 (Roviglio, Sopra Alcuni Dati Cronologici, p. 28).

[3] The Origo Gentis Langobardorum, the Chronicon Gothanum, Fredegarius and the Copenhagen Continuer of Prosper all give twelve years as the period of this interregnum. A computation of the preceding and subsequent reigns appears to sustain Paul's statement (Roviglio, id., pp. 29-31) which, however, is not free from doubt.

[4] *Duces.* It is not certain what was the Langobard name for

dukes held possession of his own city, Zaban of Ticinum (Pavia), Wallari of Bergamus (Bergamo), Alichis of Brexia (Brescia), Euin of Tridentum (Trent),[1] Gisulf of Forum Julii (Cividale).[2]   But there were thirty other dukes besides these in their own cities.[3]   In these

these rulers. Some suggest (Hodgkin, V, 183, 184) *Heretoga* (the present German *Herzog*).   The prefix and suffix *ari* which occurs frequently in Langobard names (e. g., Aripert, Arioald, Rothari) may have some connection with this dignity.   The Latin word *dux* was appropriately applied, as it meant both a leader in the field and a commander of frontier troops and of a frontier district (Hartmann, II, 1, 40).   Schmidt (p. 78) insists that the division of Italy into dukedoms was nothing else than the ancient Langobard division of their territory into cantons, only these were now connected with the former city territories of the Romans.

[1] Duke Euin (569–595) followed by Gaidoald in the latter year, and Alahis about 680 and 690, are the only three dukes of Trent mentioned in Paul's history (Hodg., VI, 23).   The duchy of Trent probably ascended by the Central Valley of the Adige as far northward as the *Mansio* of Euna, the modern town of Neumarkt, and southward to a point near the present Austro-Italian frontier where the mountains begin to slope down to the Lombard plain (Hodg., VI, 26).

[2] The dukes of Friuli were Gisulf (living in 575), Grasulf II, Taso, Cacco, Ago, Lupus (about 662), Wechtari (between 662 and 671), Landari, Rodoald, Ansfrit (between 688 and 700), Ferdulf, Corvulus, Pemmo, Anselm, Peter and Ratgaud or Hrodgaud (775 to 776) (Hodg., VI, 36).

[3] Pabst (437) gives the list of probable cities referred to:

Friuli	Parma	Cremona
Ceneda	Piacenza	Como
Treviso	Modena	Lodi
Vicenza	Brescello	Vercelli
Verona	Asti	Tortona

days many of the noble Romans were killed from

Trent	Ivrea	Alba Pompeia
Brescia	Turin	Acqui
Bergamo	Mantua	Lucca
Novara	Altino	Chiusi
Milan	Mariana	Perugia
Pavia	Feltre	Benevento
Reggio	Belluno	Spoleto (see p. 439).

This makes thirty-six cities instead of the thirty-five, and probably Pabst included one or more not yet occupied by the Langobards (Hodgkin, V, 188). Pabst also gives a very complete account of this office of duke. At first it was not hereditary (p. 414–
415) but was held for life (p. 432). Dukes were not selected on
account of their noble birth (though nobles were frequently found
among them), but on account of their military and administrative
ability. The duke was not chosen by the people but appointed
by the king (p. 414). During the interregnum of ten years when
the dukes governed different portions of the country, there
was a great increase of the ducal power. It became evident,
however, that the government could not continue thus sub-divided.
The kingly power was restored but in the meantime some of the
dukedoms, particularly Benevento and Spoleto, and in a measure
Friuli had become so powerful that they were never again wholly
subjected to the king. The succession in Benevento and Spoleto
became hereditary, and even in Friuli the rights of the ruling
family were respected (Paul, IV, 39; Pabst, 432). The duke's
jurisdiction extended, not simply over a particular city, but over
the adjoining district or province (pp. 434–435). In determining
the limits of this district the ancient boundaries were generally
observed (435). The first definite statement of the powers of the
duke is found in the laws of Rothari about the middle of the 7th
century. He had supreme military, judicial and police jurisdiction in his district (439, 440). His control of the financial administration was not so complete (440). At his side, at least in the
northern dukedoms, stood the counts and *gastaldi* who were the
immediate representatives of the king. The counts are named

love of gain, and the remainder were divided among

next after the dukes (441), though their jurisdiction nowhere (442) appears, and Pabst considers that the name is a mere honorary title for a particular *gastaldus* (or *gastaldius*). This latter word is derived, in his opinion, from the Gothic *gastaldan*, to possess, acquire. A better derivation would seem to be from *gast* and *aldius*, the "guest of the half-free" who settled as a lord on the property of the conquered Italians, and compelled them to serve him and give him a portion of the proceeds of their lands. The *gastaldi* would then be the lords or administrators of these Italian domains (Bruckner, 205). When the dukes re-established the kingly power (P. III, 16) they gave up one-half of their fortunes for royal uses. Paul tells us that at this time the oppressed people were parcelled out among their Langobard guests, and it is probable that the *gastaldi* (whose name would appear to refer to such apportionment) were first appointed at that time. In each *civitas* or city with its adjacent territory there appears to have been a *gastaldus* whose duty it was to look after the royal interests, and especially, the royal domains (p. 443). He received the king's share of inheritances when heirs were lacking and gradually came into possession of most of the financial administration (444). Dukes, counts, and *gastaldi*, are all designated by the common name of "judges" (447–448), and certain police authority is also given them—for example, to remove lepers (449), to arrest fugitives, etc. A peculiar provision of Rothari's Edict (23) is, that if a duke shall unjustly injure his soldier the *gastaldus* shall aid the latter and (24), if the *gastaldus* shall unjustly injure his soldier, the duke shall protect the injured man (443, note 3). Quite different is the position of the *gastaldi* of Benevento and Spoleto where the dukes were practically sovereign (470). We see at the courts of these dukes the same officials as at the royal court, the *cubicularius* or chamberlain, the *stolesaz*, or treasurer, etc. (472).

We find many royal expedients to limit the ducal power. Territory reconquered from the Greek empire or from rebellious dukes became the property of the sovereign (463), and *gastaldi*

their " guests " and made tributaries, that they should pay

rather than dukes were appointed to administer it.   When Liutprand endeavored to strengthen the royal power, he took advantage in Friuli of a contest between Bishop Calixtus and Duke
Pemmo and deprived Pemmo of the dukedom, but appointed
Pemmo's eldest son Ratchis in his place (see P., VI, 51).   Liutprand also deposed and appointed dukes for Spoleto and Benevento, and set aside for a time the hereditary succession, but he
did not permanently reduce these duchies to subjection.

In the other parts of the kingdom, immediately subject to him,
however (which were called Austria, Neustria and Tuscia), he appointed *gastaldi* in the cities where there had been dukes, and
greatly strengthened his own power by increasing the powers and
responsibilities of the *gastaldi*.   In his edicts he does not use the
word "duke" at all, but continually uses the word "judge" in
place of it, which latter term includes both dukes and *gastaldi*, and
the two are now no longer found side by side in a single jurisdiction.   Pabst (482–483) has given a list of the cities which, under
Liutprand, were ruled by dukes and of those which were ruled
by *gastaldi*.   The list is incomplete, and perhaps in part incorrect, yet it shows in a general way the extent of the separation of
the two offices.

There were also subordinate officials.   Among these were the
actores, who were the king's agents in administering particular
royal domains, and under the judges the *sculdahis*, or local magistrates, and the *centenarii* and *locopositi*, probably of similar
grade (500, see Hartmann, II, 2, 39).   In an ordinary judicial proceeding the complainant betook him in the first place to
the *sculdahis*, the local civil magistrate.   If the case were so important that the *sculdahis* could not decide it, he had to send the
parties to the judge (i. e., the duke or *gastaldus*) (Pabst, 485), but
if it were beyond the jurisdiction of the latter, the parties had to appear in the king's court.   If the judge could not act personally he
could appoint a deputy (*missus*) to act for him in individual cases.
The party defeated in a legal proceeding had the right to complain
to a higher jurisdiction of the decision or the conduct of the magis-

the third part of their products to the Langobards.[1] By

trate who decided against him (Hartmann, II, 2, 41), and if it were found that the judge had failed in his duties he was punished (at least until the time of king Ratchis), not by dismissal, but by a fine (Pabst, 487). In their powers, duties and responsibilities dukes and *gastaldi* at last appear to be quite alike, and while a larger domain generally appears annexed to the office of duke, the *gastaldi* usually have the administration of the royal estates (489). Possibly the king could change the *gastaldi* more quickly than the dukes whose term of office lasted for life, but this appears to be the only point in which the duke had the advantage. These arrangements suffered little change during the latter days of the kingdom.

[1] There is much controversy as to the meaning of this sentence, Does the "remainder" who were divided, refer to all the Romans, or merely to the nobles who were not killed? Hodgkin (VI, 581) believes it refers to the rest of the Roman inhabitants. Villari (Le Invasioni Barbariche, II, 32) insists that it refers grammatically to the nobles only, and asks how it would have been possible to render tributary all the Romans, thus obliging those who possessed nothing to pay one-third of the fruits of the earth? It would seem that it must be limited at least to the Roman landed proprietors who might well at this time have been roughly designated as nobles in this connection.

The word "guest" (*hospes*) expressed a relation that could exist only between the Langobard and the Roman proprietor. That of "patron" existed toward the peasants and cultivators of the lands (Villari, pp. 272, 273). The relation of "guests" also existed elsewhere between Burgundians and conquered Romans. The Roman whose land was assigned to a Burgundian was called *hospes* and *vice versa*. The land thus assigned was called *sors*, and the right to it *hospitalitas* (Savigny, Geschichte des Römischen Rechts im Mittelalter, I, p. 298).

The whole free Roman population was treated by the Langobards quite differently from the manner in which they had been treated by Theodoric and the Ostrogoths, who simply took one-

these dukes of the Langobards in the seventh year from

third of their land and left them as independent as before. The Langobards took one-third, not of the land, but of its products, and there is much dispute as to the status in which they held the Roman population. Although Villari (Le Invasioni Barbariche, pp. 265, 266, 271–272) and others deny that this population was reduced to slavery, the better opinion seems to be that during the wars of conquest and the earlier period of Langobard domination, the Romans were regarded as conquered enemies destitute of all rights (Hartmann, II, 2, 2 ; see, also, Hegel, Städteverfassung von Italien, ch. III, p. 355, and authorities there cited,) and that they very generally became *aldii* or serfs of the Lango-bards just as other subject-peoples had been during the previous wanderings of that nation. *Aldius* first meant ''man,'' then ''common man,'' then the ''half free '' man, bound to the soil (Hartmann, II, 1, 8). Rothari's Edict, though it scarcely mentions the Romans as such, contains many enact-ments concerning the *aldius*, who apparently did not differ greatly from the Roman *colonus* who cultivated the ground for his master and could not change his condition or his home, but could not have his rent raised arbitrarily, nor be sold as a slave apart from the land. We are not expressly told in the Edict that the Romans were *aldii* but this seems implied. The fine for kill-ing or crippling an *aldius* was payable to his master, probably to indemnify him for the loss of a valuable farm laborer. The con-dition of the workmen in the cities however is more doubtful and also the condition of the Romans of the higher class, if any, who survived (Hodgkin, VI, 586–592).

The third exacted by the Langobards may have been one-third of the *gross product* of the land, which would be more than half the net product and would leave a slender margin for the cultivator and his family (Hodgkin, VI, 582). This was the view originally taken by Savigny (Geschichte des Römischen Rechts, I, ch. V, p. 400), but he afterwards changed his opinion and considered that the tribute was one-third of the net produce of the land (see Hegel, Städteverfassung von Italien, I, ch. 3, p. 356, note).

the coming of Alboin [1] and of his whole people, the
churches were despoiled, the priests killed, the cities
overthrown, the people who had grown up like crops
annihilated, and besides those regions which Alboin had
taken, the greater part of Italy was seized and subjugated by the Langobards.

The Langobards were thus exempted from agricultural labor and
as absentee landlords, could live in the cities or at the court on
the tribute thus paid by their "hosts." This idleness on the one
side and servitude upon the other exercised a demoralizing influence, and the Langobard system was much more injurious than
the actual division of land under Theodoric and Odoacar where
the substantial liberty of the Romans might still be preserved.

Hartmann (II, 1, 41, 42) believes that the payment of one-
third the produce of the land was a mere temporary arrangement
while Alboin and the Langobards were acquiring possession of the
country, and that afterwards, when they were permanently settled
in the country, the Langobards took the places of the former proprietors and received all the profits of their estates. There seems
no good reason to think, however, that such complete expropria-
tion was universal.

[1] Paul scarcely means that all this occurred in the seventh year
alone but during the seven years of Langobard occupation. This
was the statement of Gregory of Tours whom Paul followed
(IV, 41), see Jacobi, 34.

BOOK III.

CHAPTER I.

Some of the dukes of the Langobards then, with a strong army invaded Gaul.[1] Hospitius, a man of God, who had been cloistered at Nicea (Nice), foresaw their invasion a long while beforehand, by revelation of the Holy Spirit, and predicted to the citizens of that city what calamities were impending. For he was a man of the greatest abstinence and of praiseworthy life, who, bound by iron chains upon his flesh and clad with goat's hair, used bread alone and a few dates for his food. But in the days of Lent he was nourished by the roots of Egyptian herbs which hermits use, the gift of some merchants. The Lord deemed it fitting that great and excellent things should be accomplished by him, which are written in the books of the reverend man Gregory, bishop of Tours. This holy man then, predicted the coming of the Langobards into Gaul in this manner: "The Langobards," he says, "will come into Gaul and will lay waste seven cities because their wickedness has waxed great in the sight of the Lord, for all the people are addicted to perjuries, guilty of thefts, intent upon plunder,

[1] An invasion of Gaul, probably a mere foray, is mentioned by Marius of Avenches as having occurred in 569, immediately after Alboin's invasion of Italy. It was evidently a failure, for it was stated that many Langobard captives were sold into slavery (Pabst, 410, note 2). The particular invasion mentioned in the text occurred not earlier than 570 (Hodgkin, V, 216).

(94)

ready for murders; the fruit of justice is not in them, tithes are not given, the poor man is not fed, the naked is not clothed, the stranger is not received in hospitality. Therefore is this blow about to come upon that people." Also advising his monks, he said: "Depart also from this place, taking away with you what you have, for behold, the nation I foretold is approaching." And when they said, "We will not abandon thee, most holy Father," he replied, "Fear not for me, it will come to pass that they will inflict injuries upon me, but they will not harm me to my death."

CHAPTER II.

And when the monks had departed, the army of the Langobards drew near. And while it was destroying all it found, it came to the place where the holy man was cloistered. He showed himself to them through the window of a tower. But when they, going around the tower, sought an entrance through which they could pass in to him, and found none at all, two of them climbed upon the roof and uncovered it. And seeing him bound with chains and clad in goat's skin, they said: "He is a malefactor and has committed murder, therefore he is held bound in these fetters," and when they had called an interpreter they inquired from him what evil deed he had committed that he was bound in such punishment, and he declared that he was a murderer and guilty of all crimes. Then one of them drew his sword to cut off his head, but straightway his right hand stiffened while suspended in the act of striking, nor could he draw it back. So he let go of the sword and dropped it upon the ground. His companions seeing these things raised a cry to heaven entreating the saint that he would graciously make known what they should do. And he indeed, having made the sign of salvation, restored the withered arm to health. And the Langobard who had been healed was converted to the faith of Christ and was straightway made a priest and then a monk, and remained in that same place up to the end of his life in the service of God. But when the blessed Hospitius had spoken the word of God to the Langobards, two dukes who heard him reverently, returned safe and sound to their own country, but certain ones who had despised his words perished miserably in that same Provincia.[1]

CHAPTER III.

Then while the Langobards were devastating Gaul, Amatus, the patrician of Provincia, a subject of Gunthram, king of the Franks, led an army against them, and when the battle began, he fled and was there killed. And the Langobards made so great a slaughter of the Burgundians that the number of the slain could not be reckoned, and enriched with incalculable booty they returned to Italy.

CHAPTER IV.

When they had departed, Eunius, who was also called Mummulus, being summoned by the king, acquired the

[1] Provence, a district on the Mediterranean at the mouth of the Rhone, the first part of Gaul to become, and the last to remain a Roman province (Hodgkin, V, 200).

honor of the patriciate, and when the Langobards again invaded Gaul [1] and came as far as Mustiascalmes (Moutiers),[2] which place lies near the city of Ebredunum (Embrun), Mummulus moved his army and set out thither with the Burgundians. And when the Langobards were surrounded by his army and trees were felled in their way [3] among the winding paths of the woods, he rushed upon them and killed many of them and captured some and sent them to Gunthram his king.[4] And the Langobards, when these things were done, returned to Italy.

CHAPTER V.

Afterwards the Saxons who had come with the Langobards into Italy, broke into Gaul and established their camp within the territory of Regia, that is, at the villa Stablo (Establon),[5] dispersing themselves among the villas of the neighboring cities, seizing booty, taking off captives and laying all things waste. When Mummulus learned this, he attacked them with his army and killed many of them, and did not cease slaying them until night made an end, for he found men ignorant and understanding nothing of what had come upon them. But when morning came, the Saxons put their army in

[1] By way of the Col de Genèvre (Hodgkin, V, 217).

[2] In the department of the Basses Alpes.

[3] *Factis concisis*—See Du Cange, *concisa*.

[4] In this battle, Salonius, bishop of Embrun, and Sagittarius, bishop of Gap, two brothers, fought and slew many (Hodg., V, 217).

[5] Near Moutiers (Abel).

order, preparing themselves bravely for war but by means of messengers they made peace, presents were given to Mummulus, the captives and all the booty were abandoned, and they returned to Italy.

Chapter VI.

After the Saxons had returned to Italy and had taken with them their wives and children and all their household goods, they planned to go back again to Gaul, in order that they might be received by king Sigispert and by his aid might return to their own country. For it is certain that these Saxons had come to Italy with their wives and children that they might dwell in it, yet as far as can be understood they were unwilling to be subject to the commands of the Langobards. But it was not permitted to them by the Langobards to live according to their own laws,[1] and therefore they determined to go back to their own country. When they were about to enter Gaul they formed themselves into two troops, and one troop indeed entered through the city of Nicea (Nice), but the other, through Ebredunum (Embrun), returning the same way they had gone the year before. Because it was the time of the harvests they collected and threshed grain

[1] This statement, which is accepted without question by most of the commentators, is discredited by Hartmann (II, 1, 80), who remarks that it is an addition made by Paul himself to the account of Gregory of Tours from whom he takes this part of his history, and that it comes from Paul's knowledge of the Langobard state in the eighth century which is quite unreliable for events occurring two centuries earlier.

and ate it and gave it to their animals to eat. They plundered flocks, nor did they abstain from burnings, and when they had come to the river Rodanus (Rhone), which they had to cross to reach the kingdom of Sigispert, Mummulus met them with a powerful multitude. Then seeing him they feared greatly, and giving him many coins of gold for their release, they were permitted to cross the Rodanus. While they were proceeding to king Sigispert they deceived many on the way in their dealing, selling bars of brass which were so colored, I know not how, that they imitated the appearance of proved and tested gold,[1] whence many were deceived by this fraud and giving gold and receiving brass, were made paupers. When they came at length to king Sigispert, they were allowed to go back to the place from which they had first come.

Chapter VII.

And when they had come to their own country they found it was held by Suavi (Suabians) and other peoples, as we have before related.[2] Bestirring themselves against these, they attempted to drive them out and destroy them. The Suavi however offered them a third

---

[1] Gregory of Tours (IV, 42) places this event at Arverni (Clermont), which seems out of the way for an army proceeding to Sigispert in Austrasia, whose capital was Metz, and Gregory says it was then spring-time, which is hard to reconcile with the statements about the threshed grain, unless indeed the Saxons wandered through Gaul until the following spring (Hodgkin, V, 192, note 1).

[2] Book II, chapter 6.

part of the region, saying: "We can live together and dwell in common without strife," and when they in no way acquiesced, the Suavi offered them a half and afterwards two parts, reserving only a third for themselves. And when they were unwilling, the Suavi offered with the land also all the flocks if only they would cease from war, but the Saxons, not content with this, sought a contest, and they had a strife among themselves beforehand in what way they should divide the wives of the Suavi. But it did not turn out with them as they thought, for when battle was joined 20,000 of them were killed, but of the Suavi four hundred and eighty fell, and the rest obtained a victory. And six thousand of the Saxons who survived the war made a vow that they would cut neither beard nor hair until they avenged themselves upon their Suabian enemies. And again going into battle, they were grievously wasted and so they ceased from war.

Chapter VIII.

After these things three dukes of the Langobards, that is, Amo, Zaban, and Rodanus, invaded Gaul,[1] and Amo indeed, taking the way of Ebredunum (Embrun), approached as far as Machoavilla (Manosque)[2] which Mummulus had acquired by gift of the king, and there he fixed his tents. Zaban however, going down by way

[1] A. D. 575. Zaban had invaded the Swiss dominions of Gunthram the year before but had been defeated and escaped to Italy (Hodgkin, V, 219).

[2] On the river Druentia (Durance), (Abel) near Avignon (Hodgkin, V, 221).

of the city of Dea (Die),[1] came to Valentia[2] (Valence),
while Rodanus approached the city of Gratianopolis
(Grenoble). Amo indeed subdued the province of
Arelate (Arles) with the cities which lie around, and
coming up to Stony Field itself, which lies by the city
of Massilia (Marseilles), he laid waste everything he
could find, and laying seige to Aquae (Aix)[3] he received twenty-two pounds of silver[4] and departed from
that place. Rodanus also and Zaban in like manner
destroyed by fire and rapine the places to which they
had come. When these things were reported to Mummulus the patrician, he came with a strong band and
fought first with Rodanus who was besieging Gratianopolis and killed many of his army, and compelled Rodanus himself, wounded by a lance, to flee to the tops of
the mountains, from whence, dashing through the winding ways of the woods with five hundred men who had
remained to him, he came to Zaban, who was then be-
seiging the city of Valentia (Valence), and reported to
him all the things that had been done. And when they
had come to the city of Ebredunum, in like manner
plundering everything, Mummulus came to meet them
with a countless army, and when battle was joined he
overcame them. Then Zaban and Rodanus making
their way again to Italy came to Secusium (Susa), which
city Sisinnius, then master of soldiers, was holding on

---

[1] In the department of Drome (Abel), on the Drome.

[2] On the Rhone at the confluence of Isère (Hodgkin, V, 221).

[3] Aquae Sextiae near Marseilles.

[4] Only £66 sterling, a small ransom (Hodgkin, V, 221, note 2).

behalf of the emperor. The servant of Mummulus, coming to him, handed him a letter sent by Mummulus and said that the latter was quickly approaching. When they learned this, Zaban and Rodanus at once departed thence to their own homes. When Amo heard these things, having collected all his booty, he set out to return to Italy, but being hindered by the snows, he abandoned the greater part of his booty and was able with difficulty to break through the Alpine path with his followers, and thus he came to his own country.[1]

CHAPTER IX.

In these days upon the approach of the Franks the fortress of Anagnis (Nano),[2] which was situated above Tridentum (Trent) within the boundary of Italy, surrendered to them. For this reason the count[3] of the Langobards from Lagaris (Lägerthal), Ragilo by name, came and plundered Anagnis. While he was returning with his booty he was slain with many of his followers in the field of Rotalian[4] by Chramnichis, the leader of

[1] These incursions seem to have been followed by an extension of the territory of king Gunthram to the Italian side of the Alps, including both Susa and Aosta. The Langobard invasions of Gaul were not renewed (Hodg., V, 223, 4). Mummulus afterwards rebelled against Gunthram and was slain (id., 224).

[2] In the Val. di Non. A. D. 577, see Muratori Annals, Vol. III, p. 498. Hartmann (II, 1, 81) believes that this was a Byzantine (not Langobard) fortress when surrendered.

[3] As to the rank, powers, etc., of a count of the Langobards, see note to Book II, ch. 32.

[4] The date of this invasion of the Franks is placed by Hodgkin at 575–584 (VI, 27; V, 227). The chronology is very doubtful,

the Franks, who went to meet him. And this Chramnichis shortly afterwards came and devastated Tridentum.[1] And Euin, duke of Tridentum, followed and
killed him with his companions in the place which is
called Salurnis (Salurn), and shook out of him all the
booty he had taken, and when the Franks had been
driven out he took again the whole territory of Tridentum.

CHAPTER X.

At this time Sigispert, king of the Franks, was killed
by the treachery of Hilperic, his brother, with whom he
had waged war, and Childepert his son, still a little
boy, with Brunihilde his mother, took up the management of his kingdom.[2] Euin, also, duke of the

but it preceded the elevation of Authari to the throne (Hartmann,
II, 1, 81). The Rotalian field is the meadow plain at the confluence of the Noce and the Adige.

[1] That is the land around Trent. It is not likely the city was
taken (Hodgkin, VI, 28).

[2] See *supra*, II, 10. The Frankish kingdom was, after the death
of Theudepert in 548 (see note to II, 2, *supra*), of his child Theudebald in 555, and of Childepert in 558, again united under one
monarch, Chlotochar I (Lothair), who ruled for three years over
the whole kingdom and died in 561, whereupon it was divided
among his four sons, one of whom, Charibert, died in 567, and the
number of sovereigns was reduced to three.

There were four great divisions of the monarchy :

(1) Austrasia, assigned to Sigispert, which extended from
Rheims across the Rhine an unknown distance into Germany.

(2) Neustria, the portion of Chilperic or Hilperic, comprising
the Netherlands, Picardy, Normandy and Maine.

(3) Burgundy, the domain of Gunthram, embracing the region

people of Tridentum, of whom we have spoken, took

watered by the Rhone (except Provence), also Switzerland and
some land in the center of Gaul.

(4) Aquitaine, stretching from the Loire to the Pyrenees, which
was split up and contended for by all (Hodgkin, V, 199, 203).

Sigispert, the youngest and best of the three brothers, determined to wed a princess of his own rank and married, in 566,
Brunihilde, daughter of Athanagild, the Visigothic king of Spain,
whom he seems to have loved with genuine affection.   Chilperic,
cruel, lustful, avaricious, "the Nero and Herod of the time,"
took to himself many mistresses, but at last determined to follow
his brother's example and sought the hand of Galswintha, another
daughter of Athanagild, who reluctantly came from Spain to
become his bride, and received as her "morning gift" Bordeaux
and four other cities in southwestern Gaul.   But Fredegundis, one
of Childperic's former concubines, a fiend incarnate, but incom-
parable in her powers of fascination, recovered the king's affec-
tions.   Galswintha was strangled, and Chilperic married her rival.
His brothers endeavored to cast out so wicked an offender, and it
was determined that the "morning gift" of the murdered queen
should be given to her sister Brunihilde in atonement for the crime
(Hodgkin, V, 204–208).   Chilperic refused, and Sigispert and Gunthram sought to dethrone him.   He was shut up in Tournay, and
a large portion of his subjects determined to acclaim as their sovereign, Sigispert, who was raised on a shield and hailed as king
by the army, but almost in the moment of his triumph, two serving-
men rushed upon him and dealt him a mortal wound.   The
weapon, it was said, had been poisoned by Fredegundis.   Sigispert's son Childepert, a child of five years, was carried back to
Metz, the capital of Austrasia, was accepted as his father's successor, and reigned for twenty-one years under the tutelage of the
Austrasian nobles and of his mother Brunihilde, who now lived
to avenge her husband's death.   She sought to accomplish this
by a marriage with Merovech, the son of Chilperic by a former
wife.   Merovech was afterwards suspected of conspiring against
his father, and died, some say at his own desire, and others that

as his wife the daughter of Garibald, king of the
Bavarians.

it was by order of Fredegundis.   Chilperic's rule became detestable, and in 584 he too was murdered by an unknown assassin,
leaving a child three years old, Chlotochar, destined at a later
time to reunite the Frankish dominions (Hodgkin, 208–214).

  The Langobard invasion of Italy (A. D. 568) occurred just after
the murder of Galswintha (A. D. 567), and the subsequent forays
into Gaul were made possible by the dissensions among the Frankish sovereigns.   These invasions appear to be mere robber raids.
Most of them occurred during the ten years' interregnum while the
dukes were ruling the cities of Italy without a king, and the feud
between the Franks and the Langobards which thus began, ripened
into an indelible national instinct and prepared the way, after the
lapse of two centuries, for the destruction of the kingdom of the
Langobards by Charlemagne (Hodgkin, V, 198, 199).

  An interesting question arises whether there is any connection
between the characters and scenes in this Frankish drama of
intrigue and revenge, and the legend of Siegfried as developed in
the Elder Edda, the Saga of the Volsungs and the Niebelungen
Lied.   The resemblance of some of the names of the heroes is
very striking; that of Sigispert, for instance, to Siegfried or Sigurd,
Gunthram to Gunther, Brunihilde to Brunhild.   Gunther in the
legend, as well as in the history, is king of Burgundy; Siegfried
is treacherously slain; there is a bitter jealousy and feud between
two rival queens, and in the Niebelungen Lied the character of
Siegfried's widow becomes transformed by his death, and she de-
votes her life to avenge his assassination, and marries a foreign
prince for the purpose.   It is well known that certain historical
characters were actually introduced into the legend.   Etzel or
Atli was Attila the Hun, and the Dietrich of Berne of the Niebelungen, was Theoderic the Great.   Moreover, the setting of the
legend recalls the times not only of the migration of the nations,
but of the Merovingians, and it is this latter period which exercised the best influence upon the story.   The kings are like the

Chapter XI.

During these times, as was stated above,[1] Justin the younger ruled at Constantinople, a man given to every kind of avarice, a despiser of the poor, a despoiler of senators.   So great was the madness of his cupidity that he ordered iron chests made in which to collect those talents of gold which he seized.   They also say that he

Merovingians, and their management of the state resembles that of the times of Gunthram and Sigispert (Scherer, Hist. German Lit., ch. 5).   On the other hand, the parts are differently assigned. In the poem, Siegfried marries Kriemhild, not Brunhild, though according to the Icelandic version, it is the latter to whom his love was first pledged.   The stories vary from the history in nearly all their details, and there may be reason for the belief that the Siegfried legend in some form was of earlier origin than the time of Sigispert.   Still it can hardly be doubted that much of the coloring, if not the principal incidents of the story, came from this dark period in the history of the Frankish monarchy, and there seems quite as much reason to identify Siegfried and Brunhild with the sovereigns of Austrasia as to consider them, as many do, the mere personifications of natural phenomena, the development of the season myth!

Referring to the legend of buried treasure discovered by Gunthram (see chap. 34 *infra*), Hodgkin (V, 202) remarks: "Treasures buried in long departed days by kings of old, mysterious caves, reptile guides or reptile guardians—are we not transported by this strange legend into the very atmosphere of the Niebelungen Lied? And if the good king Gunthram passed for the fortunate finder of the Dragon-hoard, his brothers and their queens, by their wars, their reconciliations and their terrible avengings, must surely have suggested the main argument of that most tragical epic, the very name of one of whose heroines, Brunichildis, is identical with the name of the queen of Austrasia."

[1] See Book II, Chap. 5.

fell into the Pelagian heresy.[1]   When he turned away
the ear of his heart from the Divine commands he became mad, having lost the faculty of reason by the just
judgment of God.   He took Tiberius as his Caesar to
govern his palace and his different provinces, a man just,
useful, energetic, wise, benevolent, equitable in his
judgments, brilliant in his victories, and what was more
important than all these things, a most true Christian.
From the treasures which Justin had collected he
brought out many things for the use of the poor, and the
empress Sophia often upbraided him that he would reduce the state to poverty, saying, " What I have been
collecting through many years you are scattering prodi-
gally in a short time."   But he said: " I trust to the
Lord that money will not be lacking in our treasury
so long as the poor receive charity and captives are
ransomed.   For this is the great treasure, since the Lord
says, ' Lay up for yourselves treasures in heaven where
neither moth nor rust doth corrupt and where thieves
do not break through nor steal.'   Therefore of these
things which God has furnished us let us gather treasures
in heaven, and God will deign to give us increase in this
world."   Then when Justin had reigned eleven years,[2] he
ended at last the madness he had fallen into together
with his life.   During his time indeed were waged the
wars which, as we before said in advance, were carried

[1] That there was no original sin and that God's grace was not
indispensable.   So called from the monk Pelagius, by whom it was
taught, who died about A. D. 420.

[2] Almost thirteen years (Waitz).

on by Narses the patrician against the Goths and the Franks.[1]   In fine also, when Rome at the time of pope Benedict was suffering the privation of hunger, while the Langobards were destroying everything on every side, he[2] sent many thousand bushels of grain in ships straight from Egypt and relieved it by the effort of his benevolence.

CHAPTER XII.

When Justin was dead[3] Tiberius Constantine, the fiftieth of the Roman emperors, assumed the sovereignty.   While he was still Caesar under Justin as we said above, and was managing the palace and performing many acts of charity every day, God furnished him a great abundance of gold.   For while walking through the palace he saw on the pavement of the house a marble slab on which the cross of our Lord was carved, and he said: "We ought to adorn our forehead and our breast with our Lord's cross and behold we trample it under our feet," and this said, he quickly ordered the slab to be lifted up.   And underneath the slab when it was dug out and set up, they found another having the same device.   And he ordered this also to be raised, and when it was moved they found also a third, and when this too was taken away by his command, they found a great treasure, containing more than a thousand cente-

[1] Incorrect; these wars were waged under Justinian (II, 1 *et seq. supra;* Waitz), although it was to Justin that the complaints were afterwards made of Narses' administration.

[2] That is, Justin (see Muratori Annals, A. D. 578, vol. 3, p. 501).

[3] He died October 5, 578 (Hodgkin, V, 197).

naria [1] of gold, and the gold was carried away and distrib-
uted among the poor yet more abundantly than had been
customary. Also Narses the patrician of Italy, since he
had a great dwelling in a certain city of Italy, came to
the above-mentioned city with many treasures, and there
in his dwelling he secretly dug a great cistern in which
he deposited many thousand centenaria of gold and
silver. And when all who knew of the matter had been
killed, he entrusted these to the care of one old man
only, exacting from him an oath. And when Narses
had died, the above-mentioned old man, coming to
Caesar Tiberius, said, "If it profit me anything, I will
tell you, Caesar, an important thing." The latter said
to him, "Say what you will. It will be of advantage
to you if you shall tell anything which will profit us."
"I have," he said, "the treasure of Narses hidden away,
which I, being near the end of my life, cannot longer
conceal." Then Caesar Tiberius was delighted and sent
his servants up to the place, and the old man went ahead [2]
and they followed in astonishment, and coming to the cistern, when it was opened they entered it. So much gold
and silver was found in it that it could with difficulty be
emptied in many days by those carrying its contents.
Almost all of this he bestowed upon the needy in bountiful distribution according to his custom. When he was
about to accept the imperial crown, and the people were

[1] The centenarium is a hundred pounds weight (Du Cange).
According to Hodgkin (V, 196) this thousand centenaria would
equal four million pounds sterling, an incredible sum.

[2] Literally "withdrawing."

expecting him at the spectacle in the circus according
to usage, and were preparing an ambuscade for him
that they might raise Justinian, the nephew of Justin, to
the imperial dignity, he first proceeded through the
consecrated places, then he called to him the pontiff of
the city and entered the palace with the consuls and
prefects, and clad in the purple, crowned with the diadem and placed upon the imperial throne, he was confirmed with immense applause in the honor of the
sovereignty. His adversaries hearing this, and not being able in any way to injure him who had placed his
hope in God, were covered with great shame and confusion. And after a few days had elapsed, Justinian
came and cast himself at the foot of the emperor bringing him fifteen centenaria of gold for the sake of
pardon. Tiberius, raising him up in his patient way,
commanded him to place himself in the palace at his
side. But the empress Sophia, unmindful of the promise she had previously made to Tiberius, attempted to
carry on a plot against him. And when he proceeded
to his villa according to imperial custom, to enjoy for
thirty days the pleasures of the vintage, she secretly
called Justinian and wished to raise him to the sovereignty. When this was discovered, Tiberius returned
in great haste to Constantinople, arrested the empress
and despoiled her of all her treasures, leaving her only
the nourishment of her daily food. And when he had
separated her servants from her he put others at her service of those devoted to himself, commanding absolutely
that none of the former ones should have access to her.
But Justinian, whom he punished only by words, he

afterwards cherished with so great a love that he promised his own daughter to his son, and on the other hand
asked Justinian's daughter for his own son. But this
thing, from what cause I know not, did not at all come
to pass. The army sent by him completely subdued
the Persians, and returning victorious, brought, together
with twenty elephants, so great a quantity of booty as
would be thought enough to satisfy human cupidity.

Chapter XIII.

When Hilperic, king of the Franks, sent messengers
to this sovereign, he received from him many trinkets,
and gold pieces too, of a pound each, having on the one
side the image of the emperor and the words written in a
circle, "Of Tiberius Constantine Universal Emperor," and
having on the other side a quadriga with a driver[1] and
containing the inscription "The glory of the Romans."
In his days while the blessed Gregory, the deacon who
afterwards became Pope, was papal delegate at the same
imperial city, he composed books of Morals[2] and
vanquished in debate in the presence of the emperor himself, Euthicius,[3] a bishop of that city who fell into
error regarding the resurrection.[4] Also at this time

[1] *Ascensor*, literally, one who went up in it.

[2] The object of this treatise was to show that the book of Job
comprehended all natural theology and morals.

[3] Not the same as Eutyches, leader of the Eutychian heresy,
who lived in the preceding century.

[4] Euthicius maintained that the resurrection body of the saints
will be more subtile than ether and too rare to be perceived by the
senses, a view which Gregory contested (Hodgkin, V, 293).

Faroald, first duke of the Spoletans, invaded Classis [1] with an army of Langobards and left the rich city stripped, plundered of all its wealth. [2]

CHAPTER XIV.

The patriarch Probinus, having died at Aquileia after he had ruled the church one year, the priest Helias (Elias) was set over that church.

[1] The harbor of Ravenna.

[2] While Paul has been narrating many events which took place in Gaul or at Constantinople, he has been neglecting the transactions in Italy, to which he now for a moment returns. Among the events of the interregnum, while the dukes held sway over the Langobards, and Longinus, the prefect, governed the Roman portion of Italy, was the first serious resistance offered to the Langobard invasion. Alboin had encountered little opposition, for the inhabitants of the open country fled to the cities which held out for a shorter or longer period, the Romans hoping, no doubt, that this invasion, like others which had preceded it, would soon be over and that the barbarians would retire. But in 575 or 576, Baduarius, the son-in-law of the emperor Justin II, assembled in Ravenna a considerable body of troops, and went forth and gave battle to the invaders. He was overthrown and died. It is not known what part of the forces of the various Langobard dukedoms were his antagonists. Probably it was those who were advancing towards the south and who, not far from this time, established the important dukedoms of Spoleto and Benevento under dukes Faroald and Zotto respectively (Hartmann, II, 1, 47). The taking of Classis by Faroald mentioned in the text probably occurred about 579, while Longinus was still prefect (Hodgkin, V, 197; VI, 90, 91, note). The city was afterwards retaken from the Langobards by Droctulft (III, 19, *infra*).

Chapter XV.

After Tiberius Constantine had ruled the empire seven years, he felt the day of his death impending and with the approval of the empress Sophia, he chose Maurice, a Cappadocian by race, an energetic man, for the sovereignty, and gave him his daughter adorned with the royal decorations, saying, "Let my sovereignty be delivered to thee with this girl. Be happy in the use of it, mindful always to love equity and justice." After he had said these things he departed from this life to his eternal home, leaving great grief to the nation on account of his death.[1] For he was of the greatest goodness, ready in giving alms, just in his decisions, most careful in judging, despising no one, but including all in his good will; loving all, he was also beloved by all. When he was dead, Maurice, clad in the purple and encircled with the diadem, proceeded to the circus, and his praises having been acclaimed, gifts were bestowed upon the people, and he, as the first (emperor) of the race of the Greeks, was confirmed in the imperial power.

Chapter XVI.

But the Langobards indeed, when they had been under the power of dukes for ten years, determined at length by common consent that Authari, the son of their sovereign Cleph, above mentioned, should be their king. And they called him also Flavius[2] on account of

[1] A. D. 582 (Hodgkin, V, 227).

[2] A title borrowed from the family name of Vespasian and Titus, afterwards used by a number of their successors and by the em-

his high office.   All those who were afterwards kings
of the Langobards auspiciously used this name.   In his
days on account of the re-establishment of the kingdom, those who were then dukes gave up half of their
possessions for royal uses that there might be the means
from which the king himself and those who should attend him and those devoted to his service throughout
the various offices might be supported.[1]   The oppressed
people, however, were parcelled out among their Langobard guests.[2]   There was indeed this admirable thing in

perors of the East and thence transferred to other sovereigns,
for example, to Odoacar (Hodgkin, V, 234) and to the Visigothic
kings of Spain after Recared (Abel, p. 60).   It was used to
signify that the Langobard king had succeeded to the imperial
dignity.

[1] The powers of the king are nowhere clearly defined.   It should
be noted that he was king of the Langobard people (not king of
Italy), and that the Romans, who were not free subjects, were not
taken into consideration (Hartmann, II, 2, 30).   It would seem
(Hodgkin, VI, 568) that the laws were devised by him after con-
sultation with the principal men and nobles, and then accepted
by the army, which formed the assembly of the people.   The king
was the supreme judge, but was assisted by jurors in coming to
his conclusions.   The highest criminal jurisdiction was exercised
by him, sometimes immediately in cases of great importance, but
more frequently by means of his officers.   He had the highest
police jurisdiction.   Without his permission no free man accompanied by his clan (*fara*) might change his residence.   Churches
and convents were under his protection.   He represented a woman
as against her guardian and a retainer as against his lord.

[2] "*Populi tamen adgravati per Langobardos hospites partiuntur.*"
This is one of the most important passages in Paul's history, as it
furnishes almost the only existing statement of the condition of
the Roman population under the early Langobard kings.   It has

the kingdom of the Langobards. There was no vio-

been considered very obscure, and various interpretations have
been given. Giansvero renders it: "And the people, oppressed
by their Langobard guests, are divided." Abel translates nearly
as in the text. Hodgkin (V, 232) renders it thus: "(In this
division) the subject populations who had been assigned to their
several guests were included." This departs widely from the
Latin text, though it may well be the actual meaning. Capponi
(Sui Langobardi in Italia 18, see Scritti Editi e Inediti, 75, 77) believes that the sentence means that the tributary populations
remained divided among the Langobard guests, and that the
property only was ceded to the king. But Hodgkin asks (VI,
585) why the lands should be given to the king stripped of the
Roman *aldii* to cultivate them, and what the dukes who surrendered part of their land would do with the increased population
now thrown wholly upon the remainder. Villari insists (Le
Invasioni Barbariche in Italia, pp. 265, 266) that the property
which the Langobard dukes divided with the king was that which
they had taken from the Roman nobles they had killed (II, 32
supra), or which they had confiscated in other ways, and that
there still remained to these dukes the third of the products of the
lands possessed by the Romans, and he adds (p. 273) that the
"oppressed people" were the same as those who had been made
tributaries before (II, 32 *supra*), and who, therefore, had been
and still remained divided among the Langobard proprietors who
surrendered to the king half of the lands which were their free
and full property. Savigny says (Geschichte des Römischen
Rechts, I, chap. 5, p. 401): "The king was endowed by the nobles.
The Romans were in the meantime divided among the individual
Langobards as their *hospites* and the old relation between them
remained unchanged." Hegel says: "There was no change in
the general condition of the conquered Romans. They remained
divided among their *hospites*." Troya (Storia d'Italia, I, 5 ccccx)
contends that the true reading is *patiuntur* for *partiuntur*. "The
dukes gave one-half of their property to the king, nevertheless
the populations oppressed by the Langobard guests suffered for it."

lence, no ambuscades were laid, no one constrained another unjustly, no one took spoils, there were no thefts,

The dukes made up for their patriotic surrender by screwing a
larger tribute out of the oppressed Romans.   But Hodgkin remarks (VI, 586, note) that this does not agree with the sentence
that follows about the golden age.   Since Paul no longer speaks
of the products of the land, some think (see Villari, pp. 265, 266,
273) that the third of the rents was changed into a third of the
lands, and believe that since the Langobards had made new
acquisitions of territory, a division was made of the new lands
for the benefit of those who had to give the king part of their own
possessions.

It does not seem to me that the above passage is as difficult as
it has been considered.   In the parcelling out of the people among
their Langobard guests, the king, through his representative (his
actor, or perhaps his *gastaldus*), may well have been one of these
"guests," a word which, as we have seen, was the euphemistic
name assumed by the Langobards who settled upon the lands of
the Romans and took a share of the products.   In that case the
literal translation given in the text would be entirely appropriate,
and yet there would be no shifting of the population nor any
change in the system of dividing the products of the land.

One great difficulty with the passage has been to explain the
use of the word *tamen* (however), the usual meaning of which is
adversative.   Crivellucci (Studii Storici, 1899, 255) shows that out
of forty-eight instances in which this conjunction is used by Paul
in this history, there are six places where it might properly be
given a copulative meaning equivalent to "and" or "also,"
and one place where such a meaning is required, viz., at the beginning of chapter 23, book II.   It is certain that this conjunction
as well as *nihilominus*, its equivalent, was often used by Paul,
either with a variable meaning or else most inexpressively, and
that its use here ought not to interfere with a translation of this
passage, which is in other respects both reasonable and literal.

As to the condition of this subject Roman population see note
to II, 32, *supra*.

no robberies, every one proceeded whither he pleased, safe and without fear.[1]

CHAPTER XVII.

At this time the emperor Maurice sent by his ambassadors to Childepert, king of the Franks, 50,000 solidi[2] to make an attack with his army upon the Langobards and drive them from Italy, and Childepert suddenly entered Italy with a countless multitude of Franks.[3] The Langobards indeed intrenched themselves in their towns and when messengers had passed between the parties and gifts had been offered they made peace with Childepert.[4] When he had returned

[1] This description of the golden age is not borne out by the facts (Pabst, 425, note 2).

[2] The value of the gold solidus (here referred to) differed at different times. Hodgkin places it at twelve shillings, so that this 50,000 solidi was equal to £30,000 (V, 228). He also (VI, 413, 414) gives a table of the purchasing power of the solidus about the time of Liutprand, which was more than a century later than the period in question. The average value of a slave varied from sixty solidi to sixteen ; a new olive garden sold for eight solidi ; half a house in Pisa for nine; a garden in Lucca for fifteen; a bed, tunic and mantle for ten solidi each; a horse with trappings for one hundred solidi, etc. Personalty seems to have had a high value in comparison with real estate.

[3] Paul erroneously places the elevation of Authari to the throne before the arrangement made by the emperor Maurice with Childpert II, A. D. 582, for a common enterprise against the Langobards. In fact, it was the threatened danger of foreign invasion which induced the dukes to strengthen their military power by the creation of a king (Jacobi, 35).

[4] Gregory of Tours, from whom Paul took this statement, says

to Gaul, the emperor Maurice, having learned that he
had made a treaty with the Langobards, asked for the
return of the solidi he had given in consideration of the
overthrow of the Langobards.   But Childepert, relying
upon the strength of his resources, would not give an
answer in this matter.

CHAPTER XVIII.

When these things had been done in this way,
king Authari approached the city of Brexillus (Brescello), situated on the bank of the Po,[1] to capture it.
Thither duke Droctulft had fled from the Langobards
and surrendering to the emperor's party, and being
joined by his soldiers, resisted bravely the army of
the Langobards.   This man was descended from the
race of Suavi (Suabians), that is, of the Alamanni, and
had grown up among the Langobards, and because he
was of an excellent figure, had acquired the honor of a
dukedom, but when he found an occasion of avenging his
captivity[2] he suddenly rose against the arms of the
Langobards.   The Langobards waged grievous wars
against him and at length overcame him together with
the soldiers he was aiding, and compelled him to withdraw to Ravenna.   Brexillus was taken and its walls were

the Langobards submitted to Childepert's dominion (H. F., 6, 42).
Probably these gifts were considered as tribute.

[1] Twelve miles from Parma and on the Aemilian way (Hodgkin,
V, 243).

[2] He had apparently been taken prisoner by the Imperial troops,
and resented his lack of support by the other Langobard dukes,
to whom he considered he owed his captivity (Hodgkin, V, 242).

levelled to the ground. After these things king Authari made peace for three years with the patrician Smaragdus,[1] who was then in authority at Ravenna.

CHAPTER XIX.

With the support of this Droctulft, of whom we have spoken, the soldiers of the Ravenna people often fought against the Langobards, and after a fleet was built, they drove out with his aid the Langobards who were holding the city of Classis.[2] And when he had filled the limit of life, they gave him an honorable sepulcher in front of the church of the holy martyr Vitalis,[3] and set forth his praises in the following epitaph:

Drocton lies buried within this tomb, but only in body,
  For in his merits he lives, over the orb of the world.
First with the Langobards he dwelt, for by race and by nature
  Sprung from Suavian stock, suave to all people was he.

[1] Smaragdus had been appointed in 585 to succeed the incapable Longinus (Hodgkin, V, 242). This treaty was made very shortly afterwards (Waitz).

[2] The port of Ravenna. The dates conjectured for this event vary from A. D. 584 to 588 (Hodgkin, VI, 91, 92).

[3] This church, an octagonal building in the Byzantine style, was completed in the year 547, with the aid of contributions made by the emperor Justinian and the empress Theodora. Its walls were adorned with exquisite mosaics which are still in an excellent state of preservation. St. Vitalis was the patron saint of Ravenna. He came to that city from Milan during the persecution under Nero, A. D. 62, at a time when St. Ursicinus was about to suffer martyrdom. He sustained and encouraged Ursicinus, who was terrified at the torments he was compelled to undergo, and after his death Vitalis buried him, and was thereupon arrested, tortured, and buried alive (Larousse).

Terrible to be seen was his face, though in heart he was kindly,
  Long was the beard that grew down on his vigorous breast.
Loving the standards of Rome and the emblems of the republic,
  Aid unto them he brought, crushing the power of his race.
Love unto us he bore, despising the claims of his kindred,
  Deeming Ravenna his own fatherland, dear to his heart.
First of his valiant deeds was the glory of captured Brexillus.
  There for a time he remained, dreadful to all of his foes.
Later when here his power brought aid to the Roman standards
  First within his hands rested the banner of Christ.
Afterwards when Faroald withheld by treachery Classis,
  " Fleet-town " [1] in hope to avenge, arms for the fleet he prepares,
Struggles in tiny ships on the flowing stream of Badrinus. [2]
  Conquers and overcomes numberless Langobard [3] bands,
Vanquishes also in lands of the East the impetuous Avar,
  Seeking to win for his lords victory's sovereign palm.
Often to them as a conq'ror, sustained by the aid of Vitalis,
  Martyr and holy saint, honored with triumphs he came.
And in the fane of Vitalis he sought the repose of his body,
  Pleased that this place should hold, after his death, his remains
When he died, he implored these things of the priest Joannes, [4]
  By whose pious love he had returned to these lands. [5]

---

[1] *Classis*, "a fleet" being the name of the town.

[2] Padoreno, say some, (Waitz) but this was one of the mouths of the Po more than thirty miles distant (Hodg., V, 247 note).

[3] In the original the Langobards are called *Bardi*, a name which recalls the Bardengau and Bardowick of the Elbe region.

[4] Johannes III, bishop of Ravenna, 578–595 (Hodgkin V, 248 note 2).

[5] A somewhat freer translation in rhyme is given in Hodgkin (V, 247).

Chapter XX.

Finally, after pope Benedict, Pelagius[1] was ordained pontiff of the Roman church without the authority of the emperor, because the Langobards had besieged and surrounded Rome, and no one could leave the city. This Pelagius sent to Helias (Elias), bishop of Aquileia, who was unwilling to respect the Three Chapters[2] of the

[1] The second of that name. This election of Pelagius actually occurred in 578–579 (Hodgkin, V, 195), and is placed by Paul at too late a period, after the elevation of Authari to the throne (Jacobi, 48, 49).

[2] Paul is mistaken in calling them the "Three Chapters of the Synod of Chalcedon." The Three Chapters were the doctrines of three bishops, Theodore of Mopsuestia, Theodoret of Cyrrhus and Ibas of Edessa, which were condemned by the Synod of Constantinople in 532 (Waitz, P. III, 26, note). It was, however, considered by many that this condemnation affected the validity of the decrees of the previous Council of Chalcedon. Paul is also in error in saying that Elias was unwilling to respect the Three Chapters. It was Elias who supported these doctrines and it was Pope Pelagius who condemned them.

The controversy regarding the Three Chapters which agitated the church from the time of Justinian (543) to that of Cunincpert (698), had its origin in still older disputes concerning the incarnation of the Messiah. Apollinaris, bishop of Laodicea, taught that there was one incarnate nature of Christ ; that the God-head was united to the body of a man, and the *Logos*, the Eternal Wisdom, supplied in him the place of a human soul. These teachings were condemned as heresy, and at the beginning of the fifth century the combination of two natures was the prevailing doctrine of the church, yet the mode of the co-existence of these natures could not be represented by our ideas nor expressed by our language, and contention began between those who most dreaded to confound, and those who most feared to separate the divinity and the

Synod of Chalcedon, a very salutary letter which the

humanity of Christ. Cyril, patriarch of Alexandria, was at the head of one faction and Nestorius, patriarch of Constantinople, at the head of the other. Both were fanatical and intolerant. Nestorius abhorred the confusion of the two natures and repudiated the doctrine that the Virgin was the mother of God. Cyril espoused the side of a greater unity in Christ's nature. Pope Celestine approved his creed and condemned the doctrine of Nestorius. The first Council of Ephesus was called, and amid much tumult and violence Cyril was upheld and Nestorius pronounced a heretic. Cyril, however, softened to some extent his previous anathemas, and confessed with some ambiguity the union of a twofold nature in Christ. Eutyches, an abbot of Constantinople, was the head of a sect that was so extreme in its opposition to the doctrine of Nestorius that it incurred itself the reproach of heresy. Flavian, bishop of Constantinople, condemned the doctrine of Eutyches. A second council was summoned at Ephesus, but it was dominated like the first by the patriarch of Alexandria and it accepted his doctrine. A furious multitude of monks and soldiers broke into the church. Flavian was buffeted and kicked and trampled until he expired from his wounds, and the Council of Ephesus has passed into history as "The Robber Synod." Pope Leo the Great was not in accord with the doctrine of Eutyches. His famous *Tome* or epistle on the mystery of the Incarnation had been disregarded at the last Council of Ephesus, but upon the death of the emperor Theodosius, the decrees of that council were overthrown, the *Tome* of Leo was subscribed by the Oriental bishops, and a new council was summoned at Chalcedon, near Constantinople. (Gibbon, ch. 47.) In this council (Hodgson, Early History of Venice, pp. 44 and 45) Leo's letter was accepted as the orthodox doctrine and as a refutation of Eutyches, and it was declared that the two natures of Christ existed without any "confusion, conversion, division or separation." At the same time certain letters of Cyril were accepted as a refutation of Nestorius, and the controversy was now regarded as settled. This council was held in the year 451. Nearly a century

blessed Gregory composed while he was still a deacon.

afterwards when Justinian came to the throne, he and his wife
Theodora re-opened the question by issuing an edict against certain writings of three men long dead—Theodore of Mopsuestia,
whose orthodoxy had always been doubtful, Theodoret of Cyrrhus,
who had been condemned by the Robber Synod and reinstated
by the Council of Chalcedon, and a bishop of Edessa named Ibas.
The emperor's edict set forth certain passages from the writings
of these men and anathematized them as infected with Nestori-
anism.   The condemned doctrines were known as "The Three
Chapters."   The papacy was then held by the weak and irresolute
Vigilius, a creature of Theodora, whose election to office had been
tainted with simony.   When the imperial decree was promulgated
against the Three Chapters, the Western church which had supported the Council of Chalcedon, naturally opposed it, and Vigilius
came to Constantinople in 547 pledged against the emperor's
edict.   But when he had been in that city a little more than a
year, he was induced by flattery and promises to issue his *Judicatum*, which assented to the emperor's doctrine, "saving, however, the Council of Chalcedon."   The remonstrances of the
western bishops led him again to reconsider his position.   In 550,
the *Judicatum* was withdrawn; in 551, the pope pronounced a
solemn condemnation of Justinian's advisers in the matter.   The
emperor now resorted to violence, Vigilius was roughly handled,
a general council was summoned at Constantinople which was attended almost exclusively by eastern bishops.   The pope took
no part except to send to that body a *Constitutum* in which he
asserted his right to guide the opinions of all churchmen and an-
nul all decrees inconsistent with his teachings.   He did not defend the orthodoxy of Theodore, but in regard to Ibas and Theodoret, he adhered to the approval given them at Chalcedon.   But
after the Council of Constantinople had disregarded his authority
and anathematized the Three Chapters, and the emperor was proceeding to banish him for contumacy, he retracted, finding that
the decrees of this council were not irreconcilable with those of
Chalcedon (Hodgson, 46, 47), and after his death Pelagius I, his

CHAPTER XXI.

Meanwhile Childepert, king of the Franks, waged war

successor, ratified the condemnation of the Three Chapters. After the papacy had thus committed itself to the views of Justinian, it became very earnest in its advocacy of these views, although the churches of Spain and Gaul refused to condemn the Three Chapters, while Milan, Aquileia and the churches of Istria went further and refused communion with all who held with the Council of Constantinople (Hodgson, 48, 49).

Paulinus, who was bishop of Aquileia from about 558 to 570, assembled a synod in which Pelagius, Justinian and Narses were all excommunicated (Filiasi, V, 255). John III, the successor of Pelagius, tried to convert the schismatics, but failed, whereupon Narses proceeded by command of Justinian against the rebellious bishops. After two years of turmoil Justinian died, whereupon the tumult partly subsided, and Narses sought to quiet it rather by skill than by violence (Hodgson, 48, 49). After the invasion of the Langobards in 568 Paulinus moved the See of Aquileia from that city to Grado, and soon afterwards died (P. II, 10). Probinus, who followed him, was also a schismatic, as well as Elias, his successor, who held a synod in Grado, which sent legates to Constantinople, and prevailed upon the emperor to leave the schismatics in peace (Hodgson, 48, 49). John III was succeeded by Benedict, and he by Pelagius II (Hodgkin, V, 460), who wrote to Elias exhorting the Istrians to abandon the schism, and inviting them to send bishops and presbyters to Rome to receive satisfaction on all the points upon which they were in doubt (Hodgkin, V, 462, 3). The messengers were sent, but evidently not to receive the promised explanation, for they brought with them a sharp definition of the views of the schismatics, demanding in effect that the pope himself should give way. Pelagius in a second letter argued the question with them and demanded that they should send instructed persons able to give and receive a reason in debate. The Istrian bishops sent another letter announcing their own authoritative decision, and it was to this second let-

against the Spaniards and overcame them in battle.[1] And this was the cause of the struggle: King Childepert had given Ingundis his sister in marriage to Herminigild, son of Levigild, king of the Spaniards. And this Herminigild, by the preaching of Leander, bishop of Hispalis (Seville), and by the exhortation of his wife, had been converted from the Arian heresy, in which his father was languishing, to the Catholic faith, and his impious father had caused him put to death by the axe upon the very holiday of Easter.[2] Ingundis indeed fled from the Spaniards after the death of her husband and martyr,[3] and when she sought to return to Gaul, she

ter that Pelagius sent as his answer the "useful epistle" composed by Gregory, and referred to in the text (Hodgkin, V, 465). The argument insists that Pope Leo had not confirmed *all* the decrees of the Council of Chalcedon, but had rather reserved private and personal matters; that the acts of the three Syrian bishops might be considered as included in this reservation; that the Council had impliedly condemned these bishops since it had approved of Cyril and the Council of Ephesus which they opposed; that there was good authority for anathematizing heretics even after their death, and that the long reluctance by Vigilius and the Western bishops to accept the decrees of the Council of Constantinople, arose from their ignorance of Greek and gave all the more value to their final conclusions. The letter however, did not convert the schismatics, and more violent measures were soon taken (Hodgkin V, 565–567) as we shall see hereafter (Book III, ch. 26 and note).

[1] Paul is in error regarding this war. It was conducted not by Childepert, but by Gunthram, and was unsuccessful (Jacobi, 36).

[2] This fact is doubtful (Hodgkin, V, 255). He was probably assassinated, although he seems to have raised the standard of rebellion against his father (Hartmann, II, 1, 66).

[3] He was not regarded as a martyr by Gregory of Tours (VI, 43), but as a rebel against his father.

fell into the hands of the soldiers who were stationed on the boundary opposite the Spanish Goths, and was taken with her little son and brought to Sicily and there ended her days.[1] But her son was sent to Constantinople to the emperor Maurice.

Chapter XXII.

The emperor Maurice on the other hand dispatched ambassadors to Childepert and persuaded him to send his army into Italy against the Langobards.[2] Childepert, thinking that his sister was still living at Constantinople, gave his assent to the ambassadors of Maurice and again sent the army of the Franks to Italy against the Langobards so that he could get his sister. And when the army of the Langobards hastened against them, the Franks and Alamanni, having a quarrel among themselves, returned to their own country without securing any advantage.

Chapter XXIII.

At this time [3] there was a deluge of water in the territories of Venetia and Liguria, and in other regions of Italy such as is believed not to have existed since the time of Noah. Ruins were made of estates and country seats, and at the same time a great destruction of men and animals. The paths were obliterated, the highways demolished, and the river Athesis (Adige)

---

[1] The soldiers into whose hands Ingundis fell were Greeks. She probably died at Carthage in Africa (Hodgkin, V, 256), not in Sicily.

[2] About 587 (Hodgkin, V, 258).   [3] 589 (Hodgkin, V, 261).

then rose so high that around the church of the blessed
martyr Zeno, which is situated outside the walls of the
city of Verona, the water reached the upper windows,
although as St. Gregory, afterwards pope, also wrote, the
water did not at all enter into that church.   Likewise
the walls of the city of Verona itself were partly demolished by the same inundation.   And this inundation
occurred on the 16th of the calends of November
(Oct. 17th), yet there were so many flashes of lightning and peals of thunder as are hardly wont to occur
even in the summer time.   Also after two months this
city of Verona was in great part consumed by fire.

CHAPTER XXIV.

In this outpouring of the flood the river Tiber at
the city of Rome rose so much that its waters flowed
in over the walls of the city and filled great regions in
it.   Then through the bed of the same stream a great
multitude of serpents, and a dragon also of astonishing
size passed by the city and descended to the sea.
Straightway a very grievous pestilence called inguinal [1]
followed this inundation, and it wasted the people with
such great destruction of life that out of a countless
multitude barely a few remained.   First it struck Pope
Pelagius, a venerable man, and quickly killed him.   Then
when their pastor was taken away it spread among the
people.   In this great tribulation the most blessed
Gregory, who was then a deacon, [2] was elected Pope by

[1] Of the groin.
[2] *Levita*.   See DuCange.

the common consent of all.   He ordained that a seven-
fold litany should be offered, but while they were
imploring God, eighty of them within the space of one
hour fell suddenly to the earth and gave up the ghost.
The seven-fold litany was thus called because all the
people of the city were divided by the blessed Gregory
into seven parts to intercede with the Lord.   In the first
troop indeed was all the clergy; in the second, all the
abbots with their monks; in the third, all the abbesses
with their companies; in the fourth, all the children;
in the fifth, all the laymen; in the sixth, all the widows;
in the seventh, all the married women.   And we omit
to say anything more concerning the blessed Gregory
because some years ago with the help of God we composed his life in which, according to our slender ability,
we sketched in writing what was to be told.[1]

[1] Gregory the Great, the descendant of a noble Roman family,
was born about the year 540.   In 573 he became prefect of the
city, but two years afterwards he laid down this office, founded
six Benedictine convents in Sicily and converted his ancestral
palace on the Coelian hill at Rome into a monastery dedicated to
St. Andrew, in which he himself became a monk.   It was at this
time that walking through the Forum he saw exposed for sale the
fair-haired boys from Britain of whom he said that they were not
Angles but angels, and he obtained from Pope Benedict I, leave to
undertake a mission to that island for the conversion of its people.
He was recalled, however, while upon the way and was appointed
deacon to the Pope.   When Benedict died, his successor, Pelagius II, sent Gregory as his nuncio or *apocrisarius* to the Imperial
Court at Constantinople, where, as Paul states (III, 13), he composed his book of Morals.   With the emperor Maurice his relations were not always cordial, although the emperor asked him to
stand sponsor for his son, the infant Theodosius.   After remain-

CHAPTER XXV.

At this time the same blessed Gregory sent Augustine

ing some six years in Constantinople he returned (A. D. 585 or 586) to Rome and became the head of the monastery of St. Andrew which he had established (Hodgkin, V, 287 to 296). He now placed his pen at the service of the Pope in the controversy between that pontiff and the bishops of Istria concerning the condemnation of the Three Chapters (See III, 20, *supra*, and note). In 589 the inundation mentioned at the beginning of this chapter occurred, and in 590 the plague ravaged Italy. On the 8th of February of the latter year Pope Pelagius II died and Gregory was chosen to succeed him. The seven-fold litany described by Paul occurred after Gregory was elected, but before he was confirmed in the papal dignity. A fuller account of this litany is given in Hodgkin (V, 298–302).

Gregory's Epistles, composed during his pontificate, form a rich mine for the investigator of the history of that period. They treat of the care of the vast patrimony of St. Peter which included the largest and richest domains in Sicily as well as considerable estates in Rome, in the Sabine country, in the neighborhood of Ravenna, in Campania, Apulia, Bruttium, Gaul, Illyricum, Sardinia and Corsica, embracing property some 1800 square miles in extent. Gregory's letters show a conscientious regard for the just and careful management of these estates, as well as for the useful expenditure of the papal revenues and the efficient administration of the church, not only in these regions, but in Africa, Spain and elsewhere. It was in 596 that he sent St. Augustine, abbot of his own monastery of St. Andrew, to Britain on the mission mentioned in the following chapter, which resulted in the conversion of Ethelbert and a great part of his nobles and people to Christianity, and in 601 the second mission under Mellitus was dispatched to reenforce Augustine and his co-laborers. Gregory reformed the music of the church and remodeled the Roman liturgy, giving the service of the mass nearly the form which it bears at the present day (Hodgkin, 307–329). He also took an important part in the

and Mellitus and John with many other monks who

political affairs of Italy and in the defense of Naples, Rome and
other cities of the empire against "the unspeakable Langobards."
He made a separate treaty with duke Ariulf of Spoleto (id., p.
363), and was, as we shall see hereafter, the efficient agent in pro-
curing the peace between Agilulf and the empire which relieved
Italy from the devastations of a protracted war.

He made an earnest and even daring remonstrance to the emperor Maurice against the decree forbidding the servants of the
state to enter monasteries (pp. 374–376); he reproached the emperor for preventing the peace for which he had long been striving
(pp. 382–387), and he bitterly resented the claim of the patriarch
John of Constantinople to be called the Ecumenical or Universal
Bishop (pp. 390–400). While the contest over the title was at
its height, John died. He was succeeded by Cyriacus, a man of
gentler nature, who, while he did not renounce, would not obtrude
a title which Gregory had declared to be "the precursor of Anti-
christ," but which the patriarchs of Constantinople continued to
use until the Roman pontiffs nearly a century afterwards began to
adopt it for themselves (pp. 401–403). In 602 Maurice was overthrown by Phocas, and with his four youngest children was put to
death ; later the same fate befell his eldest son Theodosius, and
three years afterwards it overtook his widowed empress Constan-
tina and her daughters. Phocas proved to be a tyrant, imbecile
and brutal, a monster of lust and cruelty. In April 603 he was
formally proclaimed emperor in Rome, and Gregory, unmindful
of the horrors incident to his accession to the throne, addressed to
the usurper a pæan of praise and thanksgiving that has cast a
stain upon the memory of this great pope (pp. 434–447). But the
judgment of his critics is perhaps too severe. He was slowly
dying of the gout, from which he had suffered many years.
Maurice had appeared to him as the oppressor of the church and
the enemy of the true religion. The detestable character of
Phocas was probably not yet manifest to Gregory, his responsibility for the assassination of the children of Maurice may well
have been unknown or disbelieved. Within a year Gregory died,

feared God into Britain and he converted the Angles to
Christ by their preaching.

CHAPTER XXVI.

In these days when Helias (Elias), patriarch of Aquileia, had died after holding his holy office fifteen
years, Severus succeeded him and undertook the management of the church.   Smaragdus the patrician, coming from Ravenna to Gradus (Grado), personally
dragged him out of the church, and brought him with
insults to Ravenna together with three other bishops
from Istria, that is, John of Parentium (Parenzo),
Severus [1] and Vendemius [2] and also Antony, [3] now an old

and although Hodgkin considers (V, 452) that it is safer to judge
him as a great Roman than as a great saint, it seems just to his
memory that the splendid qualities he exhibited throughout a life
of intense activity should not be too greatly dimmed by a single
mistake at its close.   As Hodgkin rightly says, his generosity, his
justice, his courage, entitle him to a high place among the noblest
names of his imperial race.   The secular power he wielded over
the vast property owned by the church, as well as his political influence in Italy, his negotiations and treaties with the Langobards,
his administration of the affairs of Rome and the surrounding territories at a time when the empire, weakened and beset by numerous enemies, could give no protection to its subjects—all these
things tended to change the character of the Holy See, to make
Gregory the true founder of the mediæval papacy and to pave the
way for the subsequent establishment under Charlemagne of the
temporal power of the popes.

[1] Of Tergeste (Trieste) (Waitz).

[2] Of Cissa (Pago) (Waitz).

[3] Of Grado (Waitz).

man and trustee[1] of the church. Threatening them
with exile and inflicting violence, he compelled them to
hold communion with John, the bishop of Ravenna, a
condemner of the Three Chapters, who had separated
from the communion of the Roman church at the time
of Pope Vigilius or Pelagius.[2] After the expiration of
a year[3] they returned from Ravenna to Grado. And the
people were not willing to hold communion with them
nor did the other bishops receive them. The patrician
Smaragdus became not unjustly possessed of a devil,
and being succeeded by the patrician Romanus, returned
to Constantinople.[4] After these things a synod of ten

---

[1] *Defensor ecclesiae*, a functionary often mentioned in the church
annals, nominated by the emperor on presentation of the bishop
to protect the temporal interests of a particular church.

[2] Vigilius, A. D. 538–555; Pelagius, 555–559 or 560 (Muratori
Ann. III, 455). It was at the time of Vigilius, in 553, that the
second Council of Constantinople was held. The words of Paul
appear to be written from the standpoint of the schismatics. In
point of fact the Roman church was now supporting the condemnation of the Three Chapters. Paul seems to have believed
that orthodoxy lay upon the other side (see Cipolla, Atti del Congresso in Cividale, 1899, p. 144).

Cipolla believes (p. 145) that the reference to Vigilius was taken
by Paul from a petition of the schismatic bishops of the synod of
Marano to the emperor Maurice in which they declared that their
predecessors held firmly to the instruction they had received from
Pope Vigilius and the Council of Chalcedon, and kept themselves
faithful to the Three Chapters. This would explain his distorted
view of the controversy. If Paul took this statement from
Secundus, the latter may well have derived it from the petition of
the schismatic bishops.

[3] A. D. 588 or 589 (Waitz).   [4] A. D. 590 (Waitz).

bishops was held in Marianum (Marano) [1] where they took back Severus, the patriarch of Aquileia, upon his giving a written confession of his error in taking communion at Ravenna with those who had condemned the Three Chapters. [2] The names of the bishops who had withheld themselves from this schism are these: Peter of Altinum (Altino); Clarissimus; [3] Ingenuinus of Sabione (Seben); [4] Agnellus of Tridentum (Trent); Junior of Verona; Horontius of Vicentia (Vicenza); Rusticus of Tarvisium (Treviso); Fonteius of Feltria (Feltre); Agnellus of Acilum (Asolo); Laurentius of Bellunum (Belluno); Maxentius of Julium (Zuglio); [5] and Adrian of Pola. [6] But the following bishops held communion with the patriarch; Severus, John of Parentium (Parenzo), Patricius, Vendemius and John. [7]

[1] About twelve miles west of Aquileia. The council was held about 589 (Hodgkin, V, 468, 470).

[2] This part of Paul's narrative is taken in all probability from the lost work of Secundus, bishop of Trent, who was himself a schismatic and defender of the Three Chapters, and it may be due to this that Paul's narrative is colored in their favor (Hodgkin, V, 468, note).

[3] Of Concordia (Waitz).

[4] Near Brixen (Waitz).

[5] On the Tagliamento above Tolmezzo (Abel).

[6] These bishops came largely from places under Langobard protection and could well afford to defy the pope and the exarch (Hodgkin, V, 469).

[7] This Severus was bishop of Tergeste (Trieste); Patricius, of Æmona (Laybach); Vendemius, of Cissa (Pago), and John, of Celeia (Cilli) (Waitz). It is not clear whether they held com-

Chapter XXVII.

At this time king Authari sent an army to Istria,

munion with the patriarch before or after his recantation (Hodgkin, V, 469, 470, note 2), probably before.

Paul does not tell the rest of the story. In the following year
Gregory the Great became pope and wrote a letter summoning
the patriarch and his followers to Rome to be judged by a synod
as to the matters in controversy (Hodgkin, V, 470). Upon re-
ceipt of this letter two councils were assembled, one composed of
the bishops of the territory occupied by the Langobards, and the
other of the bishops in the coast cities subject to the empire.
Each of these councils sent a letter to the emperor, and Severus
the patriarch sent a third. One of these letters, that of the Langobard bishops, has been preserved. They congratulated Maurice
upon his victories in Italy, and predicted that the day would soon
come when the "Gentiles" would be overthrown and they would
again become subjects of the empire. Then they would gladly
present themselves before a synod in Constantinople, but they
asked that they should not be compelled to appear before Gregory, who was a party to the cause, and whose communion they
had renounced. If their enemies were allowed to persecute them
the result would be that their churches would be alienated from
the imperial authority (p. 471). This was an unpleasant prospect
for the emperor, so Maurice ordered the Pope not to molest them
(p. 472). Gregory, thus restrained, had now to confine himself
to argument.

When Callinicus became exarch, about 579, the schismatic
bishops found it harder to preserve their independence, and we
hear of certain secessions from their ranks (pp. 474, 477).

The schism had extended beyond the confines of Venetia and
Istria. Constantius, bishop of Milan and a friend of Gregory,
was urged to declare that he had never condemned the Three
Chapters and when he refused, three of his suffragans renounced
his communion and induced Theudelinda, the Langobard queen,
a Catholic and the friend of Pope Gregory to do the same.

which army Euin, duke of Tridentum (Trent), commanded.[1] And they, after plunderings and burnings,
when peace had been made for one year, brought back
a great sum of money to the king. Other Langobards
too, besieged in the island of Comacina,[2] Francio,

" Here, indeed, was a blow for the Catholic cause, if the royal influence which had been won with difficulty after the contest with
Arianism was to be lost again over the souls of the three Syrians "
(Hodgkin, V, 479). Upon the entreaties of the Pope, the breach
seems to have been healed and the queen's relations with Gregory
remained friendly, although she probably sympathized with the
schismatics. In December, 603, shortly before his death, he
wrote congratulating her upon the birth and Catholic baptism of
her son Adaloald, and said that sickness prevented him from
answering " his dearest son, the abbot Secundus," who appears
to have also been on the side of heresy (p. 480).

At the time of Gregory's death the schism had assumed a geo-
graphical character. In Istria, at Grado, and among the lagoons
of Venice, " in fact, wherever the galleys of Constantinople could
penetrate, churchmen were desirous to return into unity with the
Emperor and the Pope, and were willing to admit that Theodoret,
Theodore and Ibas were suffering the vengeance of eternal fire.
On the mainland . . . wherever the swords of the Lombards
flashed, men took a more hopeful view of the spiritual prospects
of the three Syrians " (p. 481). On the death of Severus two sets
of patriarchs were appointed, one for each section (IV, 33. *infra*).
The schism continued until the end of the 7th century, when king
Cunincpert summoned a council at Pavia in which the schismatics
" with shouts of triumph " renounced their heresy and asked to
be restored to the church (Hodgkin, V, 483; VI, 14, *infra*, see
note).

[1] Probably 587 (Hodgkin, V, 244).

[2] Read *Comacina* instead of *Amacina* (Waitz). Comacina was
a small island in lake Como, a little Roman stronghold amid
Langobard surroundings.

master of soldiers, who had been hitherto of the party of Narses and had already maintained himself for twenty years. This Francio, after he had been besieged six months, surrendered that island to the Langobards but he himself was released by the king, as he had desired, and hastened with his wife and his household goods to Ravenna. In this island many riches were found which had been deposited there by particular cities.

Chapter XXVIII.

The king Flavius Authari sent an embassy to Childepert asking that the sister of the latter should be united to him in marriage. But while Childepert accepted gifts from the ambassadors of the Langobards, and promised to give his sister to their king, yet when ambassadors of the Goths came from Spain he promised this same sister over again, because he had learned that that nation had been converted to the Catholic faith.[1]

Chapter XXIX.

In the meantime he dispatched an embassy to the emperor Maurice sending him word that he would now undertake the war against the nation of the Langobards, which he had not done before, and in concert with the emperor, he would drive them out of Italy. And without delay he dispatched his army into Italy for the sub-

---

[1] This was probably due to the intrigues of the queen mother Brunihilde, who, after suppressing an insurrection of the nobles of Austrasia, pursued a policy of alliance with the empire and the church rather than with the Langobards (Hartmann, II, 1, 67, 68).

jugation of the Langobards.[1] King Authari and the troops of the Langobards quickly went forth to meet him and fought bravely for their freedom. In that fight the Langobards won the victory; the Franks were vanquished by main force, many were captured, very many also escaped by flight and returned with difficulty to their own country. So great a slaughter was there made of the army of the Franks as is not related anywhere else. And it is truly astonishing why Secundus, who wrote a number of things concerning the doings of the Langobards, should pass over so great a victory of theirs as this, since these things of which we have spoken concerning the destruction of the Franks may be read in their own history, described in almost these very words.[2]

Chapter XXX.

But after these events king Flavius Authari sent ambassadors to Bavaria to ask for him in marriage the daughter of Garibald[3] their king.[4] The latter received them kindly and promised that he would give his

[1] Probably in 588 (Hodgkin, V, 260, 261).

[2] Hartmann (II, I, 83) suggests that the silence of Secundus is due to the fact that the latter narrates principally the events that occurred in his own immediate neighborhood (in the valley of the Adige) and that the Franks probably crossed the Alps by some other route.

[3] From this name comes Garibaldi.

[4] That is, king of the Bavarians. He was more probably duke as he owed some sort of allegiance to Childepert, the Frankish king of Austrasia (Hodgkin, V, 236, note 3).

daughter Theudelinda [1] to Authari.   And when the
ambassadors on their return announced these things to
Authari, he desired to see his betrothed for himself and
bringing with him a few but active men out of the
Langobards, and also taking along with him, as their
chief,[2] one who was most faithful to him, he set forth
without delay for Bavaria.   And when they had been
introduced into the presence of king Garibald according
to the custom of ambassadors, and he who had come
with Authari as their chief had made the usual speech
after salutation, Authari, since he was known to none of
that nation, came nearer to king Garibald and said :
" My master, king Authari has sent me especially on
this account, that I should look upon your daughter,
his betrothed, who is to be our mistress, so that I may
be able to tell my lord more surely what is her appearance."   And when the king, hearing these things, had
commanded his daughter to come, and Authari had
gazed upon her with silent approval, since she was of a
very beautiful figure and pleased him much in every
way, he said to the king : " Since we see that the person of your daughter is such that we may properly wish
her to become our queen, we would like if it please your
mightiness, to take a cup of wine from her hand, as she
will offer it to us hereafter."   And when the king had
assented to this that it should be done, she took the cup

[1] Theudelinda had been betrothed to Childepert (id.), and her
sister was the wife of the Langobard duke Euin of Trent (III, 10,
supra).

[2] *Senior*, see DuCange.

of wine and gave it first to him who appeared to be the chief. Then when she offered it to Authari, whom she did not know was her affianced bridegroom, he, after drinking and returning the cup, touched her hand with his finger when no one noticed, and drew his right hand from his forehead along his nose and face.[1] Covered with blushes, she told this to her nurse, and her nurse said to her: " Unless this man were the king himself and thy promised bridegroom, he would not dare by any means to touch thee. But meanwhile, lest this become known to thy father, let us be silent, for in truth the man is a worthy person who deserves to have a kingdom and be united with thee in wedlock." For Authari indeed was then in the bloom of his youth, of becoming stature, covered with yellow hair and very comely in appearance. Having received an escort from the king, they presently took their way to return to their own country, and they speedily departed from the territories of the Noricans. The province of the Noricans indeed, which the Bavarian people inhabits, has on the east Pannonia, on the west Suavia (Swabia), on the south Italy and on the northern side the stream of the Danube. Then Authari, when he had now come near the boundaries of Italy and had with him the Bavarians who up to this time were conducting him, raised himself as much as he could upon the horse he was managing, and with all his strength he drove into a tree that

---

[1] Hodgkin translates more freely (V, 238): " Secretly intertwined her fingers with his, and bending low, guided them over the profile of his face from the forehead to the chin." According to Abel's version he stroked *her* face.

stood near by, a hatchet which he carried in his hand and left it fixed there, adding moreover these words: "Authari is wont to strike such a blow." And when he had said these things, then the Bavarians who accompanied him understood that he was himself king Authari.[1] Then after some time, when trouble had come to king Garibald on account of an invasion by the Franks, Theudelinda his daughter with her brother, Gundoald by name, fled to Italy and announced to Authari, her promised bridegroom, that she was coming. And he straightway went forth to meet her with a great train to celebrate the nuptials in the field of Sardis[2] which is above Verona, and received her in marriage amid the rejoicing of all on the ides (15th) of May.

[1] In spite of this romantic legend it is probable that political considerations played no small part in the wooing of Authari. Theudelinda was, on her mother's side, the granddaughter of the former Langobard king Waccho, of the race of the Lethingi, with which Authari, who sprang from the later stock of Beleos, desired an alliance to give an additional sanction of legitimacy to his royal title. The relations of the Langobards to their northern neighbors the Bavarians had long been friendly, and after Authari had been compelled to renounce his intended alliance with the Franks by a marriage with Chlotsuinda, the sister of Childepert, he may well have desired to retain the friendship of the Bavarians, who although nominally subject to Childepert, had control of the passes over the eastern Alps, and could offer no slight obstacle to an invasion of Italy by the Franks. The powerful Duke of Trent had married a sister of Theudelinda, and his hearty support in resisting the Franks was also necessary to the king (Hartmann, II, 1, 68).

[2] This name cannot be identified. The place must have been near Lago di Garda (Hodgkin, V, 239, note 2).

Among other dukes of the Langobards, Agilulf, Duke of the city of Taurini (Turin) was then present. A certain tree in this place which was situated in the royal inclosures was hit during a violent gale by a stroke of lightning with great crash of thunder, and Agilulf had then as a soothsayer a certain servant of his who by diabolical art understood what future happenings strokes of lightning portended. When Agilulf was sitting down to the requirements of nature the man secretly said to him: "This woman who has just been wedded to our king is to be your wife before very long." When he heard this he threatened to cut off the man's head if he said anything further about the matter, but the man answered him: "I may be killed, indeed, but assuredly that woman has come into the country to this destiny, that she should be joined with you in marriage." And it afterwards so happened. At this time, from what cause is doubtful, Ansul, a blood kinsman of king Authari was killed at Verona.

CHAPTER XXXI.

At this time also when Grippo, the ambassador of Childepert king of the Franks, returned from Constantinople and announced to his king how he had been honorably received by the emperor Maurice and that the emperor at the desire of king Childepert promised that the insults he had endured at Carthage would be atoned for,[1] Childepert without delay sent again into

[1] This occurred in 590. Grippo had been sent some time before on an embassy to Constantinople with two noblemen, Bodigisil and

Italy an army of Franks with twenty dukes to subjugate the nation of the Langobards. Of these dukes Auduald, Olo and Cedinus were quite distinguished. But when Olo had imprudently attacked the fortress of Bilitio (Bellinzona), he fell wounded under his nipple by a dart and died. When the rest of the Franks had gone out to take booty they were destroyed by the Langobards who fell upon them while they were scattered in various places. But Auduald indeed and six dukes of the Franks came to the city of Mediolanum (Milan) and set

Evantius. On their way they stopped at Carthage, where a servant of Evantius seized in the market place some object which struck his fancy, whereupon the owner clamorously demanded its return, and one day, meeting the servant in the street, laid hold of him and said : "I will not let you go until you have returned what you stole from me," whereat the servant drew his sword and slew the man and returned to the inn where the ambassadors were staying but said nothing of the matter. The chief magistrate of the city collected an armed troop, went to the inn, and summoned the ambassadors to come out and assist in investigating the murder. Meanwhile a mob began to rush into the house. Bodigisil and Evantius were slain at the inn door, whereupon Grippo at the head of his retainers went forth fully armed, denounced the murderers of his colleagues, and said there would now never be peace between the Franks and Romans. The prefect endeavored to placate him and when Grippo reached Constantinople he was promised satisfaction by the emperor and reported this promise to his king, as appears in the text. The satisfaction afterwards given was that twelve men were sent bound to Childepert who was told that he might put them to death, or redeem their lives at the rate of 300 *aurei* (180 pounds sterling) each. Childepert, greatly dissatisfied, said there was no proof that the men sent to him had anything to do with the murder and he let them go (Hodgkin, 264, 267).

up their camp there some distance away on the plains. In this place the messengers of the emperor came to them announcing that his army was at hand to aid them and saying: " After three days we will come with them, and this shall be the signal to you ; when you shall see the houses of this country-seat which stands upon the mountain burning with fire, and the smoke of the conflagration rising to heaven, you will know we are approaching with the army we promise." But the dukes of the Franks watched for six days, according to the agreement, and saw that no one came of those whom the messengers of the emperor had promised. Cedinus indeed with thirteen dukes having invaded the left side[1] of Italy took five fortresses from which he exacted oaths (of fidelity). Also the army of the Franks advanced as far as Verona and after giving oaths (of protection), demolished without resistance many fortified places which had trusted them suspecting no treachery from them. And the names of the fortified places they destroyed in the territory of Tridentum (Trent) are these: Tesana (Tiseno), Maletum (Malè), Sermiana (Sirmian), Appianum (Hoch Eppan), Fagitana (Faedo), Cimbra (Cembra), Vitianum (Vezzano), Bremtonicum (Brentonico), Volaenes (Volano), Ennemase (Neumarkt)[2] and two in Alsuca (Val Sugana) and one in

---

[1] The eastern side.

[2] Hodgkin (VI, 30) identifies these places : Tesana and Sermiana on the Adige, ten or twelve miles south of Meran; Maletum, in the Val di Sole ; Appianum, opposite Botzen ; Fagitana, between the Adige and the Avisio, overlooking the Rotalian plain ; Cimbra, in the Val di Cembra on the lower Avisio; Vitianum, west

Verona.   When all these fortified places were destroyed by the Franks, all the citizens were led away from them as captives.   But ransom was given for the fortified place of Ferrugis (Verruca),[1] upon the intercession of the bishops Ingenuinus of Savio (Seben)[2] and Agnellus of Tridentum (Trent), one solidus per head for each man up to six hundred solidi.[3]   Meanwhile, since it was summer time, the disease of dysentery began seriously to harass the army of the Franks on account of their being unused to the climate and by this disease very many of them died.   Why say more?   While the army of the Franks was wandering through Italy for three months and gaining no advantage—it could neither avenge itself upon its enemies, for the reason that they betook them-

of Trent ; Bremtonicum, between the Adige and the head of Lago di Garda ; Volaenes, a little north of Roveredo ; Ennemase, not far south of Botzen.

[1] Close to Trent (Hodgkin, VI, 32).

[2] Not far below Brixen on the Eisach (Hodgkin, VI, 32, note 2).

[3] This chapter is a specimen of Paul's way of dovetailing his authorities together.   The campaign of the three dukes is given in the main in the words of Gregory of Tours.   Then comes a passage from the history of Secundus not agreeing with what had gone before, as it enumerates thirteen fortified places instead of five, and then, after telling of the ransom, Paul here resumes his text from Gregory (Hodgkin, VI, 31, note 1).

Hodgkin gives the price of ransom at twelve shillings a head, or for all, three hundred and sixty pounds sterling.   The language seems to indicate that the garrison were six hundred in number or it might mean that the ransom varied from one solidus for a common soldier to six hundred for a chieftain (Hodgkin, VI, 32, note 4).

selves to very strong places, nor could it reach the king
from whom it might obtain retribution, since he had fortified himself within the city of Ticinum (Pavia)—the
army, as we have said, having become ill from the un-
healthiness of the climate and grievously oppressed with
hunger, determined to go back home. And while they
were returning to their own country they endured such
stress of famine that they offered first their own clothes
and afterwards also their arms to buy food before they
reached their native soil. [1]

CHAPTER XXXII.

It is believed that what is related of king Authari occurred about this time. For the report is that that king
then came through Spoletium (Spoleto) to Beneventum
(Benevento) and took possession of that region and
passed on as far even as Regium (Reggio), the last city
of Italy next to Sicily, and since it is said that a certain
column is placed there among the waves of the sea, that
he went up to it sitting upon his horse and touched it
with the point of his spear saying: "The territories of
the Langobards will be up to this place." The column

[1] The Byzantine account of this campaign of the year 590 is
given in two letters written by the exarch Romanus to Childepert,
stating that before the arrival of the Franks, the Romans had
taken Modena, Altino and Mantua, that when Cedinus was encamped near Verona they were upon the point of joining him and
supporting him by their light vessels on the river, intending with
him to besiege Pavia and capture king Authari, and that they
were amazed to learn that Cedinus had made a ten months' truce
with the Langobards and had marched out of the country (Hodgkin, V, 271–274).

is said to be there down to the present time and to be called the Column of Authari.[1]

CHAPTER XXXIII.

But the first duke of the Langobards in Beneventum[2] was named Zotto, and he ruled in it for the space of twenty years.[3]

[1] Chapter XXXII is not believed to be historical but to belong to the domain of saga and perhaps of epic song (Bruckner, p. 18, note 3 ; and Pabst, 453, note 1 ; see Hodgkin, V, 235 and 236, note 1). Beneventum was established before Authari's time (Pabst, 453 and note 1).

[2] Benevento stands in an amphitheater of hills overlooking the two rivers Calore and Sabato, which afterwards unite and form the Voltorno. It was a city of the Samnites, possibly once inhabited by Etruscans. At the time of the third Samnite war, B. C. 298 to 290, it passed under the dominion of Rome. It was situated on the great Appian Way from Rome to Brundisium and upon the great road afterwards built by Trajan, also on a branch of the Latin Way, a road connecting it with the north-east of Latium, and it was a place of the utmost importance as a military position, commanding the southern portion of Italy (Hodgkin, VI, 63–68).

[3] No passage in Paul has given a harder task to investigators than this chapter. Five different opinions (Waitz) have arisen from it as to the origin of the important duchy of Benevento. The twenty years attributed to Zotto's reign are reckoned, as Hartmann thinks (II, 1, 54), from the year 569, which was regarded as the commencement of Langobard domination in Italy, and was thus transferred to Benevento, and he does not believe that this duchy was established at so early a period. Hodgkin (VI, 71, note 1, and 73) argues that Zotto's reign began probably about 571, and ended about 591 (see Hirsch, History of the Duchy of Beneventum, Chap. I).

The duchy of Benevento is often spoken of as the duchy of the

Chapter XXXIV.

Meanwhile king Authari dispatched an embassy with words of peace to Gunthram, king of the Franks, [1] the uncle of king Childepert. The ambassadors were received pleasantly by him but were directed to Childepert who was a nephew on his brother's side, so that by his assent [2] peace should be confirmed with the nation of the Langobards. This Gunthram indeed of whom we have spoken was a peaceful king and eminent in every good quality. Of him we may briefly insert in this history of ours one very remarkable occurrence, especially since we know that it is not at all contained in the history of the Franks. When he went once upon a time into the woods to hunt, and, as often happens, his companions scattered hither and thither, and he remained with only one, a very faithful friend of his, he was oppressed with heavy slumber and laying his head upon the knees of this same faithful companion, he fell asleep. From his mouth a little animal in the shape of a reptile came forth and began to bustle about seeking to cross a slender brook which flowed near by. Then he in whose lap (the king) was resting laid his sword, which he had drawn from its scabbard, over this brook and upon it that reptile of which we have spoken passed over to the other side. And when it had entered into a certain hole in the mountain not far off, and having re-

Samnites (IV, 44, 46; VI, 2, 29, *infra*).   It lasted until the latter part of the eleventh century (Hodgkin, VI, 69).

[1] More properly, king of Burgundy (Hodgkin, V, 275).

[2] Read *nutum* instead of *notum.*

turned after a little time, had crossed the aforesaid brook upon the same sword, it again went into the mouth of Gunthram from which it had come forth.   When Gunthram was afterwards awakened from sleep he said he had seen a wonderful vision.   For he related that it had seemed to him in his slumbers that he had passed over a certain river by an iron bridge and had gone in under a certain mountain where he had gazed upon a great mass of gold.   The man however, on whose lap he had held his head while he was sleeping, related to him in order what he had seen of it.   Why say more?   That place was dug up and countless treasures were discovered which had been put there of old. [1]   Of this gold the king himself afterwards made a solid canopy [2] of wonderful size and great weight and wished to send it, adorned with many precious gems, to Jerusalem to the sepulcher of our Lord.   But when he could not at all do this he caused it to be placed over the body of St. Marcellus the martyr who was buried in the city of Cabillonum [3] (Châlon-Sur-Saone) where the capital of his kingdom was, and it is there down to the present day.   Nor is there anywhere any work made of gold which may be compared to it.   But having touched briefly upon these things, which were worthy of the telling, let us come back to our history.

CHAPTER XXXV.

In the meantime, while king Authari's messengers

---

[1] See Chap. X, *supra*, note at the end.

[2] *Ciborium*.   Italian, *baldacchino* (Hodgkin, V, 202).

[3] Founded by Gunthram (Giansevero).

were stopping in France, king Authari, after he had reigned six years,[1] died at Ticinum (Pavia) on the Nones (5th) of September[2] from poison he had taken, as they relate. And straightway an embassy was sent by the Langobards to Childepert, king of the Franks to announce to him the death of king Authari and to ask for peace from him. And when he heard this, he received the messengers indeed but promised that he would give peace at a future time. After some days, however, he dismissed the aforesaid messengers with the promise of peace. But because queen Theudelinda pleased the Langobards greatly, they allowed her to remain in her royal dignity, advising her to choose for herself whomsoever she might wish from all the Langobards; such a one, namely, as could profitably manage the kingdom. And she, taking counsel with the prudent, chose Agilulf, duke of the people of Turin as her husband and king of the nation of the Langobards, for he was a man energetic and warlike and fitted as well in body as in mind for the government of the kingdom. The queen straightway sent word to him to come to her and she hastened to meet him at the town of Laumellum (Lumello).[3] And when he had come to her, she, after some speech with him, caused wine to be brought, and when she had first quaffed it, she handed the rest

[1] Seven years, says the Origo—six years and six months, says the Continuer of Prosper (Waitz).

[2] A. D. 590, a date which is well established (Hodgkin, V, 275, note 3).

[3] A little north of the Po, about twenty miles west of Pavia (Hodgkin, V, 283, note 2).

to Agilulf to drink.   And when he had taken the cup
and had reverently kissed her hand, the queen said smil-
ing with a blush, that he should not kiss her hand who
ought to imprint a kiss upon her lips.   And straightway
raising him up to kiss her, she unfolded to him the subject of their marriage and of the sovereign dignity.
Why say more? The nuptials were celebrated with
great rejoicing and Agilulf, who was a kinsman of king
Authari on the mother's side, [1] assumed the royal dignity
at the beginning of the month of November. [2]   Later
however, in the month of May when the Langobards
had met together in one place, he was raised to the sovereignty by all at Mediolanum.

[1] Hartmann (II, 1, 121) doubts this relationship.

[2] Waitz doubts this legend and believes that Agilulf obtained
the crown by violence, citing the Origo and the Continuer of
Prosper, but in these there is no actual contradiction of the text,
as they simply say that Agilulf married Theudelinda and became
king (Hodgkin, V, 283, note 4, 284).   The fact, however, that
the occurrences related must have taken place, if at all, within
two months of the death of her first husband, detracts much from
the charm of this otherwise delightful saga and adds something to
its improbability (Hartmann, II, 1, 98, 99).   Most likely Agilulf
seized the crown and married Theudelinda, the granddaughter of
king Waccho, to acquire for his royal title some claim to legitimacy.

Agilulf, one of the great kings of the Langobards, was said to
be of Thuringian extraction, though it is possible this statement is
due to a misunderstanding of his title as duke of Turin (Hartmann,
II, 1, 121).   Theudelinda was descended on her father's side
from the Bavarians, the former Marcomanni, who after a long
sojourn to Bohemia, were settled in the region now known as
Bavaria.   Theudelinda virtually established a new dynasty in
Italy and her descendants reigned down to the fifth generation
(Hodgkin, V, 285, 286).

BOOK IV.

CHAPTER I.

When therefore Agilulf, who was also called Ago, had been confirmed in the royal dignity[1] he sent Agnellus,[2] Bishop of Tridentum (Trent) to France for the sake of those who had been led captive by the Franks from the fortified places of Tridentum. And Agnellus, on his return thence, brought back with him a number of captives whom Brunihilde,[3] the queen of the Franks had ransomed with her own money. Also Euin, duke of the people of Trent, proceeded to Gaul to obtain peace and when he had procured it he returned.

CHAPTER II.

In this year there was a very severe drought from the month of January to the month of September and there occurred a dreadful famine. There came also into the territory of Tridentum a great quantity of locusts which were larger than other locusts, and, wonderful to relate, fed upon grasses and marsh seeds, but hardly touched

[1] May, 591 (Waitz).

[2] Hartmann (II, 1, 84) believes that the statement that Agnellus was acting on behalf of the Langobards in this matter was a mistake due to the fact that Paul considered that the Catholic bishop of Trent was in Langobard territory.

[3] Cf. III, 10 *supra*.

(151)

the crops of the fields.   And they appeared also in like
manner the following year.

CHAPTER III.

In these days king Agilulf put to death Mimulf, duke
of the island of St. Julian,[1] because he had on a previous occasion treasonably surrendered to the dukes of
the Franks.   Gaidulf indeed, the Bergamascan duke,
rebelled in his city of Pergamus (Bergamo) and fortified himself against the king, but afterwards gave hostages and made peace with his sovereign.   Again
Gaidulf shut himself up in the island of Comacina.[2]
But king Agilulf invaded this island and drove Gaidulf's
men out of it and carried away to Ticinum (Pavia) the
treasure he had found placed there by the Romans.[3]
But Gaidulf again fled to Pergamus (Bergamo) and was
there taken by king Agilulf and again received into
favor.   Also duke Ulfari rebelled against king Ago at
Tarvisium (Treviso), and was beseiged and captured by
him.

CHAPTER IV.

In this year the inguinal plague was again at Ravenna,
Gradus (Grado) and Istria, and was very grievous as it
had also been thirty years before.   At this time too
king Agilulf made peace with the Avars.   Childepert

---

[1] A small island in the Lago d' Orta (Giansevero), west of lake
Maggiore.

[2] In lake Como.

[3] Cf. III, 27 *supra.*

also waged with his cousin [1] the son of Hilperic,[2] a war in which as many as thirty thousand men fell in battle. The winter was then very cold, so that hardly anyone recalled its like before. Also in the region of the Briones (Brenner) blood flowed from the clouds, and among the waters of the river Renus [3] (Reno) a rivulet of blood arose.

CHAPTER V.

In these days [4] the most wise and holy Pope Gregory, of the city of Rome, after he had written many other things for the service of the holy church, also composed four books of the Life of the Saints. This writing he called a dialogue, that is, the conversation of two persons, because he had produced it talking with his deacon Peter. The aforesaid pope then sent these books to queen Theudelinda, whom he knew to be undoubtedly devoted to the faith of Christ and conspicuous in good works.

CHAPTER VI.

By means of this queen too, the church of God obtained much that was serviceable. For the Langobards, when they were still held in the error of heathenism, seized nearly all the property of the churches, but the king, moved by her wholesome supplication, not only

[1] On the mother's side.

[2] Chlotar II.

[3] Between Ferrara and Bologna. Or was this Rhenus the Rhine?

[4] A. D. 593 (Waitz).

held the Catholic faith,[1] but also bestowed many possessions upon the church of Christ and restored to the
honor of their wonted dignity bishops who were in a
reduced and abject condition.

CHAPTER VII.

In these days Tassilo was ordained king[2] among the
Bavarians by Childepert, king of the Franks.   And he
presently entered with his army into the province of the
Sclabi (Slavs), and when he had obtained the victory,
he returned to his own land with very great booty.

CHAPTER VIII.

Also at this time, Romanus, the patrician and exarch
of Ravenna, proceeded to Rome.   On his return to
Ravenna he re-occupied the cities that were held by the
Langobards, of which the names are as follows : Sutrium
(Sutri), Polimartium (Bomarzo), Hortas (Orte), Tuder
(Todi), Ameria (Amelia), Perusia (Perugia), Luceolis[3]
(Cantiano), and some other cities.   When this fact
was announced to king Agilulf, he straightway marched
out of Ticinum with a strong army and attacked the

[1] Paul is probably mistaken in this.   Theudelinda the queen was
a Catholic, but Agilulf, although tolerant, and allowing his son to
be baptized as a Catholic, appears from the letters of St. Gregory
and St. Columban not to have become one himself (Hodgkin, VI,
140 to 144).

[2] A. D. 595 (Giansevero).

[3] All these were later in the States of the Church.   Three of
them were important stages on the Via Flamminia connecting
Rome with Ravenna (Hodgkin, V, 367).

city of Perusia, and there for some days he besieged
Maurisio, the duke of the Langobards, who had gone
over to the side of the Romans, and without delay took
him and deprived him of life. The blessed Pope Gregory was so much alarmed at the approach of this king
that he desisted from his commentary upon the temple
mentioned in Ezekiel, as he himself also relates in his
homilies.[1] King Agilulf then, when matters were arranged, returned to Ticinum (Pavia), and not long
afterwards, upon the special suggestion of his wife,
Queen Theudelinda—since the blessed Pope Gregory
had often thus admonished her in his letters—he concluded a firm peace[2] with the same most holy man
Pope Gregory and with the Romans,[3] and that venerable

[1] See Book II on Ezekiel. The passage is given in full in
Waitz's note. See Homily XXII.

[2] Paul is in error here in his chronology, Agilulf's expedition
against Perugia and Rome was in 594, or according to Hodgkin
(V. 369) in 593. The peace was concluded in the latter part of
598 (Jacobi, 27) or more probably in 599 (Hodgkin, V, 415).

[3] In this chapter Paul gives a very short and insufficient account
of a period filled with important events. In the year 592, duke
Ariulf of Spoleto, a town on the way from Ravenna to Rome,
continually threatened the communication between these two
cities and captured a number of other places belonging to the
empire, and Arichis duke of Benevento, co-operating with Ariulf,
pressed hard upon Naples. About the end of July (Hodgkin,
V, p. 363) Pope Gregory concluded a separate peace with Ariulf
which aroused great indignation at Ravenna and Constantinople
because it was beyond the authority of the Pope to make such
peace with an independent power. It would seem that it was this
action which stirred the exarch Romanus to his campaign in which
he recovered the cities mentioned by Paul, that had probably

prelate sent to this queen the following letter in expression of his thanks:

CHAPTER IX.

" Gregory to Theudelinda, queen of the Langobards. We have learned from the report of our son, the abbot Probus, that your Excellency has devoted yourself, as you are wont, zealously and benevolently, to making peace. Nor was it to be expected otherwise from your Christianity but that you would show to all your labor and your goodness in the cause of peace. Wherefore we render thanks to Almighty God, who so rules your heart by His affection, that He has not only given you the true faith, but He also grants that you devote yourself always to the things that are pleasing to Him. For think not, most excellent daughter, that you have obtained but little reward for staying the blood which

fallen into Ariulf's possession. Now Agilulf took the field and after capturing Perugia marched on Rome, and Pope Gregory, from the battlements of the city, saw the captive Romans driven from the Campagna, roped together with halters around their necks on their way to slavery. The Pope made vigorous preparations for the defense of the city but no assault was made. One of the early chroniclers known as the Copenhagen Continuer of Prosper, says Agilulf relinquished the siege because he was melted by the prayers of Gregory. This statement has been doubted (Hodgkin, V, 372) and perhaps other causes, fever, disaffection, the impregnability of the place or the rebellion of the Langobard dukes may have led to his return. But the Pope began at once to work for peace between Agilulf and the empire. The emperor Maurice and the exarch Romanus laid many obstacles in the way, and it was not until the death of Romanus and the succession of Callinicus that peace was concluded.

would otherwise have been poured out upon both sides. On account of this thing we return thanks for your good will and invoke the mercy of our God that He may weigh out to you a requital of good things in body and soul, here and hereafter. Saluting you, moreover, with fatherly love, we exhort you that you so proceed with your most excellent husband that he may not reject the alliance of our Christian Republic. For, as we think you also know, it is expedient in many ways that he should be willing to betake himself to its friendship. Do you, therefore, according to your custom, ever busy yourself with the things that relate to the welfare of the parties and take pains to commend your good deeds more fully in the eyes of Almighty God, where an opportunity may be given to win His reward."

Likewise his letter to king Agilulf: "Gregory to Agilulf, king of the Langobards. We render thanks to your Excellency that, hearing our petition, you have declared peace (as we had faith you would), which will be of advantage to both parties. Wherefore we strongly praise the prudence and goodness of your Excellency, because in loving peace you show that you love God who is its author. If it had not been made, which God forbid! what could have happened but that the blood of the wretched peasants, whose labor helps us both, would be shed to the sin and ruin of both parties? But that we may feel the advantage of this same peace as it has been made by you, we pray, saluting you with fatherly love, that as often as occasion shall be given, you may by your letters admonish your dukes in various places and especially those stationed in these parts,

that they keep this peace inviolably, as has been promised, and that they do not seek for themselves opportu-
nities from which may spring any strife or dissatisfaction,
so that we may be able to render thanks for your good
will. We have received indeed the bearers of these
present letters, as being in fact your servants, in the affection which was due, because it was just that we should
receive and dismiss with Christian love wise men who
announced a peace made with God's approval." [1]

CHAPTER X.

Meanwhile, in the following month of January, a
comet appeared morning and evening through the whole
month. And in this month also John, archbishop of
Ravenna, died and Marianus, a Roman citizen, was substituted in his place. Also Euin, the duke of Trent,
being dead, duke Gaidoald, a good man and a Catholic
in religion, was assigned to that place. And in these
same days, while the Bavarians, to the number of thirty
thousand men, attacked the Slavs, the Cagan [2] fell upon
them and all were killed. Then for the first time wild

[1] This letter is said to have been written Dec., 598 (Hodgkin,
V, 419, note), though this was before the peace was finally concluded. Probably the preliminary negotiations had been then
completed.

[2] Thus the king of the Avars or Huns was called (Giansevero),
and this is the probable meaning of the title in this place, but the
term is also applied to the chiefs of the Russians or Muscovites
(see DuCange), hence perhaps here to the chief of the Slavs. It
was a generic name like "Cæsar," "Augustus," "Flavius"
among the Romans. The word "Khan" is evidently derived
from it (Giansevero, p. 140).

horses and buffaloes [1] were brought into Italy, and were objects of wonder to the people of that country.

CHAPTER XI.

Also at this time Childepert, king of the Franks, in the twenty-fifth year of his age, was murdered, as is said, together with his wife, by poison.[2] The Huns, too, who are also called Avars, entered Thuringia from Pannonia and waged desperate wars with the Franks. Queen Brunihilde, with her grandsons Theudepert and Theuderic who were still little boys, was then reigning over Gaul and the Huns took money from them and returned home. Also Gunthram, king of the Franks, died, and queen Brunihilde, with her grandsons, the sons of Childepert, who were still little children, assumed his royal authority.

CHAPTER XII.

At the same time the Cagan, king of the Huns, sending messengers to Mediolanum (Milan) to Agilulf, made peace with him.[3] Also the patrician Romanus died[4] and Gallicinus[5] succeeded him and entered into a treaty of peace with king Agilulf.[6]

[1] *Bubalus* is probably βούβαλος "buffalo," or possibly βουβαλίς, an African deer or antelope.

[2] A. D. 593 (Hodgkin, V, 345).

[3] Some time between 593 and 600 (Hodgkin, V, 422, note 3).

[4] A. D. 596 or 597 (Hodgkin, V, 409).

[5] His proper name was Callinicus (Hodgkin, V, 410).

[6] This was the peace in regard to which Gregory wrote the preceding letters to Theudelinda and Agilulf. It was only a peace for two years (Hodgkin, V, 418, 420. 428).

Chapter XIII.

At this time also Agilulf made perpetual peace with Theuderic, king of the Franks. Afterwards king Ago put to death Zangrulf, duke of Verona, who rebelled against him. He also slew Gaidulf, duke of Pergamus (Bergamo), whom he had already spared twice. Also in like manner he put to death Warnecautius at Ticinum (Pavia).

Chapter XIV.

At a subsequent time a very severe plague again devastated Ravenna and those places which were around the shores of the sea. Also in the following year a great mortality wasted the people of Verona.

Chapter XV.

Then also a bloody sign was seen appearing in heaven, and as it were, bloody lances and a very brilliant light through the whole night. Theudepert king of the Franks at that time waged war with his cousin Clothar and violently overthrew his army.

Chapter XVI.

In the following year duke Ariulf who had succeeded Faruald[1] at Spoletium (Spoleto) died. This Ariulf, when he had waged war against the Romans at Camerinum (Camerino)[2] and had gotten the victory,[3] began

---

[1] Faruald died about 591 (Waitz). The name is also spelled Faroald, see *infra*.

[2] A city of Picenum on the east side of the Apennines near the boundaries of Umbria.

[3] The campaign of Ariulf, including probably a siege of Rome,

to inquire of his men who that man was whom he had seen fighting so vigorously in the war he had waged. And when his men answered that they had not seen anyone there acting more bravely than the duke himself, he said: " Surely I saw another man there much and in every way better than I, and as often as any one of the opposite side attempted to strike me, that active man always protected me with his shield." And when the duke himself had come near Spoletium (Spoleto) where stands the church of the blessed martyr, the bishop Savinus, [1] in which his venerable body reposes, Ariulf asked to whom belonged this spacious abode. It was answered him by devout men that the martyr Savinus reposed there whom Christians were wont to invoke in their aid as often as they went to war against their enemies. And Ariulf, since up to this time he was a heathen, thus answered: "And can it be that a dead man can give any aid to one living?" And when he had said this, he leaped down from his horse and went into the church to look at it. And then while the others were praying he began to admire the pictures of that

had taken place some time before this in 592, and had ended in a partial peace concluded by Pope Gregory with the Langobard duke, due to the veneration aroused in the heart of Ariulf by a personal interview with the pontiff. This was the peace that exposed the pope to bitter reproaches at Constantinople (Hodgkin, VI, 93) and was possibly the occasion of the campaign of Romanus against the cities that had been taken by the Langobards (IV, 8 *supra*).

[1] Hodgkin suggests (V, 365, note 3) that this may be a mistake as Savinus (or Sabinus) was patron saint, not of Spoleto but Camerino.

church.   And when he had beheld the painted figure of
the blessed martyr Savinus he straightway said and declared with an oath that that man who had protected
him in battle had in every way such a form and bearing.
Then it was understood that the blessed martyr Savinus
had brought him help in battle.   Upon the death of
Ariulf, after two sons of Faroald the former duke had
contended between themselves for the dukedom, one of
them, Teudelapius by name, was crowned with victory
and received the dukedom.[1]

CHAPTER XVII.

About this time the monastery of the blessed father
Benedict which was situated in the stronghold of Cas-
inum (Monte Cassino) was attacked at night by the
Langobards,[2] and although they plundered everything,
they could not get hold of one of the monks.   This was
in fulfilment of a prophecy of the venerable father Benedict, which he had made long before, in which he said:
"I have been able with difficulty to obtain from God
that the souls from this place should be yielded to me."[3]

---

[1] Ariulf died in 601, about ten years after his accession and king
Agilulf appears to have had little hand in regulating the succession, since this was decided by battle between the two sons of
Faruald.   Teudelapius kept the dukedom of Spoleto for more than
half a century (601 to 653), during which time there were four
kings at Pavia (Hodgkin, VI, 95, 96).

[2] This attack actually occurred A. D. 589, not 601, the date of
Ariulf's death (Jacobi, 25, 26).   Some historians indeed place it
as early as 582 (Giansevero).

[3] The whole prophecy was (see Dialogues Gregory the Great, II,
chap. 17), "All this monastery that I built and all things that I

The monks fled from this place and made their way to Rome carrying with them the manuscript of the Holy Rule (of the order) which the aforesaid father had composed, and certain other writings and also a pound of bread and a measure of wine, and whatever of their household goods they had been able to snatch away. Subsequently to the blessed Benedict indeed, Constantine governed that fraternity; after him Simplicius; after him Vitalis; finally Bonitus under whom this destruction occurred.

CHAPTER XVIII.

On the death of Zotto, duke of Beneventum (Benevento),[1] Arigis (or Arichis), sent by king Agilulf, succeeded to his place. He had come originally from Forum Julii (Cividale) and had educated the sons of Gisulf,[2] duke of Forum Julii (Friuli), and was a blood

prepared for the brothers, have been delivered to the heathen by the judgment of God Almighty. I have been able with difficulty, etc."

[1] A. D. 591. He had pushed his ravages far into Apulia Lucania and Calabria, apparently acting independently of the Langobard kingdom in the north of Italy (Hodgkin, VI, 73).

[2] Arichis was duke in 591, as appears from a letter of Gregory the Great (Epist., II, 46). How then could Grimoald, the son of Gisulf, who was a little boy during the Avar invasion of 610 (IV, 37 *infra*), have been one of his pupils before 591 ? Even Grimoald's elder brothers Taso and Cacco were young enough for the eldest to be adopted by the exarch after his father's death about 612, and could hardly have been born before 585, six years before Arichis became duke of Beneventum. Hodgkin believes (VI, 74, note) that it was the children of an earlier generation whom

relation of that same Gisulf.   There exists a letter of
the blessed Pope Gregory to this Arigis drawn up in
the following terms:

CHAPTER XIX.

" Gregory to Duke Arogis:

" Since we trust in your Highness as indeed in our own
son, we are moved to make a request of you in a way
confidentially, thinking that you will not at all suffer us
to be disappointed, especially in a matter from which
your soul may be greatly benefitted.   We inform you
then that a considerable number of wooden beams are
needful to us for the churches of the blessed Peter and
Paul, and therefore we have enjoined our sub-deacon
Savinus to cut a number in the region of Brittii (Calabria) and to bring them to a suitable place by the
sea.   And because he needs assistance in this thing,
we ask, saluting your Highness with paternal love, that
you should charge your managers[2] who are in that place

Arichis instructed, perhaps the children of Grasulf I, and that
afterwards, when Arichis received the two young princes Radoald
and Grimoald at his court (IV, 39 *infra*), it was the sons of one of
his old pupils that he welcomed to Beneventum.   Other commentators believe that Paul was altogether wrong.

Arichis practically acted as an independent sovereign, making
war with Naples and Rome, and king Agilulf could not conclude
a peace with the empire till Arichis assented.   When Arichis died
the king of the Langobards does not seem to have been consulted
in the appointment of his successor (Hodgkin, VI, 75).

[1] Spelled thus in the oldest manuscripts and also in the letters
of Gregory.

[2] *Actionarii.*   These were subordinate officials of the king

to send the men who are under them with their oxen to his assistance, so that with your aid he can the better perform what we have enjoined upon him. And we promise that when the thing is finished, we will send to you a worthy gift which will not be displeasing, for we know how to regard and to recompense our sons who show us good will. Whence we ask again, illustrious son, that you should so act that we can be debtors to you for the favor shown and that you may have a reward for (your services to) the churches of the saints."

CHAPTER XX.

In these days the daughter of king Agilulf was taken from the city of Parma, together with her husband named Gudescalc (Gottschalk), by the army of the patrician Gallicinus (Callinicus), and they were brought to the city of Ravenna. At this time also king Agilulf sent to the Cagan, the king of the Avars, workmen for the making of ships with which that Cagan afterwards conquered a certain island in Thrace. [1]

who stood in rank under the *gastaldi*, and appear to have had charge of particular domains of the king, or (in Benevento and Spoleto) of the duke (Pabst, 493).

[1] Although these shipwrights were probably Romans, the incident shows the general acceptance by the Langobards of the industrial arts of the people they had conquered. The history of these changes is given in Hartmann, II, 2, chap. I, in detail, see pp. 19–22. See also chap. 22, *infra*, where their change in dress is noted.

Chapter XXI.

At the same time queen Theudelinda dedicated the church of St. John the Baptist, which she had built in Modicia (Monza), a place which is twelve miles above Mediolanum (Milan). And she decorated it with many ornaments of gold and silver and endowed it amply with estates. In this place also Theuderic, the former king of the Goths, had constructed his palace, because the place, since it is near the Alps, is temperate and healthful in summer time.

Chapter XXII.

There also the aforesaid queen built herself a palace, in which she caused to be painted something of the achievements of the Langobards. In this painting it is clearly shown in what way the Langobards at that time cut their hair, and what was their dress and what their appearance. They shaved the neck, and left it bare up to the back of the head, having their hair hanging down on the face as far as the mouth and parting it on either side by a part in the forehead. Their garments were loose and mostly linen, such as the Anglo-Saxons are wont to wear,[1] ornamented with broad borders woven in various colors. Their shoes, indeed, were open almost up to the tip of the great toe, and were held on by shoe latchets interlacing alternately. But later they began to wear trousers,[2] over which they put leggins of shaggy

[1] This is said to be the first appearance in literature of the word "Anglo-Saxon" (Hodgkin, V, 154, note 4).

[2] The monk of Salerno says that king Adaloald (A. D. 616–626) was the first who wore trousers (Abel, note).

woolen cloth[1] when they rode. But they had taken
that from a custom of the Romans.

CHAPTER XXIII.

Up to this time the city of Patavium (Padua) had
rebelled against the Langobards, the soldiers resisting
very bravely. But at last when fire was thrown into it,
it was all consumed by the devouring flames and was
razed to the ground by command of king Agilulf. The
soldiers, however, who were in it were allowed to return
to Ravenna.

CHAPTER XXIV.

At this time the ambassadors of Agilulf who returned
from the Cagan announced a perpetual peace made with
the Avars. Also an ambassador of the Cagan came
with them and proceeded to Gaul, demanding of the
kings of the Franks that they should keep peace with
the Langobards the same as with the Avars. Meanwhile the Langobards invaded the territories of the
Istrians[2] with the Avars and the Slavs, and laid waste
everything with burnings and plunderings.

---

[1] *Tubrugos birreos.* Hodgkin considers (V, 154, 155) that the
explanation quoted in Waitz's note " *Byrrus vestis est amphimallus
villosus*" (having the nap on both sides), according to which the
birrus was a sort of waterproof cape thrown over other garments
when it rained, seems to throw most light on this passage. (See
DuCange).

[2] Istria still remained under Byzantine dominion up to the year
751 (Abel). This raid was probably about 601 (Hodgkin, V,
430, note 1).

CHAPTER XXV.

There was then born to Agilulf the king, by his queen Theudelinda, in the palace of Modicia (Monza), a son who was called Adaloald.   At a subsequent time the Langobards attacked the fortress of Mons Silicis (Monselice).[1]   During the same period, at Ravenna, after Gallicinus (Callinicus) had been driven away, Smaragdus, who had before been patrician of Ravenna, returned.[2]

CHAPTER XXVI.

Then the emperor Maurice, after he had ruled the empire twenty-one years, was killed, together with his sons Theodosius and Tiberius and Constantine, by Focas (Phocas) who was the master of horse of Priscus the patrician.   But he had been very useful to the state for he had often obtained victory when contending against the enemy.   The Huns too, who are also called Avars, were subjugated by his prowess.[3]

[1] A little south of Padua (Abel).

[2] A. D. 602 (Hodgkin, V, 431).

[3] During the reign of Maurice a radical change began to take place in the permanent government of those parts of Italy which remained subject to Byzantium.   The invasion of the Langobards, which was at first believed to be a mere temporary incursion, had been followed by their settlement in the country, and although Maurice would not abandon the hope of expelling them, it was found more and more necessary to accept their presence as a permanent condition.   The continual wars had given rise to special military jurisdiction conferred upon the chief officers of the empire, which was temporary at first, then often renewed, and at last permanent.   The exarch remained the personal representative of the

Chapter XXVII.

Gaidoald duke of Tridentum (Trent) and Gisulf of

emperor, with full powers, including the right to conclude a temporary truce with the Langobards, though not a lasting peace and alliance (Hartmann, II, 1, 125). The frontier towns were fortified and permanent garrisons were established in them which were recruited from the neighborhood; the civil municipalities became transformed into military governments; each of the larger fortified places had a tribune as a special commandant of the city, and the tribunes were under the authority of a *magister militum* or of a duke who commanded the frontier district and who was named by the exarch. These officers gradually took the place of the former provincial civil governors, and a military corporation, the *numerus*, succeeded the municipality (id., pp. 126 to 135). The military officials began to acquire extensive landed interests, the remnant of small land-owners became more completely subject to the large proprietors, and the foundations of something which afterwards resembled a feudal tenure began to be laid (p. 136). Under Phocas the relations between Italy and Constantinople became greatly relaxed and there was a decided weakening of the imperial power. Commerce suffered in the general disorganization of the empire, and the means of communication were neglected. On the other hand there was a growing disposition to come to terms with the Langobards, although as yet an armistice for a limited time, but often renewed, was all the concession that could be made, as the emperor was apparently still unwilling to recognize the permanency of Langobard domination (id., 198, 199). The exarch Smaragdus, whom Phocas had sent to Italy, co-operated more heartily than his predecessors with the pope (id., 200), and the new emperor issued a decree upholding the authority and primacy of the Roman See (Paul, IV, 36, *infra*). Active proceedings were renewed against the schismatics of Istria and Venetia, whose bishops now betook themselves to the protection of duke Gisulf of Friuli and of king Agilulf. The schismatic bishop John was consecrated as their patriarch in Cividale and the

Forum Julii (Friuli), who were previously separated by strife from the companionship of king Agilulf, were taken back by him this year in peace.[1] Then also was the above-named boy Adaloald, the son of king Agilulf, baptized in St. John in Modicia (Monza)[2] and was received from the font[3] by Secundus of Trent, a servant of Christ of whom we have often made mention.[4] The day of the Easter festival was at that time on the seventh day before the ides of April (April 7).

CHAPTER XXVIII.

In these days the Langobards still had a quarrel with the Romans on account of the captivity of the king's daughter.[5] For this reason king Agilulf departed from Mediolanum (Milan) in the month of July, besieged the city of Cremona with the Slavs whom the Cagan, king of the Avars, had sent to his assistance and took it

empire lost their support (IV, 33, *infra*, Hartmann, II, 1, 201). We even find some of them afterwards taking part on the side of the Arian king Arioald against the Catholic Adaloald in the contest for the Langobard crown (id., p. 208).

[1] If this year refers to the death of Maurice, it is 602; if it be connected with the baptism of Adaloald, that occurred in 603 (Hodgkin, VI, 34, note 1).

[2] Probably April 7, 603 (Hodgkin, V, 430, note 3).

[3] As his godson.

[4] Only once (III, 29, *supra*) and once afterwards (IV, 40, *infra*), but a great part of this book seems to be taken from his work. This baptism was a triumph for the Catholic faith over Arianism. Agilulf's predecessor Authari had forbidden the Langobard nobles to have their children baptized by Catholics (Hodgkin, V, 430).

[5] See chapter 20, *supra*.

on the twelfth day before the calends of September (August 21st)[1] and razed it to the ground. In like manner he also assaulted Mantua, and having broken through its walls with battering-rams he entered it on the ides (13th) of September,[2] and granted the soldiers who were in it the privilege of returning to Ravenna. Then also the fortress which is called Vulturina (Valdoria)[3] surrendered to the Langobards; the soldiers indeed fled, setting fire to the town of Brexillus (Brescello).[4] When these things were accomplished, the daughter of the king was restored by Smaragdus the patrician with her husband and children and all her property. In the ninth month peace was made up to the calends (first) of April of the eighth indiction.[5] The daughter of the king, indeed, presently returned from Ravenna to Parma; but she died immediately in the perils of a difficult child-birth. In this year[6] Teudepert and Theuderic, kings of the Franks, fought with their paternal uncle Clothar, and in this struggle many thousands fell on both sides.

[1] A. D. 603 (Hodgkin, V, 432).   [2] A. D. 603 (id).

[3] Hodgkin (V, 432) places it on the northern bank of the Po not far from Parma, which is probably correct. Thus Waitz. Giansevero, p. 134, believes that a castle named Vulturena at the upper end of lake Como at the entrance of the Valtellina is intended.

[4] Or as Waitz calls it, Bersello, and adds that it is not far from Reggio (d'Emilia). It was a town on the Po about ten miles from Parma (Hodgkin, V, 432 ; see III ,18 *supra*).

[5] April 1st, 605. This indiction began with the first of September, 604.

[6] A. D. 605 (Waitz).

Chapter XXIX.

Then also in the second year of the reign of Focas (Phocas), during the eighth indiction, the blessed Pope Gregory journeyed to Christ. [1]   In his place Savinianus was appointed to the office of the papacy. [2]   There was then a very cold winter and the vines died in nearly every place.   Also the crops failed, partly destroyed by mice and partly smitten by the blight.   And indeed the world was then bound to suffer from famine and drouth when, upon the departure of so great a leader, a lack of spiritual nourishment and the dryness of thirst attacked the souls of men.   I may well put a few things in this little work from a certain letter of this same blessed Pope Gregory that it may more clearly be known how humble this man was and of how great innocence and holiness.   When then he had been accused by the emperor Maurice and his sons [3] of killing in prison for money a certain bishop Malchus, he wrote a letter on this subject to Savinianus his legate, who was at Constantinople, and said to him among other things the following: "There is one thing you may briefly suggest to our Most Serene Lords, that if I, their servant, had chosen to mix myself up with the death even of Langobards, the people of the Langobards would to-day have neither king nor dukes nor counts and would be split

---

[1] Paul, following Bede as his authority, errs as to this date. Gregory died March, 604, in the seventh indiction—Phocas began to reign near the end of 602 in the sixth indiction (Waitz).

[2] *Apostolicatus* (see DuCange, tit. *Apostolicus*).

[3] I read *filios* for *filio*.

up in the utmost confusion. But because I fear God
I dread to take part in the death of any man. This
bishop Malchus indeed was neither in prison nor in any
suffering but on the day on which he pleaded his cause
and was adjudged, he was taken without my knowledge,
by Boniface, a notary, to his home to dine there and
was honorably treated by him and at night he suddenly
died." Look! how great was the humility of this man
who called himself a servant when he was the supreme
pontiff! how great was his innocence, when he was unwilling to take part in the death of Langobards who indeed were unbelievers and were plundering everything!

CHAPTER XXX.

In the following summer then,[1] in the month of July,
Adaloald was raised as a king over the Langobards, in
the circus at Mediolanum (Milan) in the presence of his
father, king Agilulf, and while the ambassadors of Teudepert, king of the Franks[2] were standing by; and the
daughter of king Teudepert was betrothed to the same
royal youth and perpetual peace was established with
the Franks.[3]

[1] A. D. 604. Paul must have been mistaken in this date since
Pope Gregory in Dec., 603, had written to Theudelinda sending
certain gifts to "Adaloald the king" (Hodgkin, V, 447).

[2] Teudepert II, king of Austrasia (Hodgkin, VI, 108).

[3] A few years later (A. D. 607) Agilulf joined Teudepert as well
as Clothar of Neustria, and Witterich, king of the Visigoths in an
alliance against Theuderic II, of Burgundy, who had repudiated
and divorced the daughter of Witterich. There is no record of
the result of this alliance and in 612 war broke out again. Theu-

Chapter XXXI.

At the same time the Franks fought with the Saxons and there was a great slaughter on both sides. At Ticinum (Pavia) also, in the church of St. Peter the Apostle, Peter the director of the choir [1] was struck by lightning.

Chapter XXXII.

Afterwards, on the following month of November, king Agilulf made peace with Smaragdus the patrician for one year, receiving from the Romans [2] twelve thousand solidi. [3] Cities of Tuscany too, that is, Balneus Regis [4] (Bagnarea) and Urbs Vetus [5] (Orvieto) were

---

deric overcame Teudepert and put him to death, but what became of his daughter, the affianced bride of Adaloald, we are not informed. Theuderic then turned against Clothar, but suddenly died, leaving four illegitimate children. The eldest of these was Sigibert and in his name, his great grandmother, the old queen Brunihilde aspired to rule over Burgundy and Austrasia, but Arnulf, bishop of Metz, and Pepin, a great noble, went over to the side of Clothar, and in 613 Brunihilde and her great-grandchild were captured. She was tied to a vicious horse and trampled to death (Hodgkin, VI, 108–110).

[1] *Cantor* who instructed the choristers and younger clerics in music and directed the singing of the service. Sometimes this office was of considerable dignity and had a prebend attached to it. See DuCange.

[2] That is, the Greeks (Waitz).

[3] See III, 17, note 2, *supra*, as to the value of the solidus.

[4] "The King's Bath."

[5] "Old City." Both these places were afterwards in the States of the Church.

seized by the Langobards.[1]   Then also in the month of
April and May there appeared in the heavens a star
which they call a comet.   Afterwards king Agilulf again
made peace with the Romans for three years.[2]

CHAPTER XXXIII.

In these days after the death of the patriarch Severus,
the abbot John was ordained in his place[3] as patriarch
in old Aquileia with the consent of the king and of duke
Gisulf.   In Gradus (Grado) also Candidianus was ordained bishop by the Romans.[4]   Again in the months
of November and December a comet appeared.   When
Candidianus also died, Epiphanius, who had been chief
of the secretaries,[5] was ordained patriarch at Gradus by
the bishops who were under the Romans.   And from
that time there began to be two patriarchs.[6]

[1]The seizure of these cities seems to have been in April, 605,
before the commencement of the year of truce just mentioned
(see Hartmann, II, 1, 197) which began in November of that
year.

[2] 607 to 610 (Hartmann, II, 1, 197.

[3] In the Chronicle of the Patriarchs of New Aquileia (see Monticolo's ed., 1890, p. 9), Marcianus is placed between Severus and
John, and it is stated that he held the office 3 years, 1 month and
5 days.   Otherwise the list corresponds with that of Paul (Cipolla
in Atti del Congresso in Cividale, 1899, p. 136).

[4] *Antistes*, a name given, not only to bishops and abbots, but
also to priors and then to parish priests.   Andrea Dandolo, a
doge and chronicler of Venice in the 14th century, says that Marcianus preceded Candidianus (see Dandolo's Chronicle, Bk. VI,
Ch. 3).

[5] *Primicerius notariorum*, Abel translates '' Papal chief notary.''

[6] The division in the patriarchate was due to the schism in

Chapter XXXIV.

At this time John of Consia[1] (Conza) took possession of Naples, but not many days afterwards Eleutherius, the patrician, drove him from that city and killed him. After these things that same patrician Eleutherius, a eunuch, assumed the rights of sovereignty. While he was proceeding from Ravenna to Rome he was killed[2] in the fortress of Luceoli[3] by the soldiers and his head was brought to the emperor at Constantinople.[4]

regard to the Three Chapters (III, 20 and 26, *supra*). The effect of the division was to throw the schismatics into the arms of the Langobards. The patriarch John, mentioned in the text, complained to Agilulf of the persecutions of the Greeks and said that three Istrian bishops had been dragged away by imperial soldiers and forced to hold communion with Candidianus at Grado, and he asked the king, now that that worthless man had gone to eternal torment, to prevent a new patriarch from being ordained at Grado. This, however, was not done. Some time later, one Fortunatus was made patriarch there, and being at heart a schismatic, he seized the treasure of the church and fled to the mainland, where he was made patriarch of Aquileia and the Langobards were asked in vain to give back the treasure. Finally the emperor Heraclius sent a large sum of money to Grado to make up for the loss (Hodgkin, V, 482, 483).

[1] Or "Compsa," a city in ancient Samnium on the Aufidus.

[2] Paul places the death of John of Consia and Eleutherius 10 or 12 years too early. According to the Liber Pontificalis, Eleutherius was killed A. D. 619 (Jacobi, 53), after Agilulf's death. See Hodgkin, VI, 156.

[3] Or "Luciuolo," which is believed to be located between Gubbio and Cagli, hence north of Perugia and south of Urbino (Muratori Ann., 4, 40).

[4] The usurpation of Eleutherius was one of a series of efforts to

Chapter XXXV.

Also at this time king Agilulf sent his secretary Stablicianus to Constantinople to the emperor Focas, and when he returned with the ambassadors of the emperor, peace was made for a year, and the ambassadors presented to king Agilulf imperial gifts.[1]

Chapter XXXVI.

Focas then, as has been already set forth, usurped the sovereignty of the Romans after the death of Maurice and his sons, and reigned during the course of eight years. Because the church of Constantinople was calling itself in writing the first of all churches, he ordained, at the request of Pope Boniface,[2] that the See of

separate Italy from the East, occasioned by the growing weakness of the empire. The exarch John, the immediate successor of Smaragdus had been killed with a number of other officers, and Eleutherius his successor had punished those who had been guilty of the crime, and had then become involved in an unsuccessful war with the Langobards with whom he had concluded an armistice in consideration of an annual tribute of 500 pounds of gold. Now he raised the standard of revolt with the design of establishing a new Western empire with Rome as its capital. He assumed the purple in Ravenna, and intended to be crowned in that city, but changed his purpose and was proceeding to Rome for his coronation when he was killed (see Hartmann, II, 1, 202, 203).

[1] This is the first instance of direct negotiations between the Langobards and Constantinople. Prior to this a truce had been made on several occasions with the exarch. These ''imperial gifts'' were probably in the nature of a tribute (Hartmann, II, 1, 198).

[2] Boniface III, A. D. 606, 607 (Abel).

the Roman and Apostolic Church should be the head of all. He commanded, at the request of another pope Boniface,[1] that the Church of the Ever-blessed Virgin Mary and of all the Martyrs should be established in the old temple which was called the Pantheon, after all the uncleannesses of idolatry had been removed, so that where formerly the worship, not of all the gods, but of all the devils was performed, there at last there should be a memorial of all the saints. At this time the Prasini and the Veneti[2] carried on a civil war throughout

[1] Boniface IV, A. D. 607–615 (Abel).

[2] So called from the colors of the contestants in the circus.   At first a chariot race was a contest of two chariots with drivers in white and red liveries.   Two additional colors, a light green (*prasinus*) and a cerulean blue (*venetus=caeruleus*, " the sky reflected in the sea ") were afterwards introduced.   The four factions soon acquired a legal establishment and their fanciful colors typified the various appearances of nature in the four seasons, or according to another interpretation, the struggle of the green and blue represented the conflict of the earth and sea.   These contests disturbed the spectacles in the circus of imperial Rome and later, raged with redoubled fury in the hippodrome of Constantinople. Under Anastasius the Greens massacred at a solemn festival three thousand of the opposite faction.   The Blues, favored by Justinian I, were the authors of widespread disorders and outrages at the capital, and in 532 a sedition called that of *Nika* was excited by the mutual hatred and momentary reconciliation of these factions, in which many of the most important buildings of the city were consumed, some thirty thousand persons slain, and the reign of Justinian himself was brought to the brink of destruction.   The hippodrome closed for a time, but when it was opened again the disorders were renewed, (Gibbon, ch. 40,) and the text shows how widespread were the disturbances some three-quarters of a century later.

the East and Egypt and destroyed each other with mutual slaughter. The Persians also waged a very severe war against the empire, took away many provinces of the Romans, including Jerusalem itself, [1] and destroying churches and profaning holy things they carried off among the ornaments of places sacred and secular, even the banner of the cross of Christ. Heraclian, who was governing Africa, rebelled against this Focas and coming with his army, deprived him of his sovereignty and his life, and Heraclius, the son of Heraclian, undertook the government of the Roman state. [2]

CHAPTER XXXVII.

About these times the king of the Avars, whom they call Cagan in their language, came with a countless multitude and invaded the territories of Venetia. [3] Gisulf the duke of Forum Julii (Friuli) boldly came to meet him with all the Langobards he could get, but although

[1] This actually occurred later (A. D. 614) under Heraclius (Giansevero).

[2] A. D. 610 (Hartmann, II, 1, 200).

[3] The date usually assigned to the Avar invasion is 611, though some place it as early as 602. Phocas reigned from 602 to 610. If the death of Severus, patriarch of Aquileia, occurred in 606, the Avar invasion took place after that date, since Gisulf concurred in the nomination of his successor (Hodgkin, VI, 51, note). The previous relations between the Langobards and Avars had been of the most friendly character. There had been treaties of alliance, joint invasions of Istria, injunctions sent by the Avars to the Franks to keep peace with the Langobards and Agilulf had furnished the Cagan with shipwrights for a naval expedition against the Eastern empire (IV, 24, 20, *supra;* Hodgkin, VI, 50, 51).

he waged war with a few against an immense multitude with indomitable courage, nevertheless, he was surrounded on every side, and killed with nearly all his followers. The wife of this Gisulf, by name Romilda, together with the Langobards who had escaped and with the wives and children of those who had perished in war, fortified herself [1] within the enclosures of the walls of the fortress of Forum Julii (Cividale). She had two sons, Taso and Cacco, who were already growing youths, and Raduald and Grimuald, who were still in the age of boyhood. And she had also four daughters, of whom one was called Appa and another Gaila, but of two we do not preserve the names. The Langobards had also fortified themselves in other fortresses which were near these, that is, in Cormones (Cormons), Nemas (Nimis), Osopus (Ossopo),[2] Artenia (Artegna),[3] Reunia (Ragogna), Glemona (Gemona),[4] and also in Ibligis (Iplis)[5] whose position was in every way impregnable. Also in the same way they fortified themselves in the remaining castles, so that they should not become the prey of the Huns, that is, of the Avars. But the Avars, roaming through all the territories of Forum Julii, devastating everything with burnings and plunderings, shut up by siege the town of Forum Julii and strove with all their

[1] I insert *se* after *muniit.*

[2] On the river Tagliamento (Waitz).

[3] In Carnia (Waitz).

[4] In Friuli (Waitz).

[5] Near Cividale on the way to Cormons (Waitz). According to others, Invilino (Abel).

might to capture it.   While their king, that is the Cagan, was ranging around the walls in full armor with a great company of horsemen to find out from what side he might more easily capture the city, Romilda gazed upon him from the walls, and when she beheld him in the bloom of his youth, the abominable harlot was seized with desire for him and straightway sent word to him by a messenger that if he would take her in marriage she would deliver to him the city with all who were in it.   The barbarian king, hearing this, promised her with wicked cunning that he would do what she had enjoined and vowed to take her in marriage.   She then without delay opened the gates of the fortress of Forum Julii and let in the enemy to her own ruin and that of all who were there.   The Avars indeed with their king, having entered Forum Julii, laid waste with their plunderings everything they could discover, consumed in flames the city itself, and carried away as captives everybody they found, falsely promising them, however, to settle them in the territories of Pannonia, from which they had come.   When on their return to their country they had come to the plain they called Sacred,[1] they decreed that all the Langobards who had attained full age should perish by the sword, and they divided the women and children in the lot of captivity.   But Taso and Cacco and Raduald, the sons of Gisulf and Romilda, when they knew the evil intention of the Avars, straightway mounted their horses and took flight.   One of them

[1] The Sacred Plain has not been identified (Hodgkin, VI, 53, note 2).

when he thought that his brother Grimoald, a little boy, could not keep himself upon a running horse, since he was so small, considered it better that he should perish by the sword than bear the yoke of captivity, and wanted to kill him. When therefore, he lifted his lance to pierce him through, the boy wept and cried out, saying: " Do not strike me for I can keep on a horse." And his brother, seizing him by the arm, put him upon the bare back of a horse and urged him to stay there if he could; and the boy, taking the rein of the horse in his hand, followed his fleeing brothers. The Avars, when they learned this, mounted their horses and followed them, but although the others escaped by swift flight, the little boy Grimoald was taken by one of those who had run up most swiftly. His captor, however, did not deign to strike him with the sword on account of his slender age, but rather kept him to be his servant. And returning to the camp, he took hold of the bridle of the horse and led the boy away, and exulted over so noble a booty—for he was a little fellow of elegant form with gleaming eyes and covered with long blonde hair—and when the boy grieved that he was carried away as a captive,

Pondering mighty thoughts within his diminutive bosom,[1]

he took out of the scabbard a sword, such as he was able to carry at that age, and struck the Avar who was leading him, with what little strength he could, on the

[1] Virgil, Georgics, IV, 83, where it is applied to the soldier bees. In Paul's quotation *versant* is changed to *versans*.

top of the head. Straightway the blow passed through
to the skull and the enemy was thrown from his horse.
And the boy Grimoald turned his own horse around and
took flight, greatly rejoicing, and at last joined his
brothers and gave them incalculable joy by his escape
and by announcing, moreover, the destruction of his
enemy. The Avars now killed by the sword all the
Langobards who were already of the age of manhood,
but the women and children they consigned to the yoke
of captivity. Romilda indeed, who had been the head
of all this evil-doing, the king of the Avars, on account
of his oath, kept for one night as if in marriage as he
had promised her, but upon the next he turned her over
to twelve Avars, who abused her through the whole
night with their lust, succeeding each other by turns.
Afterwards too, ordering a stake to be fixed in the
midst of a field, he commanded her to be impaled upon
the point of it, uttering these words, moreover, in reproach: "It is fit you should have such a husband."
Therefore the detestable betrayer of her country who
looked out for her own lust more than for the preservation of her fellow citizens and kindred, perished by such
a death. Her daughters, indeed, did not follow the sen-
sual inclination of their mother, but striving from love
of chastity not to be contaminated by the barbarians,
they put the flesh of raw chickens under the band
between their breasts, and this, when putrified by the
heat, gave out an evil smell. And the Avars, when they
wanted to touch them, could not endure the stench that
they thought was natural to them, but moved far away
from them with cursing, saying that all the Langobard

women had a bad smell. By this stratagem then the
noble girls, escaping from the lust of the Avars, not
only kept themselves chaste, but handed down a useful
example for preserving chastity if any such thing
should happen to women hereafter. And they were
afterwards sold throughout various regions and secured
worthy marriages on account of their noble birth; for
one of them is said to have wedded a king of the Alamanni, and another, a prince of the Bavarians.

The topic now requires me to postpone my general
history and relate also a few matters of a private
character concerning the genealogy of myself who write
these things, and because the case so demands, I must
go back a little earlier in the order of my narrative. At
the time when the nation of the Langobards came from
Pannonia to Italy, my great-great-grandfather Leupchis
of the same nation of Langobards came with them in
like manner. When he ended his last day after he had
lived some years in Italy, he left five sons begotten by
him who were still little boys. That misfortune of captivity of which we have spoken included these, and they
were all carried away as exiles from the fortress of
Forum Julii into the country of the Avars. After they
had borne in that region for many years the misery of
bondage, and had already come to the age of manhood,
although the four others, whose names we do not retain,
remained in the constraint of captivity, the fifth brother,
Lopichis by name, who was afterwards our great-grandfather, determined (at the inspiration as we believe of
the Author of Mercy) to cast off the yoke of bondage,
and to direct his course to Italy, where he had remem-

bered that the race of the Langobards was settled, and
he made an effort to regain the rights of freedom.
When he had gone and betaken himself to flight, carrying only a quiver and bow and a little food for the journey, and did not at all know whither he was proceeding, a wolf came to him and became the companion of
his journey and his guide. Seeing that it proceeded
before him, and often looked behind and stood with
him when he stood, and went ahead when he advanced,
he understood that it had been given to him from
heaven to show to him the way, of which he was ignorant. When they had proceeded in this manner for
some days through the solitudes of the mountains, the
bread, of which the traveler had had very little, wholly
failed him. While he went on his way fasting, and had
already become faint with exhaustion from hunger, he
drew his bow and attempted to kill with his arrow this
same wolf so that he could use it for food. But the
wolf, avoiding the stroke that he cast, slipped away from
his sight. And he, not knowing whither to proceed,
when this wolf had gone away, and made very weak
moreover by the privation of hunger, now despaired of
his life, and throwing himself upon the earth, he went to
sleep. And he saw in his dreams a certain man saying
to him the following words: "Arise! why are you
sleeping? Take your way in that direction opposite to
which your feet are turned, for there is Italy which you
are seeking." And straightway rising he began to proceed in that direction which he had heard in his dreams,
and without delay he came to a dwelling place of men;
for there was a settlement of Slavs in those places.

And when an elderly woman now saw him, she straight-way understood that he was a fugitive and suffering from the privation of hunger. And taking pity upon him, she hid him in her dwelling and secretly furnished him food, a little at a time, lest she should put an end to his life altogether if she should give him nourishment to repletion. In fine, she thus supplied him skillfully with food until he was restored and got his strength. And when she saw that he was now able to pursue his journey, she gave him provisions and told him in what direction he ought to go. After some days he entered Italy and came to the house in which he had been born, which was so deserted that not only did it have no roof but it was full of brambles and thorns. And when he had cut them down he found within the walls a large ash-tree, and hung his quiver upon it. He was after-wards provided with gifts by his relatives and friends, and rebuilt his house and took a wife. But he could obtain nothing of the property his father had had, being now excluded by those who had appropriated it through long and continuous possession. This man, as I already said before, was my great-grandfather, and he begot my grandfather Arichis,[1] and Arichis, my father Warnefrit, and Warnefrit, from Theudelinda his wife, begot me, Paul, and my brother Arichis who was named after my grandfather.[2] These few things having been con-

[1] Henry.

[2] Paul has probably omitted some links in his family genealogy. Four generations are very few for the period between Leupchis who came into Italy with Alboin, 568, and Paul, who was born between 720 and 730. It is remarkable too that Leupchis, a

sidered concerning the chain of my own genealogy, now let us return to the thread of the general history.

CHAPTER XXXVIII.

After the death, as we said, of Gisulf, duke of Forum Julii, his sons Taso and Cacco undertook the government of this dukedom. They possessed in their time the territory of the Slavs which is named Zellia (Gail-thal),[1] up to the place which is called Medaria (Windisch Matrei), hence, those same Slavs, up to the time of duke Ratchis, paid tribute to the dukes of Forum Julii. Gregory the patrician of the Romans killed these two brothers in the city of Opitergium (Oderzo) by crafty treachery. For he promised Taso that he would cut his beard,[2] as is the custom, and make him his son, and this Taso, with Cacco his brother, and some chosen youths came to Gregory fearing no harm. When presently he had entered Opitergium with his followers, straightway the patrician ordered the gates of the city to be closed and sent armed soldiers against Taso and his companions. Taso with his followers perceiving this, boldly prepared for a fight, and when a moment of quiet was given, they bade each other a last fare-

grown man in 568, should leave five little children at the time of the Avar invasion in 610 (Hodgkin, VI, 58, note 1).

[1] Hodgkin, VI, 59, note, and Hartmann, II, 1, 236. The valley of the Gail in Carinthia and eastern Tyrol.

[2] A ceremony indicating that he whose beard is shaved and whose hair is cut has arrived at the state of manhood. Thus king Liutprand performed a similar ceremony for the son of Charles Martel (Book VI, Chap. 53, *infra*).

well, and scattered hither and thither through the
different streets of the city, killing whomsoever they
could find in their way, and while they made a great
slaughter of the Romans, they also were slain at last.
But Gregory the patrician, on account of the oath he
had given, ordered the head of Taso to be brought to
him, and, perjured though he was, cut off his beard as
he had promised.[1]

CHAPTER XXXIX.

When they were thus killed, Grasulf, the brother of
Gisulf, was made duke of Forum Julii.[2]   But Radoald and
Grimoald, as they were now close to the age of manhood, held it in contempt to live under the power of
their uncle Grasulf, and they embarked in a little boat
and came rowing to the territories of Beneventum.

[1] Fredegarius (IV, 69) tells a story (which is considered by some
to be a variation of this) as to the murder of Taso, duke of Tuscany, by the patrician Isaac.   King Arioald offered Isaac to re-
mit one of the three hundredweights of gold which the empire
paid yearly to the Langobards if he would kill Taso, who was a
rebel (see chap. 49).   Isaac invited Taso to Ravenna with a troop
of warriors who were prevailed upon to leave their arms outside
the walls, and when they entered the city they were assassinated.
The tribute was accordingly reduced.   Soon afterwards Arioald
died.   As Arioald reigned from 626 to 636 and Isaac did not become exarch until 630, this story can not be reconciled with Paul's
account of an event which must have happened many years
earlier.   Either Fredegarius got hold of an inaccurate version, or
the coincidence of name is accidental and the story relates to some
different event (Hodgkin, VI, 59, 60, note 2; Pabst, 429).

[2] De Rubeis (Appendix, p. 63) says this occurred A. D. 616.

Then hastening to Arichis, duke of the Beneventines, their former preceptor, they were received by him most kindly and treated by him in the place of sons. In these times, upon the death of Tassilo, duke of the Bavarians, his son Garibald was conquered by the Slavs at Aguntum (Innichen), and the territories of the Bavarians were plundered. The Bavarians, however, having recovered their strength, took away the booty from their foes and drove their enemies from their territories.

CHAPTER XL.

King Agilulf, indeed, made peace with the emperor for one year, and again for another, and also renewed a second time the bond of peace with the Franks. In this year, nevertheless, the Slavs grievously devastated Istria after killing the soldiers who defended it. Also in the following month of March, Secundus, a servant of Christ of whom we have already often spoken, died at Tridentum (Trent). He composed a brief history of the deeds of the Langobards up to his time.[1] At that time king Agilulf again made peace with the emperor. In those days Theudepert, king of the Franks, was also killed, and a very severe battle occurred among them. Gunduald too, the brother of queen Theudelinda, who was duke in the city of Asta (Asti), died at this time, struck by an arrow, but no one knew the author of his death.

[1] After the death of Secundus in 612 Paul's source for the history of Trent becomes exhausted and we hear little more about that duchy.

CHAPTER XLI.

Then king Agilulf, who was called Ago, after he had reigned twenty-five years, ended his last day,[1] and his son Adaloald, who was still a boy, was left in the sovereignty with Theudelinda his mother. Under them the churches were restored and many gifts were bestowed upon the holy places. But when Adaloald, after he had reigned with his mother ten years, lost his reason and became insane, he was cast out of the sovereignty,[2] and

[1] Probably 615 or 616 (Waitz; Hodgkin, VI, 147, note 1).

[2] Fredegarius (Chron. 49) tells the story thus: that Adaloald, upon the advice of one Eusebius, anointed himself in the bath with some sort of ointment, and afterwards could do nothing except what he was told by Eusebius; that he was thus persuaded to order all the chief persons and nobles of the Langobards to be killed, and upon their death to surrender, with all his people to the empire; that when he had put twelve to death without their fault, the rest conspired to raise Arioald, duke of Turin, who had married Gundiperga, the sister of Adaloald, to the throne; that Adaloald took poison and died and Arioald straightway took possession of the kingdom.

Possibly the zeal of Theudelinda and Adaloald for the Catholic faith may have provoked a reaction among the Langobards, who had been Arians, and they may have become dissatisfied with the conciliatory policy toward the empire which was characteristic of the Bavarian line of sovereigns descended from Theudelinda. The legend of Eusebius was perhaps an expression of this dissatisfaction. Adaloald's successor was certainly an Arian. We have already seen (ch. 34, note, *supra*) that during Adaloald's time Eleutherius the exarch defeated John of Compsa who had revolted and taken possession of Naples, and put him to death. After this revolt the war with the Langobards was renewed and Sundrar the Langobard general repeatedly defeated the exarch, who finally obtained peace upon payment of a yearly tribute of

Arioald was substituted by the Langobards in his place.[1]
Concerning the acts of this king hardly anything has
come to our knowledge.[2] About these times the holy

five hundredweight of gold (Hodgkin, VI, 154, 155). We have
also seen that Eleutherius afterwards aspired to independent sovereignty and was killed (IV, 34, *supra*), though Paul incorrectly
places these occurrences during the reign of Agilulf. In 625 Pope
Honorius I addressed a letter to Isaac the new exarch saying that
some bishops beyond the Po had urged one Peter, who seems to
have been a layman high in office, not to follow the Catholic
Adaloald, but the tyrant Ariopalt (Arioald) (Hodgkin, VI, 158);
since the crime of the bishops was odious, the pope asked the
exarch to send them to Rome for punishment as soon as Adaloald
was restored to his kingdom. This contest between Adaloald
and his successor probably occurred between 624 and 626 (Hodgkin, VI, 160), and it would seem that Adaloald had taken refuge
with the exarch in Ravenna from which Wiese (p. 284) infers that
his death may have been by order of Isaac to avoid complications
with the Langobards. We do not learn what part Theudelinda
took in this contest. She died February 22nd, 628, shortly after
the death of Adaloald (Hodgkin VI, 160).

[1] Probably A. D. 626 (Hodgkin, VI, 161).

[2] Fredegarius (IV, 51) tells us that Gundiperga (wife of Arioald
and daughter of Agilulf and Theudelinda) said one day that Adalulf, a nobleman in the king's service, was a man of goodly
stature, and Adalulf hearing this, proposed to her that she should
be unfaithful to her marriage vow. She scorned his proposal
whereupon he charged that she had granted a secret interview to
Taso duke of Tuscany and had promised to poison the king and
raise Taso to the throne. Upon this Arioald imprisoned her in a
fortress. Two years afterwards Clothar II, king of the Franks,
sent ambassadors to Arioald asking why she had been imprisoned
and when the reason was given, one of the ambassadors suggested
a trial by battle to ascertain her guilt or innocence. The duel accordingly took place, Adalulf was slain by the queen's champion
and she was restored to her royal dignity (Hodgkin, VI, 161–163).

Columban, sprung from the race of Scots, after he had built a monastery in Gaul in the place called Luxovium (Luxeuil), came into Italy,[1] and was kindly received by the king of the Langobards, and built a convent in the Cottian Alps which is called Bobium (Bobbio) and is forty miles distant from the city of Ticinum.[2]   In this

[1] Probably before this time and about A. D. 612 (Giansevero).

[2] St. Columban was born, not in Scotland but in Ireland about 543 and entered a monastery at Bangor at a period when the Irish monasteries were centers of culture.   After some years he set forth to preach the gospel, first in Britain and then in Gaul.   Sigispert, king of Austrasia, the husband of Brunihilde gave him a ruined village named Anagratis where he established a monastery, but after a while he retired to a cave, and was so famed for miracles that he drew around him many disciples and found it necessary to establish another monastery at Luxovium in the domains of Gunthram of Burgundy, now the Vosges.   A third was established near by at Ad Fontanas (Hodgkin VI, 110, 113).   Afterwards he incurred the enmity of Brunihilde and her grandson Theuderic of Burgundy (pp. 121-123) and was expelled from that kingdom.   Under the protection of Theudepert of Austrasia he found a retreat at Bregenz on the Lake of Constance (p. 126) where he put an end to the worship of heathen gods, which had been practiced in the neighborhood.   Upon Theudepert's death, which the saint had foretold, he betook himself to Italy where he was received with honor by Agilulf and Theudelinda (p. 131).   He remained some months at Milan at the royal court and argued there with Arian ecclesiastics, until a certain Jocundus came to king Agilulf and spoke of the advantages for a monastic life offered by the village of Bobium on the Trebia among the Apennines (p. 132). Columban retired thither and there built the monastery which became an important instrument in converting the Langobards from Arianism, and in the spread of Roman culture among that people (Hartmann II, 2, 25).   He was a man of great learning.   He aided Theudelinda in her conflicts with Arianism, but he also be-

place also many possessions were bestowed by particular princes and Langobards, and there was established there a great community of monks.

CHAPTER XLII.

Then Arioald, after he had held the sovereignty over the Langobards twelve years, departed this life, and Rothari,[1] of the race of Arodus, received the kingdom of the Langobards.[2] And he was brave and strong,

came an adherent of the schismatics in the controversy of the Three Chapters, and Theudelinda used him in defending their cause, which he did in a long letter to Pope Boniface IV, the third successor of Gregory the Great. Agilulf desired to heal the schism and Columban states in his letter that the king was reported to have said that he too would believe the Catholic faith if he could know the certainty of the matter! Columban died in 615, the same year as Agilulf (Hodgkin, VI, 138–147).

[1] Hartmann (II, 1, 235) considers that in this reckoning, the time is probably included in which Arioald was in insurrection against Adaloald. Rothari ascended the throne in 636 (Waitz).

[2] Fredegarius relates that after the death of Arioald his widow Gundiperga was asked, as Theudelinda had been, to choose his successor; that her choice fell upon Rothari, whom she invited to put away his wife and marry her, which he did, but afterwards confined her in one little room in the palace, while he lived with his concubines; that after five years' seclusion the Frankish king Clovis II interceded and she was restored to her queenly dignities (Hodgkin, VI, 165, 166). This story sounds like a repetition of the account of Gundiperga's disgrace during the reign of her first husband. It would seem that Rothari's marriage to Gundiperga, like that of Agilulf to Theudelinda was to add a certain claim of legitimacy to his pretensions to the throne and perhaps the fact that he was an Arian and his wife a Catholic led to the story above related (Hartmann, II, 1, 239, 240).

and followed the path of justice;[1] he did not, however, hold the right line of Christian belief, but was stained by the infidelity of the Arian heresy.[2] The Arians, indeed, say to their own ruin that the Son is less than the Father, and the Holy Spirit also is less than the Father and the Son. But we Catholics confess that the Father and Son and Holy Spirit are one and the true God in three persons, equal in power and the same in glory. In this time there were two bishops throughout almost all the cities[3] of the kingdom, one a Catholic and the other an Arian. In the city of Ticinum too there is shown, down to the present time, the place

[1] Fredegarius relates (Chron. 71) that at the beginning of his reign he put to death many insubordinate nobles and that in his efforts for peace he maintained very strict discipline (Pabst, 430, note 3).

[2] With the exception of Adaloald, all the kings of the Langobards up to this time had been Arians though their religious convictions were not strong, and they were not generally intolerant (Hodgkin VI, 144, 145). The beliefs of the invaders under Alboin were somewhat heterogeneous. Some of his followers were probably still tinctured with the remnants of heathenism, most of them were Arians, while the Noricans and Pannonians who accompanied him to Italy (II, 26 *supra*) were Catholics (Hegel, Städteverfassung von Italien I, Ch. 3, p. 364). The conversion of the Langobards to the Catholic faith was promoted by their intermarriage with Roman wives. Theudelinda, who was a Catholic, had done much to further it. Even as early as the time of Gregory the Great there were Catholic bishops under the Langobards (id., p. 363).

[3] This is doubtful. Paul knew of some Arian bishops and doubtless he presumed, erroneously, the presence of Catholic bishops in the same places (Hartmann II, 1, 278).

where the Arian bishop, who had his seat at the church of St. Eusebius, had a baptistery, while another bishop sat in the Catholic church. Yet this Arian bishop, who was in the same city, Anastasius by name, became converted to the Catholic faith and afterwards governed the church of Christ. This king Rothari collected, in a series of writings, the laws of the Langobards which they were keeping in memory only and custom,[1] and he

[1] Compare this with the Chronicon Gothanum, (M. G., LLIV, p. 641) "Rothari reigned sixteen years and by him law and justice began with the Langobards and the judges first went through them in writing. For previously lawsuits were decided by custom, (*cadarfada*) discretion and usage." Rothari's Edict was published Nov. 22d, 643. It was composed of 388 chapters. Although written in Latin, the greater part of this Edict was of purely Langobard origin. By this code the man who conspired against the king or deserted his comrades in battle must suffer death, but those accused of a capital offense might appeal to the wager of battle. If freemen conspired and accomplished the death of another they were to compound for the murder according to the rank of the person slain (Hodgkin, VI, 175 to 179). If any one should "place himself in the way" of a free woman or girl or injure her he must pay nine hundred solidi (540 pounds sterling). If any one should "place himself in the way" of a free man he must pay him twenty solidi, if he had not done him any bodily injury. These provisions indicated the high estimation in which the free women were held. If any one should "place himself in the way" of another man's slave or hand-maid or *aldius* (half-free) he must pay twenty solidi *to his lord*. Bodily injuries were all catalogued, each of the teeth, fingers and toes being specially named and the price fixed for each. Many laws dealt specially with injuries to an *aldius* or to a household slave. These were not equivalent terms and it is generally believed that the vanquished Roman population were included in the first. A still lower class were the plantation

directed this code to be called the Edict. It was now

slaves (Hodgkin, VI, 180–189). In the laws of succession, provision was made for illegitimate as well as legitimate children, though less in amount. No father could disinherit his son except for certain grievous crimes. Donations of property were made in the presence of the *thing*, an assembly of at least a few freemen, a survival of the *folk-thing* of the ancient Germans, from which comes the Latinized word *thingare*, to grant or donate, and one of the laws of Rothari provides that, if a man shall wish to " thing away " his property to another, he must make the *gairethinx* (spear donation), not secretly, but before freemen. The Langobard women always remained under some form of guardianship (pp. 193–197). If a man should commit an immorality with a female slave "belonging to the nations" he must pay her lord twenty solidi, if with a Roman, twelve solidi, the Roman bond-woman being of less value than the slave of Teutonic or other origin. This is the only reference to Romans as such in Rothari's laws. If a slave or *aldius* married a free Langobard woman, her relatives had a right to slay her or sell her and divide her substance. No slave or *aldius* could sell property without the consent of his master or patron. Slaves might be emancipated in various ways, but there were severe laws for the pursuit and restoration of fugitives (pp. 204–211). In judicial procedure, a system of compurgation prevailed as well as the wager of battle (pp. 224–230).

Rothari's code was rude and barbarous to the last degree as compared with the elaborate system of Roman jurisprudence embodied in the laws of Justinian, under which the population of Italy had been living prior to the Langobard conquest. In Rothari's laws, although the rights of the clan, so important during the migration of the Langobards, became more and more subordinated to the rights of the state (Hartmann, II, 2, 11), the authority of the family still continued to be recognized as an important feature. The general assembly of freemen continued to add solemnity to important popular acts, such as the enactment of new laws or the selection of a king, although it was now manifestly impossible that

indeed the seventy-seventh year from the time when the
Langobards had come into Italy, as that king bore wit-

such an assembly should consist, as in earlier times, of all those
capable of bearing arms (id., pp. 12–13).

Villari (Le Invasioni Barbariche in Italia, p. 310) insists that the
indirect action of Roman jurisprudence appears in Rothari's laws,
not only in the Latin language in which they were written, in some
Justinian-like phrases, and in an arrangement to some extent
systematical, but also in certain provisions which he thinks cannot
be of Germanic origin.   He adds (p. 311) that it cannot be conceived how the Langobards could have destroyed a system of
jurisprudence established for centuries which had created among
the conquered Italians a number of legal relations unknown to
their conquerors so that the laws of the latter could not provide
for them, nor how Roman law could be destroyed and afterwards
reappear in Langobard Italy, without any account of its disap-
pearance and reappearance in documents or chronicles.   He concludes that although not officially recognized, it was allowed to live
under the form of custom, in many of the private relations that
existed among the conquered Italians.   This view is confirmed by
the 204th law of Rothari which, speaking of "any free woman
living according to the law of the Langobards," would indicate
that there were others not living according to that law.   Moreover
it was declared (Hodgkin, VI, 231) that foreigners who came to
settle in the land ought to live according to the laws of the Langobards unless they obtained from the king the right to live according to some other law.   Villari also sees (p. 312) evidences of the
persistency of Roman law in the subsequent legislation of Liutprand providing that if a Langobard, after having children, should
become a churchman, they should continue to live subject to the
law under which he had lived before becoming a churchman.
This would indicate that after becoming a churchman, the father
lived under another law, which must have been the Roman law.
Villari (p. 329) also sees elsewhere in Liutprand's legislation evidences of canonical law.

ness in a prologue to his Edict.[1]   To this king, Arichis,
the duke of Beneventum sent his son Aio.   And when
the latter had come to Ravenna on his way to Ticinum,
such a drink was there given him by the malice of the
Romans that it made him lose his reason, and from that
time he was never of full and sound mind.[2]

Chapter XLIII.

Therefore when duke Arichis, the father of him of
whom we have spoken, was now ripe in years and near-
ing his last day, knowing that his son Aio was not of
right mind, he commended Radoald and Grimoald,[4] now
in the flower of their youth, as if they were his own
sons, to the Langobards who were present, and said to
them that these two could rule them better than could
Aio his son.

Chapter XLIV.

Then on the death of Arichis, who had held the
dukedom fifty years, Aio, his son, was made leader of
the Samnites,[3] and still Radoald and Grimoald[4] obeyed
him in all things as their elder brother and lord.   When

[1] Rothari says the seventy-sixth year (Edicti Codices M. G.
LL., IV, p. 1.)   As to this, see note to I, 21, note 3, pp. 39,
40, *supra;* as to the so-called prologue, see Appendix, II, A. 1.

[2] His intercourse with the Romans, as in the case of Adaloald,
seems to have led to insanity.   Was this the Langobard idea of
the effect of contact with Roman luxury and civilization upon the
princes of their race?

[3] That is the Beneventines.   This occurred A. D. 641 (Waitz).

[4] I follow here and in other places the spelling of Waitz's text
which is not uniform.

this Aio had already governed the dukedom of Beneventum a year and five months, the Slavs came with a
great number of ships and set up their camp not far
from the city of Sipontum (Siponto). They made
hidden pit-falls around their camp and when Aio came
upon them in the absence of Raduald and Grimoald and
attempted to conquer them, his horse fell into one of
these pit-falls, the Slavs rushed upon him and he was
killed with a number of others. When this was announced to Raduald he came quickly and talked famili-
arly with these Slavs in their own language,[1] and when
in this way he had lulled them into greater indolence
for war, he presently fell upon them, overthrew them
with great slaughter, revenged the death of Aio and
compelled those of his enemies who had survived to
seek flight from these territories.[2]

CHAPTER XLV.

King Rothari then captured all the cities of the
Romans which were situated upon the shore of the sea
from the city of Luna (Luni) in Tuscany up to the
boundaries of the Franks.[3]   Also he captured and de-

[1] Raduald and Grimoald had been neighbors to the Slavs in the
dukedom of Fruili from which they had come to Beneventum
(Waitz).

[2] A. D. 642 (Hartmann, II, 1, 244).

[3] Rothari was a representative of the national, anti-Roman,
Arian feeling among the Langobards; so the peace with the empire
was broken and war renewed. He thus rounded out his possessions
in the northern part of the kingdom, and Neustria, the western
portion of these dominions, began to be distinguished from Austria,
east of the Adda, which was more immediately subject to the
dukes of Trent and Friuli (Hartmann, II, 1, 243).

stroyed Opitergium (Oderzo)[1] a city placed between
Tarvisium (Treviso) and Forum Julii (Cividale).   He
waged war with the Romans of Ravenna [2] near the river
of Emilia which is called the Scultenna (Panaro).   In
this war eight thousand fell on the side of the Romans
and the remainder took to flight.   At this time a great
earthquake occurred at Rome and there was then a
great inundation of the waters.   After these things
there was a scab disease of such a kind that no one
could recognize his own dead on account of the great
swelling and inflammation.[3]

CHAPTER XLVI.

But when duke Raduald, who had managed the dukedom five years, died at Beneventum, Grimuald his
brother became duke and governed the dukedom of the
Samnites five and twenty years.   From a captive girl,
but one of high birth, however, whose name was Ita, he
begot a son Romuald and two daughters.   And since he
was a very warlike man and distinguished everywhere,
when the Greeks at that time came to plunder the
sanctuary of the holy arch-angel [4] situated upon Mount
Garganus (Gargano), Grimuald, coming upon them with
his army, overthrew them with the utmost slaughter.

[1] This destruction was not complete, but twenty-five years later
under Grimoald, the place was entirely annihilated (V, 28, *infra*).

[2] Who were under the exarch Isaac (Hodgkin, VI, 169).

[3] The earthquake and plague are placed by the Liber Pontificalis
in the sixth indiction (617–618), and incorrectly placed by Paul
during the reign of Rothari (636–652) (Jacobi, 54).

[4] Michael.

CHAPTER XLVII.

But king Rothari indeed, after he had held the sovereignty sixteen years and four months, departed from life [1] and left the kingdom of the Langobards to his son Rodoald. When he had been buried near the church of St. John the Baptist,[2] after some time, a certain man inflamed by wicked cupidity opened his sepulcher at night and took away whatever he found among the ornaments of his body. St. John appearing to him in a vision frightened him dreadfully and said to him, "Why did you dare to touch the body of that man? Although he may not have been of the true faith yet he has commended himself to me. Because therefore you have presumed to do this thing you will never hereafter have admission into my church." And so it occurred; for as often soever as he wished to enter the sanctuary of St. John, straightway his throat would be hit as if by a very powerful boxer and thus stricken, he suddenly fell down backwards. I speak the truth in Christ; he who saw with his own eyes that very thing done related this to me. Rodoald then received the kingdom of the Langobards after the death of his father, and united with himself in marriage Gundiperga the daughter of Agilulf and Theudelinda.[3] This Gundiperga in imitation of her mother, just as the latter had done in Modicia

[1] A. D. 652 (Hodgkin, VI, 241).

[2] In Modicia (Monza) or possibly in Ticinum (Waitz).

[3] If Fredegarius (Chapters 50, 51, 70) be correct Paul must be mistaken, since Gundiperga was the wife of king Arioald and after his death, of Rothari, and was now over fifty years old (Waitz).

(Monza), so the former within the city of Ticinum (Pavia) built a church in honor of St. John the Baptist, which she decorated wonderfully with gold and silver and draperies and enriched bountifully with particular articles, and in it her body lies buried.   And when she had been accused to her husband of the crime of adultery, her own slave, Carellus by name, besought the king that he might fight in single combat for the honor of his mistress, with him who had imputed the crime to the queen.   And when he had gone into single combat with that accuser he overcame him in the presence of the whole people.   The queen indeed after this was done, returned to her former dignity. [1]

CHAPTER XLVIII.

Rodoald after he had reigned five years [2] and seven days was killed as is said by a certain Langobard whose wife he had defiled, and Aripert, son of Gundoald, who had been the brother of queen Theudelinda, followed him in the government of the kingdom. [3]   He estab-

---

[1] Hartmann (II, 1, 274) believes that Paul relates here the story of the first imprisonment of Gundiperga given by Fredegarius but has transposed it to a period two decades later (see Ch. 41, note, *supra*).

[2] Paul should have written here five months instead of five years (Waitz).   He probably died about March, 653 (Hartmann, II, 1, 275).

[3] There is no record of the events which led to the succession of Aripert, a Catholic of the Bavarian house and friendly to the Romans, in place of the Arian, anti-Roman dynasty of Rothari (Hartmann, II, 1, 244).

lished at Ticinum a sanctuary of our Lord and Saviour, which lay outside the western gate that is called Marenca and he decorated it with various ornaments and enriched it sufficiently with possessions.

CHAPTER XLIX.

In these days when the emperor Heraclius had died at Constantinople,[1] his son Heraclones with his mother Martina received the rights of sovereignty and ruled the empire for two years. And when he departed from life his brother Constantine, another son of Heraclius, followed in his place and reigned six months. When he also died his son Constantine rose to the dignity of the sovereignty and held the imperial power for eight and twenty years.

CHAPTER L.

About these times the wife of the king of the Persians, Cesara by name, on account of her love of the Christian faith, departed out of Persia in private dress with a few of her faithful followers, and came to Constantinople. She was honorably received by the emperor and after some days obtained baptism as she desired and was raised from the sacred font by the empress.[2] When her husband the king of the Persians heard this, he sent ambassadors to Constantinople to the emperor in order

---

[1] The death of Heraclius (A. D. 641) is erroneously placed by Paul after the death of Rodoald 653 (Waitz) and after the taking of Oderzo by Rothari (IV, 45, *supra*). See Simonsfeld's article on Dandolo (Archivio Veneto, 14, p. 141).

[2] That is the empress became her god-mother (Abel).

that the latter should restore to him his wife. When they came to the emperor they reported the words of the king of the Persians who demanded his queen. The emperor hearing these things and being altogether ignorant of the affair, returned them an answer saying: " We confess that we know nothing concerning the queen you seek except that a woman came to us here in the dress of a private person." But the ambassadors answered saying: " If it please your Imperial Presence we would like to see this woman you speak of," and when she had come by command of the emperor, presently the ambassadors looked upon her attentively, prostrated themselves at her feet and suggested to her with reverence that her husband wanted her. She replied to them: " Go, take back the answer to your king and lord that unless he also shall so believe in Christ as I have already believed, he can now no more have me as the partner of his bed." Why say more? The ambassadors returned to their country and reported again to their king all they had heard. And he without any delay came peaceably with sixty thousand men to Constantinople to the emperor by whom he was joyfully received and in a very suitable manner. And he, with the whole of them, believing in Christ our Lord, was in like manner with all the rest sprinkled [1] with the water of holy baptism and was raised by the emperor from the font and confirmed in the Catholic faith; and having been honored by the emperor with many gifts, he took

---

[1] *Perfusus* (see DuCange) seems to indicate sprinkling rather than immersion, though the latter was at this time the more usual form except in the case of those about to die.

his wife and returned happy and rejoicing to his own country. [1] About these times upon the death of duke Grasulf at Cividale, Ago undertook the government of the dukedom of Forum Julii. At Spoletium (Spoleto) also upon the death of Theudelaupus, Atto was made commander of that city. [2]

CHAPTER LI.

Aripert then, after he had ruled at Ticinum for nine years, died,[3] leaving the kingdom to be governed by his two sons, Perctarit and Godepert who were still of youthful age.[4] And Godepert, indeed, had the seat of his kingdom at Ticinum, but Perctarit, at the city of Mediolanum. Between these brothers, at the instigation of evil men, quarrels and the kindling of hatreds arose to such a degree that each attempted to usurp the royal power of the other. Wherefore Godepert sent Garipald, duke of Turin, to Grimuald, who was then the enterprising leader of the people of Beneventum, inviting him to come as soon as possible and bring aid to him against his brother Perctarit, and promising to give him his sister, the daughter of the king. But the ambassador, acting treacherously against his master, exhorted Grim-

[1] This account is wholly fictitious. Chosroes II, although well disposed toward the Christian faith did not abjure his own (Waitz).

[2] A. D. 653–663 (Hodgkin, VI, 96).

[3] A. D. 661 (Hodgkin, VI, 241).

[4] This is the first instance of a divided inheritance of the kingdom, if indeed we can speak of inheritance at all of a kingdom where the succession varied so greatly as in that of the Langobards.

uald to come and himself seize the kingdom of the
Langobards which the two youthful brothers were dis-
sipating, since he was ripe in age, prudent in counsel
and strong in resources. When Grimuald heard these
things he presently set his mind upon obtaining the
kingdom of the Langobards, and having established his
son Romuald as duke of Beneventum, he took his way
with a chosen band to proceed to Ticinum, and in all
the cities through which his route lay he drew to himself friends and auxiliaries for getting the kingdom. He
dispatched, indeed, Count Transemund, of Capua,
through Spoletium (Spoleto) and Tuscia (Tuscany) to
attach the Langobards of those regions to an alliance
with him. Transemund carried out his orders energetically, and met him on the way in Emilia with many
auxiliaries. Therefore when Grimuald had come near
Placentia (Piacenza) with a strong body of men, he
dispatched ahead to Ticinum Garipald, who had been
sent as a messenger to him by Godepert, so as to announce his coming to this same Godepert. And when
Garipald came to Godepert he said that Grimuald was
quickly approaching. When Godepert asked him in what
place he ought to prepare entertainment for this Grimuald, Garipald answered as follows: That it was fitting
that Grimuald, who had come for his sake and was going
to take his sister in marriage, should have his place of
entertainment within the palace. And this also was so
done, for when Grimuald came, he received his lodging
within the palace. But this same Garipald, the sower
of the whole wickedness, persuaded Godepert to come
and speak with Grimuald only after putting on a cuirass

under his clothing, saying that Grimuald wanted to kill him. Again this same artist in deceit came to Grimuald and said that unless he equipped himself stoutly Godepert would kill him with his sword, declaring that Godepert was wearing a cuirass under his clothing when he came to confer with him. Why say more? When, upon the following day, they had come to conference and Grimuald, after salutation, had embraced Godepert he immediately perceived that he was wearing a cuirass under his clothing, and without delay, he unsheathed his sword and deprived him of life,[1] and usurping his kingdom and all his power, he subjugated it to his dominion. But Godepert then had a son, a little boy, Raginpert by name, who was carried away by the faithful followers of his father and brought up secretly; nor did Grimuald care to pursue him since he was still a little child. When Perctarit, who was ruling at Mediolanum, heard that his brother was killed, he took flight with what speed he could and came to the Cagan, king of the Avars, leaving behind his wife Rodelinda and a little son named Cunincpert, both of whom Grimuald sent in exile to Beneventum. When these things had been thus brought to pass, Garipald, by whose instigation and effort they had been accomplished—and not only had he done these acts, but he had also committed a fraud in his embassy, since he had not transmitted whole and entire the gifts he ought to have brought to Beneventum—the performer of such deeds then did not long rejoice. There was, indeed, in the household of

[1] A. D. 662 (Hodgkin, VI, 243; Hartmann, II, 1, 275).

Godepert a little dwarf who came from the city of Turin.
When he knew that duke Garipald, upon the very holy
day of Easter would come to pray in the church of St.
John, he got up cn the sacred font of the baptistery
and held himself by his left hand to a little column supporting the canopy[1] where Garipald was about to pass,
and having drawn his sword he held it under his clothing, and when Garipald had come near him to pass
through, he lifted his garment and struck him on the
neck with his sword with all his might and cut off his
head upon the spot.   Those who had come with Garipald fell upon him, killing him with wounds from many
blows, but although he died, he still signally avenged
the wrong done to his master Godepert.

[1] *Tugurium*, a place shut off and covered from above.   See
DuCange.   The font itself had a roof or cover supported by small
columns.

BOOK V.

Chapter I.

When therefore Grimuald had been confirmed in the sovereignty[1] at Ticinum, he married not long afterward king Aripert's daughter who had already been betrothed to him and whose brother Godepert he had killed. He sent back indeed to their own homes, supplied with many gifts, the army of Beneventines by whose aid he had acquired the sovereignty. He kept however quite a number of them to dwell with him, bestowing upon them very extensive possessions.

Chapter II.

When he afterwards learned that Perctarit had gone to Scythia as an exile and was living with the Cagan, he sent word to this Cagan, king of the Avars, by ambassadors that if he kept Perctarit in his kingdom he could not thereafter have peace, as he had had hitherto, with the Langobards and with himself. When the king of the Avars heard this, Perctarit was brought into his presence and he said to him that he might go in what direction he would, so that the Avars should not incur enmity with the Langobards on his account.[2] When Perctarit

[1] A. D. 662 (Waitz). Grimuald, whose brothers, Taso and Cacco, had been treacherously murdered by the exarch in Oderzo, represented the national, anti-Roman sentiment of his people and was continually engaged in wars against the empire.

[2] According to another account Perctarit testified to the good

heard these things he went back to Italy to return to
Grimuald for he had heard that he was very merciful.
Then when he had come to the city of Lauda[1] (Lodi
Vecchio) he sent ahead of him to king Grimuald, Unulf,
a man most faithful to him to announce that Perctarit
was approaching trusting to his protection. When the
king heard this he promised faithfully that since
Perctarit came trusting him he should suffer no harm.
Meanwhile Perctarit arrived and went forward to Grimuald, and when he attempted to fall down at his feet, the
king graciously held him back and raised him up to
receive his kiss. Perctarit said to him: "I am your
servant. Knowing you to be most Christian and pious,
although I can live among the heathen, yet relying
upon your mercy I have come to your feet." And
the king with an oath, as he was wont, promised him
again saying: "By Him who caused me to be born,
since you have come to me trusting me, you will suffer
nothing evil in any way but I will so provide for you
that you can live becomingly." Then offering him a
lodging in a spacious house, he bade him have a rest
after the toil of the journey, ordering that food and
whatever things were necessary should be supplied to
him bountifully at public expense. But when Perctarit
had come to the dwelling prepared for him by the king,
presently throngs of the citizens of Ticinum began to

faith of the Cagan who had refused a whole *modius* full of gold
solidi for his betrayal (Waitz).

[1] The ancient Roman colony Laus Pompeia, a short distance
southeast of Milan and northeast of Padua.

gather around him to see him and salute him as an old
acquaintance. But what cannot an evil tongue inter-
rupt? For presently certain wicked flatterers coming to
the king declared to him that unless he quickly deprived
Perctarit of life, he would himself at once lose his kingdom with his life, asserting that the whole city had
gathered around Perctarit for this purpose. When he
heard these things, Grimuald became too credulous and
forgetting what he had promised, he was straightway in-
cited to the murder of the innocent Perctarit and took
counsel in what way he might deprive him of life on
the following day, since now the hour was very late.
Finally in the evening he sent to him divers dishes, also
special wines and various kinds of drinks so that he
could intoxicate him, to the end that relaxed by much
drinking during the night and buried in wine, he could
think nothing of his safety. Then one who had been
of his father's train, when he brought a dish from the
king to this Perctarit, put his head under the table as if
to salute him and announced to him secretly that the
king was arranging to kill him. And Perctarit straightway directed his cup-bearer that he should give him to
drink in a silver drinking vessel nothing but a little
water. And when those who brought him drinks of
different kinds from the king asked him upon the command of the king to drink the whole cup, he promised
to drink it all in honor of the king, and took a little
water from the silver cup. When the servants announced to the king that he was drinking insatiably, the
king merrily answered: "Let that drunkard drink; but
to-morrow he will spill out the same wines mixed with

blood." And Perctarit quickly called Unulf to him and announced to him the design of the king concerning his death. And Unulf straightway sent a servant to his house to bring him bed clothing [1] and ordered his couch to be put next to the couch of Perctarit. Without delay king Grimuald directed his attendants that they should guard the house in which Perctarit was reposing so that he could not escape in any way. And when supper was finished and all had departed and Perctarit only had remained with Unulf and Perctarit's valet, [2] who in any case were entirely faithful to him, they disclosed their plan to him and begged him to flee while the valet would pretend as long as possible that his master was sleeping within that bed chamber. And when he had promised to do this, Unulf put his own bed clothes and a mattress and a bear's skin upon the back and neck of Perctarit and began to drive him out of the door according to the plan, as if he were a slave from the country, offering him many insults, and did not cease moreover to strike him with a cudgel from above and urge him on, so that driven and struck he often fell to the ground. And when the attendants of the king who had been put on guard asked that same Unulf why this was, "That worthless slave," he says, " has put my bed in the chamber of that drunken Perctarit who is so full of wine that he lies there as if he were dead. But it is enough that I have followed his

[1] According to DuCange *lectisternia* means the trappings of a bed, cushions, bolster, etc.

[2] *Vestiarius*, he who has charge of one's clothing (DuCange).

madness up to the present time. From now on, during the life of our lord the king, I will stay in my own house." When they heard these things and believed what they heard to be true, they were delighted, and making way for the two, they let pass both him and Perctarit, whom they thought was a slave and who had his head covered that he should not be recognized. And while they were going away, that most faithful valet bolted the door carefully and remained inside alone. Unulf indeed let Perctarit down by a rope from the wall at a corner which is on the side of the river Ticinum (Ticino) and collected what companions he could, and they, having seized some horses they had found in a pasture, proceeded that same night to the city of Asta (Asti) in which the friends of Perctarit were staying, and those who were still rebels against Grimuald. Thence Perctarit made his way as quickly as possible to the city of Turin, and afterwards passed across the boundaries of Italy and came to the country of the Franks. Thus God Almighty by His merciful arrangement delivered an innocent man from death and kept from offense a king who desired in his heart to do good.

CHAPTER III.

But king Grimuald, indeed, since he thought that Perctarit was sleeping in his lodging, caused a line of men to stand by on either side from this place of entertainment up to his palace, so that Perctarit might be led through the midst of them in order that he could not at all escape. And when those sent by the king had come and called Perctarit to the palace, and knocked at the door where they thought he was sleeping, the valet who was inside begged them saying: " Have pity with him and let him sleep a little because he is still wearied by his journey and oppressed by very heavy slumber." And when they had acquiesced, they announced this thing to the king, that Perctarit was sleeping up to this time in a heavy slumber. Then the king said: " Last evening he so filled himself with wine that now he cannot waken." He ordered them, however, to arouse him at once and bring him to the palace. And when they came to the door of the bed-room in which they believed that Perctarit was sleeping, they began to knock more sharply. Then the valet began to beg them again that they would let this Perctarit still, as it were, sleep a little. And they cried out in rage that that drunken man had already slept enough. Straightway they broke open the door of the bed-chamber with their heels, entered, and looked for Perctarit in the bed. And when they did not find him, they supposed he was sitting down to the requirements of nature, and when they did not find him there, they asked that valet what had become of Perctarit. And he answered them that he had fled. Furious with rage they beat him, and seized him by the hair and straightway dragged him to the palace. And conducting him into the presence of the king they said that he was privy to the flight of Perctarit and therefore most deserving of death. The king directed him to be released and asked him in due order in what way Perctarit had escaped and he related to the king all the occurrences as they had taken place. Then the king asked those who were standing around and said: "What do you think of this man who has committed such things?" Then all answered with one voice that he deserved to die, racked with many torments, but the king said: " By Him who caused me to be born this man deserves to be treated [1] well, who for the sake of fidelity to his master did not refuse to give himself up to death." And presently, he ordered that he should be among his own valets enjoining him to observe toward himself the same fidelity he had kept to Perctarit and promising to bestow upon him many advantages. And when the king asked what had become of Unulf,[2] it was announced to him that he had taken refuge in the church of the Blessed Archangel Michael. And he presently sent to him voluntarily promising that he should suffer no harm if he would only come and trust him. Unulf indeed, hearing this promise of the king, presently came to the palace and having fallen at the king's feet, was asked by him how and in what way Perctarit had been able to escape. But when he had told him everything in order, the king, praising his fidelity and prudence, graciously conceded to him all his [3]means and whatever he had been able to possess.

CHAPTER IV.

And when after some time the king asked Unulf whether he would then like to be with Perctarit, he answered with an oath that he would rather die with

[1] Read *haberi* for *habere*.

[2] *Ejus facultates.* There is doubt whether this refers to the property of Unulf or of Perctarit (Hodgkin, VI, 251, note 1).

Perctarit than live anywhere else in the greatest enjoy-
ment. Then the king also called for that valet, asking
him whether he would prefer to stay with him in the
palace or to spend his life wandering with Perctarit, and
when he had given a like answer with Unulf, the king
took their words kindly, praised their fidelity and
directed Unulf to take from his house whatever he
wanted, namely, his servants and his horses and furni-
ture of all kinds and to proceed without harm to Perctarit. And in like manner also he dismissed that valet,
and they, taking away all their goods, as much as they
needed, according to the kindness of the king, set out
with the help of the king himself into the country of the
Franks to their beloved Perctarit.

CHAPTER V.

At this time an army of the Franks, coming forth from
Provincia (Provence), entered into Italy. Grimuald
advanced against them with the Langobards and deceived them by this stratagem: he pretended indeed to
flee from their attack and left his camp with his tents
quite clear of men but filled with divers good things
and especially with an abundance of excellent wine.
When the troops of the Franks had come thither, thinking that Grimuald with the Langobards had been terrified by fear and had abandoned their whole camp, they
straightway became merry and eagerly took possession
of everything and prepared a very bountiful supper.
And while they reposed, weighed down with the various
dishes and with much wine and sleep, Grimuald rushed
upon them after midnight and overthrew them with so

great a slaughter that only a few of them escaped and were able with difficulty to regain their native country. The place where this battle was fought is called up to this time the Brook of the Franks [1] (Rivoli) [2] and it is not far distant from the walls of the little city of Asta (Asti).

CHAPTER VI.

In these days the emperor Constantine who was also called Constans, [3] desiring to pluck Italy out of the hand

[1] *Rivus Francorum.*

[2] Not the same as the scene of Napoleon's victory.

[3] Constans II, or more correctly Constantine IV, was born A. D. 631, and became emperor in 642, when only eleven years old, on the death of his father Constantine III. During his reign the Saracens conquered Armenia (Hodgkin, VI, 253) and seized Cyprus and Rhodes. He fought in person a naval battle with them off the coast of Lycia in 655 and was defeated. In his reign the doctrine of the Monotheletes or those who maintained that there was only one will in the nature of the Saviour, agitated the empire, and popes and patriarchs wrangled bitterly upon the subject. His grandfather Heraclius had declared in favor of the Monothelete heresy, even pope Honorius (Hartmann, II, 1, 217) at one time acquiesced in it though he deprecated the strife and desired the church to abide by its ancient formulas. Finally, Constans in 648 when only seventeen years of age issued his *Type*, forbidding controversy upon both sides. Pope Martin I, whose appointment lacked the confirmation of the emperor and who was regarded by the latter as a usurper, convened in 649, a council in the Lateran palace and anathematized the *Type* and its defenders (Hodgkin, VI, 255, 256). Constans regarded these proceedings as acts of rebellion and sent his chamberlain Olympius as exarch to Italy in 649 with directions to secure the acceptance of the *Type* and if possible to bring pope Martin a prisoner to Constantinople ; but the exarch found public opinion and the disposition of the

of the Langobards, left Constantinople[1] and taking his
way along the coast, came to Athens, and from there,
having crossed the sea, he landed at Tarentum.[2]   Previously, however, he went to a certain hermit who was
said to have the spirit of prophecy, and sought eagerly
to know from him whether he could overcome and
conquer the nation of the Langobards which was dwelling in Italy.   The servant of God had asked him for the
space of one night that he might supplicate the Lord for
this thing, and when morning came he thus answered

army so adverse that he was compelled to renounce the project,
and soon afterwards became the ally of the Pope and the Italians
(Hartmann, II, 1, 227), and with their support assumed independent authority and led an army in Sicily against the Saracens where
he died in 652 (id., p. 228).   These acts were naturally regarded
as an insurrection against the empire, and upon his death Constans sent Calliopas to Italy as exarch, who in June, 653, coming
to Rome with the army from Ravenna, seized the Pope, who had
taken refuge in the Lateran basilica, declared his deposition and
sent him as a prisoner to Constantinople, where he arrived after
long delays, was tried for treason, insulted, forced to stand as a
public spectacle in the Hippodrome, was loaded with irons,
immured in a dungeon and sentenced to death, but this was
commuted to banishment in the Crimea.   There he languished
and died in 655 (Hodgkin, VI, 259–268).   He was succeeded
by Eugenius (A. D. 657) who was chosen Pope while Martin
was still alive and Eugenius was followed by Vitalian (A. D.
657–672), who lived on terms of accommodation with the emperor, although there is no evidence that he abjured the doctrines
of his predecessors (Hartmann, II, 1, 232, 233).   It was under
Vitalian that Constans' visit to Italy described in this chapter
occurred.

[1] A. D. 662 (Hodgkin, VI, 270).
[2] A. D. 663 (Hodgkin, VI, 271).

the emperor: "The people of the Langobards cannot be overcome in any way, because a certain queen coming from another province has built the church of St. John the Baptist in the territories of the Langobards, and for this reason St. John himself continually intercedes for the nation of the Langobards. But a time shall come when this sanctuary will be held in contempt and then the nation itself shall perish." We have proved that this has so occurred, since we have seen that before the fall of the Langobards, this same church of St. John which was established in the place called Modicia (Monza) was managed by vile persons so that this holy spot was bestowed upon the unworthy and adulterous, not for the merit of their lives, but in the giving of spoils.

CHAPTER VII.

Therefore after the emperor Constans, as we said, had come to Tarentum, he departed therefrom and invaded the territories of the Beneventines and took almost all the cities of the Langobards through which he passed. He also attacked bravely and took by storm Luceria, a rich city of Apulia, destroyed it and leveled it to the ground. Agerentia[1] (Acerenza), however, he could not at all take on account of the highly fortified position of the place. Thereupon he surrounded Beneventum with all his army and began to reduce it energetically. At that time Romuald, the son of Grimuald, still a young man, held the dukedom there and as soon

---

[1] A fortress on one of the outlying buttresses of Monte Vulture (Hodgkin, VI, 273).

as he learned of the approach of the emperor, he sent his tutor, Sesuald by name, to his father Grimuald on the other side of the Padus (Po) begging him to come as soon as possible and strongly reinforce his son and the Beneventines whom he himself had reared. When king Grimuald heard this he straightway started to go with an army to Beneventum to bring aid to his son. Many of the Langobards left him on the way and returned home saying that he had despoiled the palace and was now going back to Beneventum not to return. Meanwhile the army of the emperor was assaulting Beneventum vigorously with various machines of war and on the other hand Romuald with his Langobards was resisting bravely, and although he did not dare to engage hand to hand with so great a multitude on account of the smallness of his army, yet frequently dashing into the camp of the enemy with young men sent out for that purpose, he inflicted upon them great slaughter upon every side. And while Grimuald his father was now hastening on, he sent to his son to announce his approach, that same tutor of his of whom we have spoken. And when the latter had come near Beneventum he was captured by the Greeks and brought to the emperor, who asked of him whence he had come, and he said he had come from King Grimuald and he announced the speedy approach of that king. Straightway the emperor, greatly alarmed, took counsel with his followers in what way he could make a treaty with Romuald so as to return to Naples.

CHAPTER VIII.

After he had taken as a hostage the sister of Romuald whose name was Gisa, he made peace with him. He ordered the tutor Sesuald indeed to be led to the walls, threatening death to him if he should announce anything to Romuald or the people of the city concerning the approach of Grimuald, and (demanding) that he should rather declare that the king could not come. He promised that he would do this, as was enjoined upon him, but when he had come near the walls he said he wanted to see Romuald. And when Romuald had quickly come thither he thus spoke to him: " Be steadfast, master Romuald, have confidence and do not be disturbed since your father will quickly come to give you aid. For know that he is stopping this night near the river Sangrus (Sangro)[1] with a strong army. Only I beseech you to have pity on my wife and children since this faithless race will not suffer me to live." When he had said this, his head was cut off by command of the emperor and thrown into the city by an instrument of war which they call a stone-thrower.[2] This head Romuald ordered brought to him and kissed it weeping and commanded that it should be buried in a suitable casket.[3]

[1] In the present province of Abruzzi (Waitz), about fifty miles from Benevento.

[2] *Petraria.*

[3] All this as well as the two following chapters, seems inconsistent with the peace with Romuald mentioned in the first sentence of this chapter. Waitz suggests that possibly the peace was made after the incidents concerning Sesuald.—Possibly Paul combined in his history accounts taken from two contradictory sources.

Chapter IX.

Then the emperor, fearing the sudden approach of king Grimuald, broke up the siege of Beneventum and set out for Neapolis (Naples). Mitola, however, the Count of Capua, forcibly defeated his army near the river Calor (Calore), in the place which up to the present time is called Pugna (the fight).[1]

Chapter X.

After the emperor came to Naples it is said that one of his chief men, whose name was Saburrus, asked for twenty thousand soldiers from his sovereign, and pledged himself to fight against Romuald, and win the victory. And when he had received the troops and had come to a place whose name is Forinus (Forino)[2] and had set up his camp there, Grimuald, who had already come to Beneventum, when he heard these things, wanted to set out against him. His son Romuald said to him: "There is no need, but do you turn over to me only a part of your army. With God's favor I will fight with him, and when I shall have conquered him a greater glory, indeed, will be ascribed of your power." It was done, and when he had received some part of his father's army, he set out with his own men likewise against Saburrus. Before he began the

[1] The Calore flows a little east of Benevento. Camiilus Peregrinius believes that the river Sabatus (Sabato) is intended, which flows close to Beneventum, and near which Peter the Deacon recognizes this place called Pugna (Waitz).

[2] Between Avellino and Nocera (Waitz), about twenty-five miles east of Naples.

battle with him he ordered the trumpets to sound on four sides, and immediately he rushed daringly upon them. And while both lines were fighting with great obstinacy, a man from the king's army named Amalong, who had been accustomed to carry the royal pike, taking this pike in both hands struck violently with it a certain little Greek and lifted him from the saddle on which he was riding and raised him in the air over his head. When the army of the Greeks saw this, it was terrified by boundless fear and at once betook itself to flight, and overwhelmed with the utmost disaster, in fleeing it brought death upon itself and victory to Romuald and the Langobards. Thus Saburrus, who had promised that he would achieve for his emperor a trophy of victory from the Langobards, returned to him with a few men only and came off with disgrace; but Romuald, when the victory was obtained from the enemy, returned in triumph to Beneventum and brought joy to his father and safety to all, now that the fear of the enemy was taken away.

CHAPTER XI.

But the emperor Constans, when he found that he could accomplish nothing against the Langobards, directed all the threats of his cruelty against his own followers, that is, the Romans. He left Naples and proceeded to Rome.[1] At the sixth mile-stone from the city, pope Vitalian came to meet him with his priests

[1] July 5, 663. No emperor had visited Rome for nearly two centuries (Hodgkin VI, 276).

and the Roman people.¹   And when the emperor had
come to the threshold of St. Peter he offered there a
pallium woven with gold; and remaining at Rome twelve
days he pulled down everything that in ancient times had
been made of metal for the ornament of the city, to
such an extent that he even stripped off the roof of the
church of the blessed Mary which at one time was called
the Pantheon, and had been founded in honor of all the
gods and was now by the consent of the former rulers
the place of all the martyrs; and he took away from
there the bronze tiles and sent them with all the other
ornaments to Constantinople.   Then the emperor returned to Naples, and proceeded by the land route to
the city of Regium (Reggio); and having entered
Sicily² during the seventh indiction³ he dwelt in Syracuse and put such afflictions upon the people—the inhabitants and land owners of Calabria, Sicily, Africa, and
Sardinia—as were never heard of before, so that even
wives were separated from their husbands and children
from their parents.⁴   The people of these regions also
endured many other and unheard of things so that the
hope of life did not remain to any one.   For even the
sacred vessels and the treasures of the holy churches of

¹ The relations between the emperor Constans and the popes
had been decidedly strained on account of the Monothelete controversy (see note to Chap. 6, *supra*).

² His purpose was to use Sicily as a base of operations against
the Saracens in Africa (Hodgkin VI, 280).

³ Commencing September, 663.

⁴ Sold into slavery to satisfy the demands of the tax gatherers
(Hodgkin VI, 280).

God were carried away by the imperial command and by the avarice of the Greeks. And the emperor remained in Sicily from the seventh to the twelfth [1] indiction, [2] but at last he suffered the punishment of such great iniquities and while he was in the bath he was put to death by his own servants. [3]

CHAPTER XII.

When the emperor Constantine was killed at Syracuse, Mecetius (Mezezius) seized the sovereignty in Sicily, but without the consent of the army of the East. [4] The soldiers of Italy, others throughout Istria, others through the territories of Campania and others from the regions of Africa and Sardinia came to Syracuse against him and deprived him of life. And many of his judges were brought to Constantinople beheaded and with them in like manner the head of the false emperor was also carried off.

[1] An error. This should be eleventh indiction. He was killed July 15, 668 (Hodgkin VI, 281, note 2).

[2] In Sicily he decreed the independence of the bishopric of Ravenna from that of Rome, thus attempting to create two heads of the church in Italy, a severe blow to the papacy (Hartmann II, 1, 250, 251), a measure which, however, was revoked after his death.

[3] His valet Andreas struck him with a soap box (Hodgkin VI, 281).

[4] Paul seems to have misunderstood the Liber Pontificalis (Adeodatus) from which he took this passage, which reads: "Mezezius who was in Sicily with the army of the East, rebelled and seized the sovereignty."

CHAPTER XIII.

The nation of the Saracens that had already spread through Alexandria and Egypt, hearing these things, came suddenly with many ships, invaded Sicily, entered Syracuse and made a great slaughter of the people—a few only escaping with difficulty who had fled to the strongest fortresses and the mountain ranges—and they carried off also great booty and all that art work in brass and different materials which the emperor Constantine had taken away from Rome; and thus they returned to Alexandria.

CHAPTER XIV.

Moreover the daughter of the king, who we said had been carried away from Beneventum as a hostage[1] came to Sicily and ended her last days.

CHAPTER XV.

At this time there were such great rain storms and such thunders as no man had remembered before, so that countless thousands of men and animals were killed by strokes of lightning. In this year the pulse which could not be gathered on account of the rains grew again and was brought to maturity.[2]

CHAPTER XVI.

But king Grimuald indeed, when the Beneventines and their provinces had been delivered from the Greeks,

[1] See Chapter 8 *supra*.

[2] These events are placed by the Liber Pontificalis in the year of the death of Pope Adeodatus (672) (Jacobi, 54, 55).

determined to return to his palace at Ticinum, and to Transamund, who had formerly been count of Capua and had served him most actively in acquiring the kingdom, he gave his daughter, another sister of Romuald in marriage, and made him duke of Spoletium (Spoleto) after Atto of whom we have spoken above.[1] Then he returned to Ticinum.

CHAPTER XVII.

When indeed Grasulf, duke of the Friulans died, as we mentioned before, Ago was appointed his successor in the dukedom;[2] and from his name a certain house situated within Forum Julii (Cividale) is called Ago's House up to this day. When this Ago had died, Lupus was made commander of the Friulans.[3] This Lupus entered into the island of Gradus (Grado) which is not far from Aquileia, with an army of horsemen over a stone highway which had been made in old times through the sea, and having plundered that city, he removed from thence and carried back the treasures of the church of Aquileia. When Grimuald set out for Beneventum, he intrusted his palace to Lupus.

CHAPTER XVIII.

Since this Lupus had acted very insolently at Ticinum

[1] IV, 50 *supra*.

[2] The date is uncertain. De Rubeis says 661, Hodgkin thinks about 645 (VI, 285).

[3] A. D. 663 according to De Rubeis, about 660 according to Hodgkin (VI, 285).

in the king's absence,[1] because he did not think he would return, when the king did come back, Lupus, knowing that the things he had not done rightly were displeasing to him, repaired to Forum Julii and, conscious of his own wickedness, rebelled against this king.

CHAPTER XIX.

Then Grimuald, unwilling to stir up civil war among the Langobards, sent word to the Cagan, king of the Avars, to come into Forum Julii with his army against duke Lupus and defeat him in war. And this was done. For the Cagan came with a great army, and in the place which is called Flovius,[2] as the older men who were in that war have related to us, during three days duke Lupus with the Friulans fought against the Cagan's army. On the first day indeed he defeated that strong army, very few of his own men being wounded; on the second day he killed in like manner many of the Avars, but a number of his own were now wounded and dead; on the third day very many of his own were wounded or killed, nevertheless he destroyed a great army of the Cagan and took abundant booty; but on the fourth day they saw so great a multitude coming upon them that they could scarcely escape by flight.

[1] That is when he went to the relief of Romuald who was besieged at Benevento by Constans.

[2] *Fluvius Frigidus* in the valley of Wippach in the province of Krain (Waitz)—"Cold River below the pass of the Pear Tree," southeast of Cividale (Hodgkin, VI, 286, note 1).

Chapter XX.

When duke Lupus then had been killed there, the rest who had remained (alive) fortified themselves in strongholds. But the Avars, scouring all their territories, plundered or destroyed everything by fire. When they had done this for some days, word was sent them by Grimuald that they should now rest from their devastation. But they sent envoys to Grimuald saying that they would by no means give up Forum Julii, which they had conquered by their own arms.

Chapter XXI.

Then Grimuald, compelled by necessity, began to collect an army that he might drive the Avars out of his territories. He set up therefore in the midst of the plain his camp and the place where he lodged the Avar (ambassadors), and since he had only a slender fragment of his army, he caused those he had to pass frequently during several days before the eyes of the envoys in different dress and furnished with various kinds of arms, as if a new army was constantly advancing. The ambassadors of the Avars indeed, when they saw this same army pass by, first in one way and then in another, believed that the multitude of the Langobards was immense. And Grimuald thus spoke to them : "With all this multitude of an army which you have seen I will straightway fall upon the Cagan and the Avars unless they shall quickly depart from the territories of the Friulans." When the envoys of the Avars had seen and heard these things, and had re-

peated them to their king, he presently returned with
all his army to his own kingdom.

CHAPTER XXII.

Finally, after Lupus was killed in this way, as we have
related, Arnefrit, his son, sought to obtain the dukedom
at Forum Julii in the place of his father.   But fearing
the power of king Grimuald, he fled into Carnuntum,
which they corruptly call Carantanum (Carinthia)[1] to
the nation of the Slavs,[2] and afterwards coming with the
Slavs as if about to resume the dukedom by their means,
he was killed when the Friulans attacked him at the fortress of Nemae (Nimis), which is not far distant from
Forum Julii.[3]

CHAPTER XXIII.

Afterwards Wechtari was appointed duke at Forum
Julii.   He was born at the city of Vincentia (Vicenza),
was a kind man, and one who ruled his people mildly.
When the nation of the Slavs had heard that he had set
out for Ticinum, they collected a strong multitude and
determined to attack the fortress of Forum Julii, and
they came and laid out their camp in the place which is
called Broxas,[4] not far from Forum Julii.   But it hap-

[1] The name given by Paul (Carnuntum), the modern Presburg,
is incorrect, Carantanum was the proper name for Carinthia
(Hodgkin, VI, 288, note 1).

[2] These Slavs belonged to the Slovene branch of the Slav race
(Hodgkin VI, 288).

[3] About 15 miles northwest of Cividale (Hodgkin, VI, 288).

[4] Bethmann believes that a certain stronghold, Purgessimus, is

pened according to the Divine will that the evening before, duke Wechtari came back from Ticinum without the knowledge of the Slavs. While his companions, as is wont to happen, had gone home, he himself, hearing these tidings concerning the Slavs, advanced with a few men, that is, twenty-five, against them. When the Slavs saw him coming with so few they laughed, saying that the patriarch was advancing against them with his clergy. When he had come near the bridge of the river Natisio (Natisone),[1] which was where the Slavs were staying, he took his helmet from his head and showed his face to them. He was bald-headed, and when the Slavs recognized him that he was Wechtari, they were immediately alarmed and cried out that Wechtari was there, and terrified by God they thought more of flight than of battle. Then Wechtari, rushing upon them with the few men he had, overthrew them with such great slaughter that out of five thousand men a few only remained, who escaped with difficulty.[2]

meant, near the bridge hereafter referred to; others say Prosascus, at the source of the Natisone; others, Borgo Bressana, a suburb of Cividale (Waitz). Musoni (Atti del Congresso in Cividale, 1899, pp. 187, 188) considers all these conjectures inadmissible, and shows that it was at the place now called Brischis, near that city.

[1] Waitz says the bridge of San Pietro dei Schiavi. Musoni (Atti, etc., p. 191), believes it was probably the present bridge of San Quirino.

[2] It is evident that this account, which is no doubt based upon oral tradition and perhaps has some historical basis, has been greatly exaggerated, if indeed there is not a mistake in the figures, as Muratori suggests, The allusion to the patriarch also appears to contain an anachronism, since it was in 737, after these events,

CHAPTER XXIV.

After this Wechtari, Landari held the dukedom at Forum Julii, and when he died Rodoald succeeded him in the dukedom.

CHAPTER XXV.

When then, as we have said, duke Lupus had died, king Grimuald gave Lupus' daughter Theuderada to his own son Romuald, who was governing Beneventum.[1] From her he begot three sons, that is, Grimuald, Gisulf, and also Arichis.

CHAPTER XXVI.

Also king Grimuald avenged his injuries (received) from all those who deserted him when he had set out for Beneventum.

CHAPTER XXVII.

But he also destroyed in the following manner Forum Populi (Forlimpopoli), a city of the Romans,[2] whose citizens had inflicted certain injuries upon him when he

that the patriarch Calixtus removed his see to Cividale. Communities of Slavs still inhabit a portion of Friuli; they are divided, according to their linguistic peculiarities, into four principal groups, and probably came into this district at different times. (Musoni, Atti del Congresso in Cividale, 1899, pp. 187, 193.)

[1] Theuderada emulated Theudelinda in piety, and established the duchy of Benevento in the Catholic faith (Hodgkin, VI, 297, 298).

[2] On the Æmilian way, twenty miles south of Ravenna (Hodgkin, VI, 290).

set out for Beneventum and had often annoyed his couriers going from Beneventum and returning. Having left Tuscany[1] through Bardo's Alp[2] (Bardi) at the time of Lent without any knowledge of the Romans, he rushed unexpectedly upon that city on the holy Sabbath of Easter itself[3] in the hour when the baptism was occurring and made so great a carnage of men slain that he killed in the sacred font itself even those deacons who were baptizing little infants. And he so overthrew that city that very few inhabitants remain in it up to the present time.

CHAPTER XXVIII.

Grimuald had indeed no ordinary hatred against the Romans, since they had once treacherously betrayed his brothers Taso and Cacco.[4] Wherefore he destroyed to its foundations the city of Opitergium (Oderzo) where they were killed, and divided the territories of those who had dwelt there among the people of Forum Julii (Cividale), Tarvisium (Treviso) and Ceneta (Ceneda).

[1] Read *e Tuscia egressus* in place of *Tusciam ingressus* (Hodgkin VI, 290, note 3).

[2] A pass of the Apennines near Parma. There is evidently some mistake, either in the text or else by Paul, as the two places are far apart (Hodgkin, VI, 290, note 3). Otto von Freising says that the whole Apennine range was so called (Abel).

[3] *Sabbato paschali.* Abel translates Easter Saturday, Hodgkin (VI, 290) Easter Sunday, which seems more probable from the context.

[4] IV, 38, *supra.*

Chapter XXIX.

During these times a duke of the Bulgarians, Alzeco by name, left his own people, from what cause is unknown, and peacefully entering Italy with the whole army of his dukedom, came to king Grimuald, promising to serve him and to dwell in his country. And the king directing him to Beneventum to his son Romuald, ordered that the latter should assign to him and his people places to dwell in. [1]   Duke Romuald, receiving them graciously, accorded to them extensive tracts to settle which had been deserted up to that time, namely, Sepinum (Sepino), Bovianum (Bojano), Isernia [2] and other cities with their territories and directed that Alzeco himself, the name of his title being changed, should be called gastaldius [3] instead of duke. And they dwell up to the present time in these places, as we have said, and although they also speak Latin, they have not at all forsaken the use of their own language.

Chapter XXX.

When the emperor Constans, as we said,[4] had been killed in Sicily and the tyrant Mezetius who had succeeded him had been punished, Constantine, the son of the emperor Constantius, undertook the government of the empire of the Romans and reigned over the Romans

[1] Theophanes (Historia Miscella) relates the story differently (Waitz).

[2] Places in the highlands of Samnium (Hodgkin VI, 284).

[3] See note II, 32, *supra*, pp. 88–91.

[4] Ch. 12, *supra*.

seventeen years. In the times of Constans indeed the archbishop Theodore and the abbot Adrian, also a very learned man, were sent by pope Vitalian into Britain and made very many churches of the Angles productive of the fruit of ecclasiastical doctrine. Of these men archbishop Theodore has described, with wonderful and discerning reflection, the sentences for sinners, namely, for how many years one ought to do penance fcr each sin.[1]

CHAPTER XXXI.

Afterwards, in the month of August, a comet appeared in the east with very brilliant rays, which again turned back upon itself and disappeared. And without delay a heavy pestilence followed from the same eastern quarter and destroyed the Roman people. In these days Domnus (Donus), Pope of the Roman Church, covered with large white blocks of marble in a wonderful manner the place which is called Paradise in front of the church of the blessed apostle Peter.

CHAPTER XXXII.

At this time Dagipert governed the kingdom of the Franks in Gaul and with him king Grimuald entered into a treaty of lasting peace.[2] Perctarit also, who had settled in the country of the Franks, fearing the power

---

[1] The book is entitled *Poenitentiale* (Giansevero).

[2] This appears to be doubtful, as Dagipert II, to whom it refers, came to the throne in 674, after Grimuald's death (Jacobi, 42). Hartmann believes that the treaty was made, though not with Dagipert (II, 1, 277). Clothar III or Childeric are suggested (Waitz).

of this Grimuald, departed from Gaul and determined to hasten to the island of Britain and the king of the Saxons.

Chapter XXXIII.

But Grimuald indeed having remained in the palace on the ninth day after the use of the lancet, took his bow and when he attempted to hit a dove with an arrow, the vein of his arm was ruptured. The doctors, as they say, administered poisoned medicines and totally withdrew him from this life. He added in the edict which king Rothari had composed certain chapters of law which seemed useful to him.[1] He was moreover very strong in body, foremost in boldness, with a bald head and a heavy beard and was adorned with wisdom no less than with strength. And his body was buried in the church of the blessed Ambrose the Confessor, which he had formerly built in the city of Ticinum. Upon the expiration of one year and three months after the death of king Aripert, he usurped the kingdom of the Langobards, reigned nine years and left as king Garibald his son, still of boyish age whom the daughter of king Aripert had borne him.[2] Then, as we had begun to say, Perctarit having departed from Gaul, embarked in

[1] In these chapters he discouraged the wager of battle and made strict provisions against bigamy, a crime which seems to have been increasing. He also incorporated the Roman principle in the succession of property, that when a father died the children should represent and take his share. His edict was issued A. D. 668 (Hodgkin, VI, 291, 292).

[2] His elder son Romuald seems to have kept the duchy of Benevento.

a ship to pass over to the island of Britain to the kingdom of the Saxons. And when he had already sailed a little way through the sea, a voice was heard from the shore of one inquiring whether Perctarit was in that ship. And when the answer was given him that Perctarit was there, he who called out added: "Say to him he may return to his country since to-day is the third day that Grimuald has been withdrawn from this life." When he heard this, Perctarit straightway turned back again and coming to the shore could not find the person who informed him of the death of Grimuald, from which he thought that this was not a man but a Divine messenger. And then directing his course to his own country, when he had come to the confines of Italy he found already there awaiting him all the retinue of the palace, and all the royal officials in readiness together with a great multitude of the Langobards. And thus when he returned to Ticinum, and the little boy Garibald had been driven away from the kingdom, he was raised to the kingly power by all the Langobards, the third month after the death of Grimuald.[1] He was moreover a pious man, a Catholic in belief,[2] tenacious of justice and a very bountiful supporter of the poor. And he straightway sent to Beneventum and called back from thence his wife Rodelinda and his son Cunincpert.

[1] A. D. 671 (Hartmann, II, 1, 255).

[2] So much a Catholic that he caused the Jews in the kingdom to be baptized, and ordered all who refused to be slain (Song of the Synod of Pavia; see Hodgkin, VI, 303). Grimuald's aggressive policy against the Romans was now abandoned.

Chapter XXXIV.

And as soon as he had taken upon himself the rights of sovereignty, he built in that place which is on the side of the river Ticinus (Ticino) whence he himself had previously escaped, a convent called the New one, to his Lord and Deliverer in honor of the Holy Virgin and Martyr Agatha.[1] In it he gathered together many virgins, and he also endowed this place with possessions and ornaments of many kinds. His queen Rodelinda indeed built with wonderful workmanship outside the walls of this city of Ticinum a church of the Holy Mother of God which is called "At the Poles," and adorned it with marvelous decorations. This place moreover was called "At the Poles" because formerly poles, that is beams, had stood there upright which were wont to be planted according to the custom of the Langobards for the following reason: if any one were killed in any place either in war or in any other way, his relatives fixed a pole within their burial ground upon the top of which they placed a dove made of wood that was turned in that direction where their beloved had expired so that it might be known in what place he who had died was sleeping.

Chapter XXXV.

Then Perctarit, when he had ruled alone for seven years, now in the eighth year took his son Cunincpert

[1] It is said his escape occurred in the night before the festival of St. Agatha (Waitz).

as his consort in the government and with him he reigned in like manner for ten years.[1]

CHAPTER XXXVI.

And while they were living in great peace and had tranquility around them on every side, there arose against them a son of iniquity, Alahis by name, by whom the peace was disturbed in the kingdom of the Langobards, and a great slaughter was made of the people. This man, when he was duke of the city of Tridentum (Trent), fought with the count of the Bavarians that they call "gravio"[2] who governed Bauzanum (Botzen) and other strongholds, and defeated him in an astonishing manner. Elated from this cause, he also lifted his hand against Perctarit his king, and rebelling, fortified himself within the stronghold of Tridentum. King Perctarit advanced against him and while he besieged him from the outside, suddenly Alahis rushed unexpectedly out of the city with his followers, overthrew the king's camp and compelled the king himself to seek flight. He afterwards however returned to the favor of king Perctarit through the agency of Cunincpert, the king's son, who loved him now for a long time. For when the king had at different times wanted to put him to death, his son Cunincpert always prevented this being done, thinking that he would thereafter be faithful, nor did he refrain from getting his

---

[1] This seems to be a mistake. The period was something more than eight years (Hodgkin, VI, 304).

[2] Or *grafio*, the German *Graf*.

father also to bestow upon Alahis the dukedom of Brexia (Brescia), although the father often protested that Cunincpert did this to his own ruin, since he offered his enemy the means of obtaining the kingly power. The city of Brexia indeed had always a great multitude of noble Langobards and Perctarit feared that by their aid Alahis would become too powerful. In these days king Perctarit built with wonderful workmanship in the city of Ticinum, a gate adjoining the palace which was also called the " Palace Gate."

Chapter XXXVII.

When he had held the sovereignty eighteen years,[1] first alone and afterwards with his son, he was withdrawn from this life and his body was buried hard by the church of our Lord the Saviour which Aripert his father had built. He was of becoming stature, of a corpulent body, mild and gentle in all things. But king Cunincpert indeed took to wife Hermelinda, of the race of the Anglo-Saxons.[2] She had seen in the bath Theodote, a girl sprung from a very noble stock of Romans, of graceful body and adorned with flaxen hair almost to the feet, and she praised the girl's beauty to king Cunincpert, her husband. And although he concealed from his wife that he had heard this with pleasure, he

[1] But see chapter 35, *supra* and note.

[2] Egbert, king of Kent from 664 to 673, had a sister Eormengild and an uncle Eormenred, whose daughters' names all begin with " Eormen." Eormenlind or Hermelinda probably came from one of these families (Hodgkin, VI, 305, note 3).

was inflamed, nevertheless, with great love for the girl, and without delay he set forth to hunt in the wood they call "The City," and directed his wife Hermelinda to come with him. And he stole out from there by night and came to Ticinum, and making the girl Theodote come to him he lay with her. Yet he sent her afterwards into a monastery in Ticinum which was called by her name.

CHAPTER XXXVIII.

Alahis indeed gave birth to the iniquity he had long since conceived, and with the help of Aldo and Grauso, citizens of Brexia, as well as many others of the Langobards, forgetful of so many favors that king Cunincpert had conferred upon him, forgetting also the oath by which he had engaged to be most faithful to him, he took possession, while Cunincpert was absent, of his kingly power and of the palace that stood at Ticinum. Cunincpert, hearing this at the place where he was, straightway fled to an island which is in Lake Larius (Como), not far from Comum (Como), and there fortified himself strongly.

But there was great grief among all who loved him and especially among the priests and clergy, all of whom Alahis held in hatred. There was indeed at that time a bishop of the church of Ticinum, Damianus, a man of God, distinguished for sanctity and well instructed in the liberal arts. When he saw that Alahis had taken possession of the palace, in order that neither he nor his church should suffer harm from him, he dispatched to him his deacon Thomas, a wise and religious man and

sent by him to this same Alahis the blessing[1] of his holy
church.   It was announced to Alahis that Thomas the
deacon stood before the door and had brought the bene-
diction from the bishop.   Then Alahis, who as we said,
held all churchmen in hatred, thus spoke to his servants :
" Go, say to him if he has clean breeches he may come
in but if otherwise let him keep his foot outside."
Thomas, indeed, when he had heard these expressions
thus answered : " Say to him that I have clean breeches,
since I put them on washed to-day."   Alahis sent word
to him again as follows : " I do not speak of the breeches
but of the things that are inside the breeches."   To
these things Thomas thus made answer : " Go, say to
him God only can find blame in me for these causes,
but that man can by no means do so."   And when
Alahis had made this deacon come in to him he spoke
with him very bitterly and with reproaching.   Then fear
and hatred of the tyrant took possession of all the
churchmen and priests, since they deemed they could
not at all bear his rudeness ; and they began to wish for
Cunincpert so much the more as they had in execration
the haughty usurper of the kingdom.   But not very long
did rudeness and rough brutality keep the sovereignty
they had usurped.

Chapter XXXIX.

In fine, on a certain day when he was counting solidi
upon a table, one tremisses[2] fell from that table, which

---

[1] *Benedictio*, perhaps " the bread of the Eucharist " the " blessed
bread " (Waitz).   See DuCange *Benedictiones*, *Eulogia*.

[2] A coin, the third part of a solidus, and worth, says Hodgkin,

the son of Aldo, who was yet a little boy, picked from the floor and gave back to this Alahis. Thinking that the boy understood but little, Alahis spoke to him as follows: "Your father has many of these which he is soon going to give me if God shall so will." When this boy had returned to his father in the evening, his father asked him if the king had said anything to him that day, and he reported to his father all the things as they had happened and what the king had said to him. When Aldo heard these things he was greatly concerned; and

(VI, 308), about four shillings. Soetbeer (Forschungen zur Deutschen Geschichte, II, pp. 374 to 383) gives an account of the coins used by the Langobards. The mode of computation was the same as in the Greek jurisdiction of Ravenna (p. 374). The tremisses, not the whole solidus, was the common coin and those coined at Lucca after the time of the Ostrogothic kingdom (both before that city fell under the Langobards and afterwards down to 797), were an important medium of circulation. The average weight of the oldest of these coins was 1.38 grammes—corresponding with the Byzantine coins of the same period, while the coins of Lucca varied much in the fineness of the gold, from 23 carats, the Byzantine standard, down to 15—the average being perhaps 17 or 18 (pp. 375, 376, 380). After the subjection of Lucca (about the year 640) and before the names of the last Langobard kings, Aistulf and Desiderius were placed upon the coins, that is during the period described in the text, the average weight was 1.33 grammes, while the fineness of the gold was very slightly reduced. Under Aistulf and Desiderius the average weight was 1.12 grammes. It is not possible to say which Langobard king first began to coin money. Rothari in his Edict made provision for the punishment of false coinage, but the first king whose monogram appears upon a tremisses is Grimuald (Hartmann, II, 2, 33), and the first king's portrait is that of Cunincpert. The duchy of Benevento had also a special coinage of its own (id).

joining his brother Grauso he reported to him all the things the king had ill-naturedly said. And they presently took counsel with their friends and with those they could trust, in what way they might deprive the tyrant Alahis of his sovereignty before he could do them any injury. And later they set out to the palace and spoke to Alahis as follows: "Why do you deign to stay in town? See! all the city and the whole people are faithful to you, and that drunken Cunincpert is so broken up that he cannot now have any further resources. Depart and go to the hunt and exercise yourself with your young men, and we, with the rest of your faithful subjects, will defend this city for you. But we also promise you that we will soon bring you the head of your enemy, Cunincpert." And he was persuaded by their words and departed from the city and set out for the very extensive City forest, and there began to exercise himself with sports and huntings. Aldo and Grauso, however, went to Lake Comacinus (Como), embarked in a boat and proceeded to Cunincpert. When they came to him they threw themselves at his feet, acknowledged that they had acted unjustly against him and reported to him what Alahis had knavishly spoken against them and what counsel they had given him to his ruin. Why say more? They shed tears together and gave oaths to each other fixing the day when Cunincpert should come that they might deliver to him the city of Ticinum. And this was done, for on the appointed day Cunincpert came to Ticinum, was received by them most willingly and entered his palace. Then all the citizens, and especially the bishop and the

priests also and the clergy, young men and old, ran to
him eagerly and all embraced him with tears, and filled
with boundless joy, shouted their thanks to God for his
return; and he kissed them all as far as he could. Suddenly there came to Alahis one who announced that
Aldo and Grauso had fulfilled all they had promised
him and had brought him the head of Cunincpert, and
not only his head, but also his whole body, for the man
declared that he was staying in the palace. When Alahis heard this he was overwhelmed with dismay, and
raging and gnashing his teeth, he threatened many
things against Aldo and Grauso, and departed thence
and returned through Placentia (Piacenza) to Austria[1]
and joined to himself as allies the various cities, partly
by flatteries, partly by force. For when he came to
Vincentia (Vicenza) the citizens went forth against him
and made ready for war, but presently they were conquered and were made his allies. Going forth from
thence he entered Tarvisium (Treviso), and in like
manner also the remaining cities. And when Cunincpert collected an army against him, and the people of
Forum Julii (Cividale),[2] on account of their fidelity,

[1] This name was used to designate the eastern part of the Langobard kingdom, and was often mentioned in the laws of king
Liutprand (Waitz). Its western boundary was the Adda, and the
land west of that stream was called Neustria, which, with a third
division, Tuscia, constituted the main kingdom immediately subject to the king, as distinguished from the duchies of Spoleto and
Benevento.

[2] It will be noticed here that the people of Forum Julii and not
the duke is mentioned. This is one of the signs of the gradual

wished to march to Cunincpert's assistance, Alahis himself lay hid in the wood which is called Capulanus by the
bridge of the river Liquentia (Livenza), which is distant
forty-eight miles from Forum Julii and is in the way of
those going to Ticinum, and when the army of the
people of Forum Julii came, a few at a time, he compelled them all as they arrived to swear allegiance to
him, diligently watching lest anyone of them should
turn back and report this thing to the others who were
approaching; and thus all those coming from Forum
Julii were bound to him by oath. Why say more?
Alahis with the whole of Austria, and on the other hand
Cunincpert with his followers came and set up their
camps in the field whose name is Coronate (Kornate).[1]

CHAPTER XL.

Cunincpert dispatched a messenger to him, sending
him word that he would engage with him in single combat; that there was no need of using up the army of
either. To these words Alahis did not at all agree.
When one of his followers, a Tuscan by race, calling
him a warlike and brave man, advised him to go forth
boldly against Cunincpert, Alahis replied to these words:
" Cunincpert, although he is a drunkard and of a stupid
heart, is nevertheless quite bold and of wonderful
strength. For in his father's time when we were boys
there were in the palace wethers of great size which he

decrease in the power of the dukes in the northern portions of the
Langobard kingdom. (See note 3, Bk. II, Ch. 32 *supra*.)

[1] By the Adda, about ten miles southwest of Bergamo (Hodgkin, VI, 311).

seized by the wool of the back and lifted from the
ground with outstretched arm, which, indeed, I was not
able to do." That Tuscan hearing these things said to
him: " If you do not dare to go into a fight with Cunincpert in single combat you will not have me any longer
as a companion in your support." And saying this he
broke away and straightway betook himself to Cunincpert and reported these things to him. Then, as we
said, both lines came together in the field of Coronate.
And when they were already near, so that they were
bound to join in battle, Seno, a deacon of the church of
Ticinum, who was the guardian of the church of St.
John the Baptist (which was situated within that city
and which queen Gundiperga had formerly built), since
he loved the king very much, and feared lest his sovereign should perish in war, said to the king: " My lord
king, our whole life lies in your welfare. If you perish
in battle that tyrant Alahis will destroy us by various
punishments; therefore may my counsel please you.
Give me a suit of your armor and I will go and fight
with that tyrant. If I shall die, you may still re-estab-
lish your cause, but if I shall win, a greater glory will be
ascribed to you, because you will have conquered by
your servant." And when the king refused to do this,
his few faithful ones who were present began to beg
him with tears that he would give his consent to those
things the deacon had said. Overcome at last, since he
was of a tender heart, by their prayers and tears, he
handed his cuirass and his helmet, and his greaves and
his other arms to the deacon, and dispatched him to the
battle to play the part of the king. For this deacon

was of the same stature and bearing, so that when he had gone armed out of the tent he was taken for king Cunincpert by all. The battle then was joined and they struggled with all their might. And when Alahis pressed the harder there where he thought the king was, he killed Seno the deacon, and imagined that Cunincpert had been slain. And when he had ordered his head cut off so that after it was lifted upon a pike they should cry out "Thanks to God," when the helmet was removed, he learned that he had killed a churchman. Then crying out in his rage he said: "Woe is me! We have done nothing when we have brought the battle to this point that we have killed a churchman! Therefore, I now make this kind of a vow that if God shall give me the victory I will fill a whole well with the members of churchmen."

Chapter XLI.

Then Cunincpert, seeing that his men had lost, straightway showed himself to them, and taking away their fear, strengthened their hearts to hope for victory. Again the lines of battle formed and on the one side Cunincpert, and on the other, Alahis made ready for the struggles of war. And when they were already near so that both lines were joining to fight, Cunincpert again sent a message to Alahis in these words: "See how many people there are on both sides! What need is there that so great a multitude perish? Let us join, he and I, in single combat and may that one of us to whom God may have willed to give the victory have and possess all this people safe and entire." And when his

followers exhorted Alahis to do what Cunincpert enjoined him he answered: "I cannot do this because
among his spears I see the image of the holy archangel
Michael[1] by whom I swore allegiance to him." Then
one of them said: "From fear you see what is not, and
anyhow, it is now late for you to think of these things."
Then when the trumpets sounded, the lines of battle
joined, and as neither side gave way, a very great slaughter was made of the people. At length the cruel tyrant
Alahis perished, and Cunincpert with the help of the
Lord obtained the victory. The army of Alahis too,
when his death was known, took the protection of flight.
And of these whomsoever the point of the sword did not
cut down the river Addua (Adda) destroyed. Also the
head of Alahis was cut off and his legs were cut away
and only his deformed and mangled corpse remained.
The army of the people of Forum Julii was not in this
war at all because, since it had unwillingly sworn allegiance to Alahis, for this reason it gave assistance neither
to king Cunincpert nor to Alahis, but returned home
when the two engaged in war. Then Alahis having
died in this manner, king Cunincpert commanded that
the body of Seno the deacon should be buried in great
splendor before the gates of the church of St. John
which the deacon had governed. The reigning sovereign himself indeed returned to Ticinum with the rejoicing of all and in the triumph of victory.

[1] The patron saint of the Langobards (Hartmann, II, 2, 25;
Waitz).

BOOK VI.

Chapter I.

While these things were occurring among the Langobards across the Po, Romuald, duke of the Beneventines
after he had collected a great multitude of an army,
attacked and captured Tarentum (Taranto) and in like
manner Brundisium (Brindisi) and subjugated to his dominion all that very extensive region which surrounds
them.[1] His wife Theuderata, too, built at the same time,
a church in honor of the blessed apostle Peter outside
the walls of the city of Beneventum and in that place
she established a convent of many nuns.

Chapter II.

Romuald, too, after he had governed the dukedom
sixteen years was withdrawn from this life. After him
his son Grimuald ruled the people of the Samnites[2]
three years. Wigilinda, a sister of Cunincpert and daughter of king Perctarit was united to him in marriage.
When Grimuald also died, Gisulf his brother was made
duke[3] and ruled over Beneventum seventeen years.

[1] This probably refers to the "heel of Italy," the land around
Otranto, which now passed under the Langobard sway (Hodgkin,
VI, 335).

[2] Thus were the Beneventines called (IV, 44, 46, *supra*).

[3] His mother Theuderata governed the dukedom during his
minority (Waitz).

Winiperga was married to him and bore him Romuald. About these times, when a great solitude existed for a number of years past in the stronghold of Cassinum (Monte Cassino) where the holy body of the most blessed Benedict reposes, there came Franks from the regions of the Celmanici (Cenomannici)[1] and of the Aurelianenses,[2] and while they pretended to keep a vigil by the venerable body they bore away the bones of the reverend father and also of the revered Scolastica his sister, and carried them to their own country where two monasteries were built, one in honor of each, that is, of the blessed Benedict and of St. Scolastica. But it is certain that that venerable mouth, sweeter than all nectar, and the eyes beholding ever heavenly things, and the other members too have remained to us, although decayed.[3] For only the body of our Lord alone did not see corruption; but the bodies of all the saints have been subjected to corruption, to be restored afterwards to eternal glory, with the exception of those which by divine miracles are kept without blemish.

CHAPTER III.

But when Rodoald indeed, who as we said before,[4] held the dukedom at Forum Julii, was absent from that

[1] Inhabitants of Le Mans.

[2] Inhabitants of Orleans.

[3] A long controversy between the French and Italian Benedictine monks has arisen from this passage, as to the genuineness of the relics of St. Benedict (Waitz).

[4] V, 24 *supra.*

city, Ansfrit from the fortress of Reunia (Ragogna) [1]
swept through his dukedom without the consent of the
king.   Rodoald, when he learned this, fled into Istria
and thence came by ship through Ravenna to Ticinum
to king Cunincpert.   Ansfrit indeed, not content to rule
the dukedom of the Friulans, but rebelling against
Cunincpert besides, attempted to usurp his sovereignty.
But he was seized in Verona and brought to the king,
his eyes were torn out and he was cast into banishment.
After these things Ado, the brother of Rodoald, governed the Friulan dukedom a year and seven months
under the name of caretaker.[2]

CHAPTER IV.

While these things occurred in Italy, a heresy arose
at Constantinople which asserted that there was one will
and mode of action in our Lord Jesus Christ.   Georgius [3]
the patriarch of Constantinople, Macharius, Pyrrus, Paul
and Peter stirred up this heresy.   Wherefore the em-

[1] About thirty miles west of Cividale (Hodgkin, VI, 328, note 1).

[2] *Loci servator*.   The only instance of this title during the Langobard period.   Later it frequently occurs (Pabst, 460, note).
There is no date for these events except that they occurred under
Cunincpert, 688–700 (Hodgkin, VI, 328, note 3).   By these occurrences the dukedom of Friuli, which had been semi-independent,
seems to have been placed directly under the power of the king
(Hartmann, II, 1, 267).

[3] This is a mistake.   Georgius was used by the emperor as an
instrument of reconciliation (Hartmann, II, 1, 259).   It was the
former patriarchs, Sergius, Pyrrus, Paul and Peter, who stirred up
the heresy, and Macharius, bishop of Antioch, supported it (p. 260).

peror Constantine[1] caused to be assembled a hundred and fifty bishops[2] among whom were also the legates of the holy Roman Church sent by Pope Agatho—John the Deacon and John the bishop of Portus (Porto)[3]—and they all condemned this heresy.[4] At that hour so many spider webs fell in the midst of the people that they were all astonished, and by this it was signified that the uncleanesses of heretical depravity were driven away. And Georgius the patriarch indeed was rebuked,[5] the

[1] See V, 30, *supra*. He was also called Pogonatus.

[2] Paul erroneously places the time of this general council (A. D. 680) in the reign of Cunincpert, which began 688 (Jacobi, 56).

[3] At the mouth of the Tiber.

[4] We have seen (V, 6, note, *supra*) that the so-called Monothelete heresy had succeeded the controversy regarding the Three Chapters. Four successive patriarchs of Constantinople had approved the Monothelete doctrine, but the church in the west was united against it, and the emperor, desirous of a reconciliation, issued an invitation to the Pope to send deputies to a council. Pope Agatho accordingly dispatched three legates and three bishops to a conference at Constantinople, which became the Sixth Œcumenical Council. It lasted from November, 680, to September, 681. Macharius, patriarch of Antioch, undertook to prove that the dogma of " one theandric energy " was in harmony with the decisions of the Fourth and Fifth Councils, but the genuineness of some of his quotations was denied and the relevancy of others disputed. Gregory, patriarch of Constantinople, formally announced his adhesion to the cause of the Pope, who insisted that there were two wills in Christ. The decrees of Pope Agatho and the Western Synod were ratified, Macharius was deposed and the upholders of the Monothelete heresy were condemned, including Honorius, former pope of Rome (Hodgkin, VI, 345, 346),

[5] A mistake. See note above.

others, however, who persisted in their defense were
visited by the penalty of excommunication. At this
time Damianus, bishop of the church of Ticinum [1] composed in the name of Mansuetus archbishop of Mediolanum (Milan) an epistle upon this question, quite
useful to correct belief, which in the aforesaid synod,
won no ordinary approbation. For the correct and
true belief is this, that as there are in our Lord Jesus
Christ two natures, that is of God and of man, so also
there may be believed to be two wills or modes of action.
Will you hear what there is of the Deity in him? He
says, "I and my Father are one." [2] Will you hear what
there is of humanity? "My Father is greater than I." [3]
Behold him sleeping in the ship according to his human
nature! Behold his divinity when the evangelist says:
"Then he arose and rebuked the winds and the sea and
there was a great calm!" [4] This Sixth General Synod
was celebrated at Constantinople and recorded in the
Greek language at the time of Pope Agatho, and the
emperor Constantine conducted it while remaining
within the enclosures of his palace.

Chapter V.

In these times during the eighth indiction (A. D.
680) the moon suffered an eclipse; also an eclipse of
the sun occurred at almost the same time on the fifth

---

[1] At this time Damianus was only a presbyter (Waitz).

[2] John x. 30.

[3] John xiv. 28.

[4] Matt. viii. 26.

day before the Nones of May [1] about the tenth hour of
the day. And presently there followed a very severe
pestilence for three months, that is, in July, August and
September, and so great was the multitude of those dying that even parents with their children and brothers
with their sisters were placed on biers two by two and
conducted to their tombs at the city of Rome. And in
like manner too this pestilence also depopulated Ticinum
so that all citizens fled to the mountain ranges and to
other places and grass and bushes grew in the market
place and throughout the streets of the city. And then
it visibly appeared to many that a good and a bad angel
proceeded by night through the city and as many times
as, upon command of the good angel, the bad angel,
who appeared to carry a hunting spear in his hand,
knocked at the door of each house with the spear, so
many men perished from that house on the following
day. Then it was said to a certain man by revelation
that the pestilence itself would not cease before an altar
of St. Sebastian the martyr was placed in the church of
the blessed Peter which is called " Ad Vincula." And
it was done, and after the remains of St. Sebastian the
martyr had been carried from the city of Rome, presently the altar was set up in the aforesaid church and
the pestilence itself ceased. [2]

[1] May 2nd. Pagi says that the solar eclipse occurred in 680
and the other in 681 (Giansevero).

[2] The historians of Pavia declare that the bishop St. Damianus
begged from the Roman pontiff the remains of the holy martyr
and placed them in the church of St. Peter ad Vincula (Waitz).

CHAPTER VI.

While king Cunincpert, indeed, after these things was
taking counsel in the city of Ticinum with his master of
horse, which in their language is called "marpahis,"[1]
in what way he might deprive Aldo and Grauso of life,
suddenly in the window near which they were standing
sat a fly of the largest kind which when Cunincpert
attempted to strike with his knife to kill it, he only cut
off its foot. While Aldo and Grauso indeed, in ignorance of the evil design, were coming to the palace, when
they had drawn near the church of the holy martyr
Romanus which is situated near the palace, suddenly a
certain lame man with one foot cut off came in their
way who said to them that Cunincpert was going to kill
them if they should go on to him. When they heard
this they were seized with great fear and fled behind the
altar of that church. Presently it was announced to
king Cunincpert that Aldo and Grauso had taken refuge
in the church of the blessed martyr Romanus. Then
Cunincpert began to accuse his master of horse asking
why he had to betray his design. His master of horse
thus answered him: "My lord king, you know that
after we conferred about these things I did not go out
of your presence and how could I have said this to any
one?" Then the king sent to Aldo and Grauso, asking
them why they had taken refuge in the holy place.
And they answering said: "Because it was reported to
us that our lord the king wished to kill us." Again the
king sent to them, seeking to know who he was who had

[1] II, 9 *supra.*

given them the report, and he sent them word that unless they would report to him who had told them, they could not find favor with him. Then they sent word to the king as it had occurred, saying that a lame man had met them upon the way who had one foot cut off and used a wooden leg up to the knee, and that this man had been the one who told them they would be killed. Then the king understood that the fly whose foot he had cut off had been a bad spirit and that it had betrayed his secret designs. And straightway he took Aldo and Grauso on his word of honor from that church, pardoned their fault and afterwards held them as faithful subjects.

Chapter VII.

At that time Felix, the uncle of my teacher Flavian was renowned in the grammatical art. The king loved him so much that he bestowed upon him among other gifts of his bounty, a staff decorated with silver and gold.

Chapter VIII.

During the same time also lived John the bishop of the church of Bergoma (Bergamo), a man of wonderful sanctity.[1] Since he had offended king Cunincpert while they were conversing at a banquet, the king commanded to be prepared for him when he was returning to his inn a fierce and untamed horse who was accustomed to dash to the earth with a great snorting those who sat upon him. But when the bishop mounted him he was

[1] He took part in the council at Rome under Pope Agatho against the Monotheletes (Waitz).

so gentle that he carried him at an easy gait to his own house. The king, hearing this, cherished the bishop from that day with due honor and bestowed upon him in gift that very horse, which he had destined for his own riding.

CHAPTER IX.

At this time between Christmas and Epiphany there appeared at night in a clear sky a star near the Pleiades shaded in every way as when the moon stands behind a cloud. Afterwards in the month of February at noonday there arose a star in the west which set with a great flash in the direction of the east. Then in the month of March there was an eruption of Bebius (Vesuvius) for some days and all green things growing round about were exterminated by its dust and ashes.

CHAPTER X.

Then the race of Saracens, unbelieving and hateful to God, proceeded from Egypt into Africa with a great multitude, took Carthage by siege and when it was taken, cruelly laid it waste and leveled it to the ground.

CHAPTER XI.

Meanwhile the emperor Constantine died at Constantinople and his younger son Justinian [1] assumed the sovereignty of the Romans and held the control of it for ten years. He took Africa away from the Saracens

---

[1] Here Paul misunderstands Bede from whom he took the statement. Bede (A. M. 4649) speaks of ''Justinian the younger, a son of Constantine.'' He succeeded to the throne in 685.

and made peace with them on sea and land. He sent
Zacharias his protospatarius[1] and ordered that Pope
Sergius should be brought to Constantinople because he
was unwilling to approve and subscribe to the error of
that synod which the emperor had held at Constantinople.[2] But the soldiery of Ravenna and of the neighboring parts, despising the impious orders of the emperor, drove this same Zacharias with reproaches and
insults from the city of Rome.[3]

CHAPTER XII.

Leo seizing the imperial dignity, in opposition to this
Justinian, deprived him of his kingdom, ruled the empire
of the Romans three years and kept Justinian an exile
in Pontus.[4]

CHAPTER XIII.

Tiberius in turn rebelled against this Leo and seized

[1] Captain of the imperial body guard, a high Byzantine dignity.

[2] The Quinisextan (Fifth–Sixth) council summoned by Justinian
II in 691 (Hodgkin, VI, 354–356).

[3] A. D. 691 (Giansevero).

[4] The reign of Justinian II had been marked by oppressive exactions and great cruelties. After ten years' misgovernment
Leontius (the Leo mentioned in the text) a nobleman of Isauria,
commander of the armies of the East, who had been imprisoned
by the tyrant and then released, was proclaimed emperor in 695.
A mob assembled in the Hippodrome and demanded Justinian's
death. Leontius spared his life, but mutilated him by slitting
his nose (whence he was called *Rhinotmetus*) and banished him to
Cherson on the southwest coast of the Crimea (Hodgkin, VI,
359–361).

his sovereignty and held him in prison in the same city all the time he reigned.[1]

CHAPTER XIV.

At this time[2] the council held at Aquileia, on account of the ignorance of their faith, hesitated to accept the Fifth General Council until, when instructed by the salutary admonitions of the blessed pope Sergius, it also with the other churches of Christ consented to approve of this. For that synod was held at Constantinople at the time of pope Vigilius under the emperor Justinian against Theodorus and all the heretics who were asserting that the blessed Mary had given birth to a man only and not to a God and a man. In this synod it was established as a Catholic doctrine that the blessed Mary ever virgin should be called Mother of God since, as the Catholic faith has it, she gave birth not to a man only, but truly to a God and a man.[3]

[1] A naval armament under the command of the patrician John had delivered Carthage from the Saracens but the latter had retaken the city and the imperial troops on their return to Constantinople broke out in a mutiny against both their general and Leontius, and a naval officer named Apsimar was proclaimed emperor. When the fleet reached Constantinople, Leontius was dethroned and Apsimar under the name of Tiberius III, reigned seven years, from 698 to 705 (Hodgkin, VI, 362, 363).

[2] A. D. 698 (Giansevero).

[3] Paul is in error in saying that it was the Synod of Constantinople at the time of pope Vigilius which declared the Virgin Mary the Mother of God. Such declaration was made at Ephesus. The Council of Constantinople was the one that condemned the Three Chapters and led to the long schism described in the previ-

CHAPTER XV.

In these days [1] Cedoal king of the Anglo-Saxons who had waged many wars in his own country [2] was converted to Christ and set out for Rome, and when on the way he came to king Cunincpert he was magnificently received by him, and when he had come to Rome he was baptized by pope Sergius and called Peter and while dressed in white [3] he departed to the heavenly realms. His body was buried in the church of St. Peter and has inscribed above it this epitaph: [4]

Cedoal, mighty in arms, for the love of his God has forsaken
  Eminence, riches and kin, triumphs and powerful realms,
Arms and nobles and cities and camps and gods of the household,
  Things that the thrift of his sires gathered, or he for himself,

ous notes (III, 20, 26; IV, 33 *supra*). The return of the schismatics to the church took place according to other authorities not at Aquileia but at Pavia (Waitz, Appendix, p. 245, 248), when they declared with shouts of triumph that they renounced the heresy of Theodore and his companions and asked to be restored to the church. Legates were sent to bear the news to Pope Sergius who ordered that the manuscripts of the schismatics should be burned (Hodgkin, V, 483, 484). Possibly one council was held at Aquileia and another at Pavia. Thus all the kingdom of the Langobards was now restored to full Catholic communion.

[1] This journey and conversion of king Cedoal (or Ceadwalla of Wessex) is incorrectly placed by Paul at the time of the synod at Aquileia, 698. It actually occurred in 689 (Hodgkin, VI, 318; V, 483).

[2] He had annexed Sussex, ravaged Kent and massacred the inhabitants of the Isle of Wight (Hodgkin, VI, 318).

[3] The garment of the neophytes, worn by those just baptized.

[4] The author of this epitaph was Archbishop Benedict of Milan, A. D. 681–725 (Waitz, p. 225).

So that as king and a guest he might gaze on Peter and Peter's
   Chair, and propitiously quaff waters unstained from his spring,
Taking in radiant draught the shining light whose refulgence,
   Giving immortal life, floweth on every side!
Swift to perceive the rewards of a life restored by conversion,
   Joyful, he casts aside heathenish madness, and then
Changes his name as well, and Sergius the pontiff commanded
   Peter he should be called; until the Father himself,
Making him pure by the grace of Christ in the font of the new birth,
   Lifted him, clothed in white, up to the stronghold of heaven!
Wonderful faith of the king, and of Christ the astonishing mercy!
   His is the perfect plan—counsel that none can approach!
Coming in safety indeed from remotest regions of Britain,
   Through many nations, along ways many, over the straits,
Bringing his mystical gifts, he gazed upon Romulus' city
   Looked upon Peter's church, worthy of reverence due;
Clad in white will he go, in the flocks of Christ a companion;
   Earth his body may hold, heaven his spirit will keep.
You may the rather believe he has changed the mere badge of the
   scepters
   He whom your eyes have seen winning the kingdom of Christ.[1]

CHAPTER XVI.

At this time in Gaul when the kings of the Franks
were degenerating from their wonted courage and skill,
those who were regarded as stewards of the palace
began to administer the kingly power and to do whatever is the custom for kings, since it was ordained from
heaven that the sovereignty of the Franks should be
transferred to the race of these men. And Arnulf was
at that time[2] steward of the royal palace, a man, as was

[1] A version in rhyme, less literal than the foregoing, is found in
Giles' translation of the Ecclesiastical History of Bede, Vol. I, p. 278.

[2] Paul is in error in making Arnulf, who died August 18, 641,
contemporary with Cunincpert (Jacobi, 42).

afterwards apparent, pleasing to God and of wonderful holiness, who, after enjoying the glory of this world, devoted himself to the service of Christ and was distinguished in the episcopate and finally, choosing the life of a hermit, rendered all kinds of services to lepers and lived in the greatest abstinence. Concerning his wonderful doings at the church of Metz where he carried on the bishopric, there is a book containing an account of his miracles and the abstinence of his life. But I too, in a book which I wrote concerning the bishops of this city, at the request of Angelramnus, archbishop of the aforesaid church, a very gentle man and distinguished by holiness, have set down concerning this most holy man Arnulf, certain of his miracles which I have considered it merely superfluous to repeat here.

CHAPTER XVII.

During these occurrences Cunincpert, a ruler most beloved by all, after he had held for twelve years alone, succeeding his father, the kingdom of the Langobards, was finally withdrawn from this life. He built in the field of Coronate where he had waged war against Alahis, a monastery in honor of the holy martyr George.[1] He was moreover a handsome man and conspicuous in every good quality and a bold warrior. He was buried with many tears of the Langobards near the

[1] The city of Modena, half ruined during the insurrection of Alahis, was also restored by him (Hodgkin, VI, 314, note 2). Cunincpert was the first Langobard king whose effigy is found upon the coins (id., p. 317).

church of our Lord the Saviour which his grandfather Aripert had formerly built.[1]   And he left the kingdom of the Langobards to his son Liutpert who was yet of the age of boyhood, to whom he gave as his tutor Ansprand, a wise and distinguished man.

CHAPTER XVIII.

When eight months had elapsed from this time,[2] Raginpert, duke of Turin, whom formerly king Godepert had left as a little boy when he was killed by Grimuald, of which we have also spoken above,[3] came with a strong force and fought against Ansprand and Rotharit, duke of the Bergamascans at Novariae (Novara), and defeating them in the open field took possession of the kingdom of the Langobards. But he died the same year.

CHAPTER XIX.

Then his son Aripert, again making ready for war, fought at Ticinum with king Liutpert and with Ansprand and Ato and Tatzo and also Rotharit and Farao ; but overcoming all these in battle he took the child Liutpert alive as a prisoner of war.   Ansprand also fled and fortified himself in the island of Commacina.[4]

[1] In Ticinum, where there was an epitaph upon his tomb, referred to by Muratori in his book on the Antiquities of Este, Chapters 1–10, p. 73 (Waitz).

[2] A. D. 701 (Giansevero).

[3] IV, Ch. 51.

[4] Spelled elsewhere Comacina.

Chapter XX.

But when Rotharit indeed returned to his city of Bergamus (Bergamo) he seized the kingly power. King Aripert marched against him with a great army, and having first attacked and captured Lauda (Lodi) he beseiged Bergamus, and storming it without any difficulty with battering rams and other machines of war, presently took it and seized Rotharit the false king and shaving his hair and his beard, thrust him into exile at Turin, and there after some days he was killed. Liutpert indeed whom he had taken he deprived of life in like manner in the bath.

Chapter XXI.

He also sent an army into the island of Commacina against Ansprand. When this was known Ansprand fled to Clavenna (Chiavenna), thence he came through Curia (Chur) a city of the Rhaetians to Theutpert, duke of the Bavarians, and was with him for nine years. But the army of Aripert indeed took possession of the island in which Ansprand had been and destroyed his town.

Chapter XXII.

Then king Aripert when he was confirmed in his sovereignty, tore out the eyes of Sigiprand, the son of Ansprand, and afflicted in various ways all who had been connected with the latter by the tie of blood. He also kept Liutprand the younger son of Ansprand, in custody, but because he regarded him as a person of no importance and as yet a mere youth, he not only inflicted no punishment at all upon his body, but let him depart so that he could go to his father. There is no doubt that this was done by the command of God Almighty who was preparing him for the management of the kingdom. Then Liutprand proceeded to his father in Bavaria and caused him incalculable joy by his coming. But king Aripert caused the wife of Ansprand, Theodorada by name, to be seized; and when she with her woman's wilfulness boasted that she would get to be queen, she was disfigured in the beauty of her face, her nose and ears being cut off. Also the sister of Liutprand, Aurona by name, was mutilated in like manner.

Chapter XXIII.

At this time in Gaul, in the kingdom of the Franks, Anschis,[1] the son of Arnulf, who is believed to be named after Anchises the former Trojan, conducted the sovereignty under the title of steward of the palace.

Chapter XXIV.

When Ado who we said was caretaker[2] had died at Forum Julii, Ferdulf, a man tricky and conceited, who came from the territories of Liguria, obtained the dukedom. Because he wanted to have the glory of a victory over the Slavs, he brought great misfortune upon himself and the people of Forum Julii. He gave sums of money to certain Slavs to send upon his request an army of Slavs into this province, and it was accord-

[1] Or Ansegis. He is to be referred however to an earlier period (Waitz).

[2] VI, Chap. 3, *supra*.

ingly done. But that was the cause of great disaster in this province of Forum Julii. The freebooters of the Slavs fell upon the flocks and upon the shepherds of the sheep that pastured in their neighborhoods and drove away the booty taken from them. The ruler of that place, whom they called in their own language "sculdahis,"[1] a man of noble birth and strong in courage and capacity, followed them, but nevertheless he could not overtake the freebooters. Duke Ferdulf met him as he was returning thence and when he asked him what had become of these robbers, Argait, for that was his name, answered that they had escaped. Then Ferdulf in rage thus spoke to him: "When could you do anything bravely, you whose name, Argait, comes from the word coward,"[1] and Argait, provoked by great anger, since he was a brave man, answered as follows: "May God so will that you and I, duke Ferdulf, may not depart from this life until others know which of us is the greater coward." When they had spoken to each other

[1] See the German, *Schultheiss*, local magistrate. They were subordinate to the judges (*i. e.*, the dukes or the gastaldi). See II, 32, note 4 (pp. 86–91), *supra;* Pabst, 499.

[2] *Arga*, a Langobard word, meaning cowardly, inert, worthless. See Rothari, Edict, Chapter 381 (M. G. LL., IV, p. 88), where the word is recognized as conveying a particular insult. "If one in rage calls another an *arga*, and he cannot deny it, and says he has called him so in rage, he shall declare upon oath that he does not hold him for an *arga*, and thereupon he shall pay twelve *solidi* for the offensive word. But if he insists upon it and says he can prove it in a duel, so let him convict him, if he can, or let him pay as above."

in turn, these words, in the vulgar tongue,[1] it happened not many days afterwards, that the army of the Slavs, for whose coming duke Ferdulf had given his sums of money, now arrived in great strength. And when they had set their camp upon the very top of a mountain

---

[1] "*Vulgaria verba.*" Hartmann (II, 2, 58) regards this passage as presupposing that Ferdulf and Argait could speak Latin with one another. After the permanent settlement of the Langobards in Italy the current Latin language of the time (which was the only written language, and the only one fitted to many of the new relations imposed by their intercourse with the Roman population) gradually superseded their own more barbarous tongue. (Hartmann, II, 2, 22.) It is evident, however, from the German words used by Paul, as well as from his description of this controversy between duke Ferdulf and Argait, which must have occurred not far from A. D. 700 (Hodgkin, VI, 328, note 3), that the Langobard language was spoken in the eighth century, and there are traces of its continuance even after the Frankish invasion, A. D. 774. In a document in upper Italy the pronoun *ih* introduced by mistake before the Latin words "have subscribed myself" indicate the existence of the Langobard as a spoken language in the latter half of the ninth century. The Chronicle of Salerno, composed in 978 (Ch. 38, MGH. SS., III, 489), refers to the German language as "formerly" spoken by the Langobards, from which it would appear that in that region at least it had then become extinct. But it is quite uncertain just when it ceased to be used. Probably the language continued longest where the German population was most dense, and the period where it died out as a living language must have been preceded by a considerable time, in which those who spoke it also understood and spoke the Latin tongue. The period of its decline can be traced by numerous Latin terminations of German words and the addition of German suffixes (for example, *engo, ingo, esco-asco- atto- etto- otto*) to Latin words, combinations which have been important ingredients in the formation of modern Italian (Bruckner, Sprache der Langobarden, pp. 11-17).

and it was hard to approach them from almost any side,
duke Ferdulf, coming upon them with his army, began
to go around that mountain in order that he could attack them by more level places. Then Argait of whom
we have spoken thus said to Ferdulf: "Remember,
duke Ferdulf, that you said I was lazy and useless and
that you called me in our common speech a coward,
but now may the anger of God come upon him who
shall be the last of us to attack those Slavs," and saying
these words, he turned his horse where the ascent was
difficult on account of the steepness of the mountain,
and began to attack the fortified camp of the Slavs.
Ferdulf, being ashamed not to attack the Slavs himself,
through the same difficult places, followed him through
those steep and hard and pathless spots, and his army
too, considering it base not to follow their leader, began
also to press on after him. Consequently the Slavs,
seeing that they were coming upon them through steep
places, prepared themselves manfully, and fighting
against them more with stones and axes[1] than with arms
they threw them nearly all from their horses and killed
them. And thus they obtained their victory, not by
their own strength, but by chance. There all the
nobility of the Friulans perished. There duke Ferdulf
fell and there too he who had provoked him was killed.
And there so great a number of brave men were vanquished by the wickedness and thoughtlessness of dissension as could, with unity and wholesome counsel,

[1] *Securibus.* Hodgkin translates "tree trunks," believing that
the axes were used in felling trees to cast down upon them (VI,
330, and note 3).

overthrow many thousands of their enemies. There, however, one of the Langobards, Munichis by name, who was afterwards the father of the dukes Peter of Forum Julii and Ursus of Ceneta (Ceneda), alone acted in a brave and manly manner. When he had been thrown from his horse and one of the Slavs suddenly attacking him had tied his hands with a rope, he wrested with his bound hands the lance from the right hand of that same Slav, pierced him with it, and tied as he was, threw himself down through the steep places and escaped. We put these things into this history especially for this purpose, that nothing further of a like character may happen through the evil of dissension.

Chapter XXV.

And so duke Ferdulf having died in this way, Corvolus was appointed in his place, but he held the dukedom only a little while, and when he had offended the king, his eyes were torn out and he lived ignominiously.

Chapter XXVI.

Afterwards indeed Pemmo acquired the dukedom.[1] He was a man of talent and useful to his country. His father was Billo who had been a native of Bellunum (Belluno), but on account of a sedition he had caused at that place he afterwards came to Forum Julii, and lived there peacefully. This Pemmo had a wife, Ratperga by name, who since she was boorish in appear-

---

[1] De Rubeis (319) thinks this was in 705. He held the dukedom about twenty-six years (Hodgkin, VI, 332).

ance often asked her husband to send her away and take
another wife whom it would befit to be the spouse of so
great a duke. But as he was a wise man he said that
her behavior and humility and reverent modesty pleased
him more than beauty of body. From this wife then
Pemmo begot three sons, Ratchis and Ratchait and
Ahistulf,[1] energetic men, whose birth raised the humility of their mother to high honor. This duke collected
all the sons of all the nobles who had died in the war
of which we have spoken, and brought them up in like
manner with his own children as if they themselves had
been begotten by him.

CHAPTER XXVII.

At this time then, Gisulf the ruler of the Beneventines took Sura (Sora), a city of the Romans, and in
like manner the towns of Hirpinum (Arpino) and Arx
(Arce).[2] This Gisulf at the time of Pope John[3] came
to Campania with all his forces burning and plundering,
took many captives and set up his camp as far as in the
place which is called Horrea,[4] and no one could resist

[1] Ratchis and Aistulf were afterwards kings of the Langobards.

[2] Three towns on or near the river Liris or Garigliano and something over fifty miles southeast of Rome.

[3] John VI, A. D. 701–704. Others think, John V, A. D. 685
(Waitz).

[4] Hodgkin (VI, 336, note 2) believes that Puteoli is intended—
Duchesne, followed by Hartmann (II, 2, 116), says it was a place
at the fifth milestone of the Via Latina. It seems uncertain
whether one incursion or more was meant by this chapter of Paul
(Id).

him.   The Pontiff sent priests to him with apostolic
gifts and redeemed all the captives from the hands of
his troops, and induced the duke himself to go back
home with his army.

Chapter XXVIII.

At this time [1] Aripert king of the Langobards made
restitution by gift of the patrimony of the Cottian
Alps [2] which had formerly belonged to the jurisdiction
of the Apostolic See but had been taken away by the
Langobards a long time before, and he dispatched this
deed of gift written in golden letters to Rome.   Also in
these days [3] two kings of the Saxons [4] coming to Rome
to the footsteps of the apostles, died suddenly as they
desired.

Chapter XXIX.

Then also Benedict archbishop of Mediolanum
(Milan) came to Rome and conducted his lawsuit for
the church of Ticinum, but he was defeated because
from early times the bishops of Ticinum had been con-

[1] A. D. 707 (Giansevero).

[2] Paul does not intend to say that this patrimony included the
whole province of the Cottian Alps, but simply that part of the
papal patrimony was in that province (Hodgkin, VI, 324, note 2).

[3] This is erroneous, the king's pilgrimage did not occur during
the papacy of John VI (701–705), to whom Aripert made this gift,
but in 709 under Constantine I (Jacobi, p. 50; Hodgkin, VI, 323).

[4] Coinred king of the Mercians and Offa prince of the East
Saxons (Hodgkin, VI, 323).

secrated by the Roman Church.[1] This venerable archbishop Benedict was a man of eminent holiness, and the
fame of good opinion concerning him shone brightly
throughout the whole of Italy.

CHAPTER XXX.

Then when Transamund, the duke of the Spoletans
had died,[2] Faruald his son, succeeded to his father's
place. Moreover, Wachilapus was the brother of Transamund and governed that same dukedom equally with
his brother.

CHAPTER XXXI.

But Justinian, who had lost his imperial power and was
in exile in Pontus, again received the sovereignty by the
help of Terebellus, king of the Bulgarians, and put to
death those patricians who had expelled him. He took
also Leo and Tiberius[3] who had usurped his place and
caused them to be butchered in the midst of the circus
before all the people.[4] He tore out the eyes of Gallici-

[1] The date of this is fixed by Paul at too early a period (Jacobi,
56).

[2] He appears to have reigned forty years from 663 to 703
(Hodgkin, VI, 337).

[3] Paul has here misunderstood the language of Bede from whom
he took this statement and who said that Justinian executed Leo
(Leontius) and Tiberius (Apsimar) the patricians who had expelled him. No other patricians are referred to (Jacobi, 50).

[4] Justinian II, who had been exiled to Cherson (see ch. 12, note
supra), was rejected by the citizens of that place, whereupon he
roamed through the southern part of Russia and took refuge with

nus[1] the patriarch of Constantinople and sent him to
Rome and he appointed Cyrus the abbot who had taken
care of him when he was an exile in Pontus, as bishop
in the place of Gallicinus. He ordered Pope Constantine to come to him, and received him and sent him
back with honor. [2] Falling upon the earth he asked the
Pope to intercede for his sins and he renewed all of the
privileges of his church.[3] When he sent his army into
Pontus to seize Filippicus, whom he had held there in
bondage, this same venerable Pope earnestly forbade
him from doing this but he could not, however, prevent it.

the Cagan of the Khazars, a Hunnish tribe settled around the sea
of Azof, and the Cagan gave him in marriage his sister Theodora.
The reigning emperor Tiberius sent messengers to the Cagan
offering him great gifts to kill or surrender Justinian.   The Cagan
listened to the tempting proposals, but Theodora warned her husband, who fled to the Danube, where Terbel or Terebellus joined
him in an effort to regain the throne.   With the aid of the Bulgarians he attacked and conquered Constantinople.   His two
rivals, who had successively reigned in his absence, were now
both loaded with chains and brought before his throne in the
Hippodrome where he placed his feet upon their necks before
causing them to be beheaded at the place of public execution
(Hodgkin, 365–368).

[1] Callinicus (not Gallicinus) had preached a sermon rejoicing at
the overthrow of Justinian ten years before (Hodgkin, VI, 361).

[2] Constantine left Rome October, 710 (Hodgkin, VI, 375) and
returned October, 711 (id., p. 379).

[3] It is probable that the decrees of the Quinisextan Council were
now accepted by the pope (Hodgkin, VI, 378–379).

Chapter XXXII.

The army too which had been sent against Filippicus joined Filippicus' side and made him emperor. He came to Constantinople against Justinian, fought with him at the twelfth milestone from the city, conquered and killed him, and obtained his sovereign power. Justinian indeed reigned six years with his son Tiberius in this second term.[1] Leo in banishing him cut off his nostrils and he, after he had assumed the sovereignty, as often as he wiped off his hand flowing with a drop of rheum, almost so often did he order some one of those who had been against him to be slain.[2]

[1] In his insane fury for revenge against the people of Cherson who had rejected him when he was exiled, Justinian sent three expeditions against that city to destroy it. In the first of these its leading citizens were seized and sent for punishment to Constantinople, where some were roasted alive and others drowned ; but Justinian still accused his generals of slackness in executing his orders and sent others in their places, who were, however, compelled to give up the bloody work, and then for self-protection to join the party of revolt which gathered around one Bardanis, an Armenian, who was proclaimed emperor under the name of Filippicus, whereupon an expedition set out for Constantinople to dethrone Justinian. It was entirely successful. The tyrant was deserted by his subjects, and with his son Tiberius was captured and slain (Hodgkin, 379–384).

[2] A reign of terror had followed the restoration of Justinian and innumerable victims perished. Some were sewn up in sacks and thrown into the sea, others invited to a great repast and when they rose to leave were sentenced to execution (Hodgkin, VI, 369). He was specially infuriated against the city of Ravenna and sent a fleet thither under the patrician Theodore, seized the chief men of the city, brought them to Constantinople, blinded the arch-

CHAPTER XXXIII.

In these days then, when the patriarch Peter was dead, Serenus undertook the government of the church of Aquileia.[1] He was a man endowed with a simple character and devoted to the service of Christ.

CHAPTER XXXIV.

But Filippicus indeed, who was called Bardanis, after he was confirmed in the imperial dignity, ordered that Cyrus, of whom we have spoken, should be turned out of his patriarchate and return to Pontus, to govern his monastery. This Filippicus dispatched letters of perverted doctrine to pope Constantine which he, together

bishop Felix, and put the rest to death (pp. 373–374). Justinian then sent as exarch to Italy John Rizokopus, who went first to Rome and put to death a number of papal dignitaries and then proceeded to Ravenna, where in a struggle with the local forces he was killed. The people of Ravenna refused to recognize Justinian, and chose a leader of their own in the person of Georgius, who organized an autonomous government and established a military organization in Italy independent of Byzantium (Hartmann, II, 2, 78–81).

[1] It was afterwards, at the request of king Liutprand, that pope Gregory II sent the pallium of a metropolitan to Serenus, bishop of Aquileia (Dandolo, VII, 2, 13, see Muratori Rer. Ital. Script. XII, 131 ; Chronicle of John the Deacon, p. 96, Monticolo). Dissensions arose between the patriarchs of Aquileia and Grado, and Gregory wrote to Serenus warning him not to pass beyond the bounds of the Langobard nation and trespass upon Grado (Hodgkin, 466–467). The seat of the patriarch was subsequently removed, first to Cormons, and after Serenus had died and Calixtus had succeeded him (see Ch. 51, *infra*), to Cividale.

with a council of the Apostolic See, rejected,[1] and on account of this affair he caused pictures to be made in the portico of St. Peter representing the transactions of the six holy general councils. For Filippicus had ordered that pictures of this kind which were in the imperial city, should be carried away. The Roman people determined that they would not take the name of the heretical emperor upon their documents, nor his likeness upon their coins. Hence his image was not brought into the church, nor was his name mentioned in the solemnities of the mass. When he had held the sovereignty one year and six months, Anastasius, who was also called Artemius, rising against him, expelled him from the sovereignty and deprived him of his eyes, but did not however kill him.[2] This Anastasius sent letters to Rome to pope Constantine by Scolasticus, the patrician and exarch of Italy, in which he declared himself to be an adherent of the Catholic church and an acknowledger of the Sixth Holy Council.

Chapter XXXV.

Then after Ansprand had been in exile in Bavaria for now nine full years, in the tenth year, after Teutpert was at last prevailed upon, (to make war) the commander of the Bavarians came with his army to Italy

[1] The authorities disagree and the passage is not clear. Perhaps a partial council, summoned by the Pope, is meant. Filippicus declared in favor of the Monotheletes, who had been condemned by the Sixth Œcumenical Council at Constantinople (Giansevero).

[2] A. D. 713 (Hodgkin, VI, 386).

and fought with Aripert and there occured a great
slaughter of the people on both sides. But although at
last, night broke off the battle, it is certain that the
Bavarians had turned their backs and that the army of
Aripert had returned as a victor to its camp. But since
Aripert was unwilling to remain in camp and preferred
to go into the city of Ticinum, by this act he brought
despair upon his own people and boldness upon his
adversaries, and after he had returned to the city and
had felt that he had offended his army by this deed, he
presently took advice that he should flee to France
and carried with him from the palace as much gold
as he thought useful to him. And when weighted down
with the gold, he attempted to swim across the river
Ticinus, he sank there and, choked with the waters, expired. His body was found on the following day, was
cared for in the palace and was thence brought forth to
the church of our Lord the Saviour which the former
Aripert had built, and was there buried. In the days
when he held the kingly power, Aripert, going forth at
night, and proceeding to one place and another, inquired
for himself what was said about him by particular cities,
and diligently investigated what kind of justice the various judges rendered to the people. When the ambassadors of foreign nations came to him, he wore in their
presence mean garments and those made of skins, and
in order that they should not form designs against Italy
he never offered them precious wines nor delicacies of
other kinds. He reigned moreover with his father
Ragimpert, and alone, up to the twelfth year. He was
also a religious man, given to charities and a lover of

justice.[1] In his days there was very great fertility of the land, but the times were barbarous. His brother Gumpert then fled to France and remained there to the day of his death. He had three sons, of whom the eldest one, Ragimpert by name, governed the city of Aureliani (Orleans) in our own days. After the death of this Aripert, Ansprand obtained possession of the kingdom of the Langobards[2] but reigned only three months. He was a man distinguished in all ways and very few were to be compared with him in wisdom. When the Langobards become aware of his approaching death they set his son Liutprand on the royal throne[3] and when Ansprand, while he was living, heard this he greatly rejoiced.[4]

Chapter XXXVI.

At this time the emperor Anastasius dispatched a fleet to Alexandria against the Saracens. His army was turned to another purpose, and in the midst of its journey came back to the city of Constantinople, and hunting up the orthodox Theodosius, chose him as emperor and when he was put by force upon the throne of the empire, confirmed him. This Theodosius conquered Anastasius in a severe battle at the city of Nicea,

[1] Paul's estimate of Aripert's character is evidently too favorable.

[2] Thus a new dynasty came to the throne. The descendants of Theudelinda were set aside and ended their lives in the kingdom of the Franks (Hartmann, II, 2, 125).

[3] June 12, 712 (Pabst, 474).

[4] Ansprand was buried in Pavia in the chapel of Adrian the martyr which he is said to have built. Waitz gives his epitaph.

and having imposed an oath upon him, caused him to be ordained a churchman and a presbyter. When Anastasius received the sovereignty, he presently put up in its former place in the imperial city that revered picture in which the holy councils were painted and which had been torn down by Filippicus. In these days the river Tiber had such an inundation that having overflowed its bed it did many injuries to the city of Rome so that it rose in the Via Lata to one and a half times the height of a man, and from the gate of St. Peter to the Molvian bridge[1] the waters all mingled together as they flowed down.

Chapter XXXVII.

In these times, by the inspiration of Divine Love, many of the nobles and common people, men and women, dukes and private persons of the nation of the Angles were in the habit of coming from Britain to Rome. Pipin[2] at that time obtained the sovereignty in the kingdom of the Franks. He was a man of astonishing boldness who instantly crushed his foes in attacking them. For he crossed the Rhine and with only one of his attendants he fell upon a certain adversary of his and killed him with his followers in his bedchamber where he lived. He also courageously waged many wars with the Saxons and especially with Ratpot, king of the Frisians. He had also a number of sons but

---

[1] The Pons Mulvius (now the Ponte Molle) was built by the censor M. Æmilius Scaurus, B. C. 109.

[2] The father of Charles Martel (Abel).

among these Charles, who succeeded him afterwards in
the sovereignty, was the most distinguished.

CHAPTER XXXVIII.

But when king Liutprand had been confirmed in the
royal power,[1] Rothari, a blood relation of his, wished to
kill him.   He prepared therefore a banquet for him in
his home at Ticinum, in which house he hid some very
strong men fully armed who were to kill the king while
he was banqueting.   When this had been reported to
Liutprand he ordered Rothari to be called to his palace,
and feeling him with his hand he discovered, as had
been told him, a cuirass put on under his clothing.[2]
When Rothari found out that he was detected, he
straightway leaped backwards and unsheathed his sword
to strike the king.   On the other hand the king drew
forth his own sword from his scabbard.   Then one of
the king's attendants named Subo, seizing Rothari from
behind, was wounded by him in the forehead, but others
leaping upon Rothari killed him there.   Four of his
sons indeed who were not present were also put to death
in the places where they were found.   King Liutprand
was indeed a man of great boldness so that when two
of his armor-bearers thought to kill him and this had
been reported to him, he went alone with them into a
very deep wood and straightway holding against them

A. D. 712 (Hodgkin, VI, 389).   By this confirmation the
usurpation of the new dynasty of Ansprand was recognized (Hartmann, II, 2, 125).

[2] The story of Grimuald and Godepert seems to be here repeated
with a slight variation.

his drawn sword he reproached them because they had planned to slay him and urged them to do it. And straightway they fell at his feet and confessed all they had plotted. And he also did this thing in like manner with others, but nevertheless he presently pardoned those who confessed even a crime of such great wickedness.

Chapter XXXIX.

Then when Gisulf, the duke of the Beneventines had died, Romuald his son undertook the government of the people of the Samnites.

Chapter XL.

About these times Petronax, a citizen of the city of Brexia (Brescia) spurred by the love of God, came to Rome and then by the exhortation of Pope Gregory of the Apostolic See, proceeded to this fortress of Cassinum;[1] and when he came to the holy remains of the blessed father Benedict he began to dwell there with certain honest men who were already living there before. And they appointed this same venerable man Petronax as their superior, and not long afterwards, with the aid of Divine Mercy and through favor of the merits of the blessed father Benedict, after the lapse of about a hundred and ten years from the time when that place had become destitute of the habitation of men, he became there the father of many monks of high and low degree who gathered around him, and he began to live, when the dwellings were repaired, under the restraint

[1] Paul wrote this at Monte Cassino.

of the Holy Rule of the Order and the institutions of
the blessed Benedict, and he put this sacred monastery in
the condition in which it is now seen. At a subsequent
time Zacharias, Chief of Priests and Pontiff beloved by
God, bestowed many useful things upon this venerable
man Petronax, namely the books of Holy Scripture and
all sorts of other things that relate to the service of a
monastery and moreover he gave him with fatherly piety
the Rule of the Order which the blessed father Benedict
had written with his own holy hands.[1] The monastery
indeed of the blessed martyr Vincent, which is situated
near the source of the river Vulturnus and is now celebrated for its great community of monks, was then already founded by three noble brothers, that is, Tato,
Taso and Paldo, as the writings of the very learned
Autpert, abbot of this monastery show, in the volume
which he composed on this subject. While the blessed
Pope Gregory indeed[2] of the Roman See was still living, the fortress of Cumae was taken by the Langobards
of Beneventum, but when night came on, certain of the
Langobards were captured and others were killed by the
duke of Naples; also the fortress itself was re-taken by
the Romans. For the ransom of this fortress the Pontiff gave seventy pounds of gold as he had promised in
the first place.[3]

[1] Afterwards burned A. D. 896 (Waitz).

[2] Gregory II.

[3] A. D. 717. The recapture of this place did not occur at once
as Paul's account seems to indicate, but the duke of Naples was
urged to the act by the Pope who promised and paid him the so-
called ransom (Hodgkin, VI, 442).

CHAPTER XLI.

Meanwhile the emperor Theodosius, who had ruled the empire only one year, having died,[1] Leo was substituted as emperor in his place.[2]

CHAPTER XLII.

Among the people of the Franks, after Pipin had been released from life, his son Charles[3] of whom we have spoken took the sovereignty from the hand of Raginfrid only by means of many wars and struggles. For when he was held in prison he was set free by God's command and escaped and at first he began two or three times a struggle against Raginfrid with a few men and at last overcame him in a great battle at Vinciacum (Vincy).[4] Nevertheless he gave him one city to dwell in, that is, Andegavi (Angers)[5] while he himself undertook the government of the whole nation of the Franks.[6]

[1] An error.   Theodosius did not die but was deposed (Waitz).

[2] Leo the Isaurian, the great iconoclastic emperor, born about 670, was appointed to a place in the life-guards of Justinian II, and was afterwards sent on a desperate mission to the Alans in the Caucasus where he showed great courage and ingenuity. Anastasius, the successor of Justinian appointed him general of the forces of Anatolia in Asia Minor where he kept the Saracens at bay.   Theodosius III who succeeded Anastasius was considered incompetent to defend Constantinople against the Saracens and in 716 Leo was raised to the throne (Hodgkin, VI, 425, 426).

[3] Charles Martel.

[4] Near Cambray.

[5] In this statement Paul is not supported by other authorities and he is not well informed in Frankish history (Jacobi, 43).

[6] His title was not that of king but mayor of the palace: during

CHAPTER XLIII.

At this time king Liutprand confirmed to the Roman Church the gift of the patrimony of the Cottian Alps, and not long afterwards the same ruler took in marriage Guntrut, the daughter of Teutpert, duke of the Bavarians [1] with whom he had lived in exile, and from her he begot one daughter only.

CHAPTER XLIV.

During these times Faroald, duke of the Spoletans, attacked Classis, a city of the Ravenna people, but by command of king Liutprand it was restored to these same Romans. Against this duke Faroald his own son Transamund revolted and usurped his place and made him a churchman.[2] In these days Teudo, duke of

the latter part of his life however there was no king. He was the real founder of the Arnulfing or Carolingian dynasty, and his son Pipin assumed the title of king (Hodgkin, VI, 421, 422).

[1] The policy of the Bavarian dynasty, as to friendly relations with the Catholic church and with the neighboring Bavarians was continued by Liutprand. This marriage however afterwards led to other complications. After Teutpert's death, his brother Grimoald attempted to rob his son Hucbert of the sovereignty. Charles Martel, who had established his dominion over the Frankish kingdom, now seized the opportunity to restore his own suzerainty over the Bavarian dukedom, while Liutprand (probably about 725) invaded the Bavarian territories and pushed forward the boundaries of the Langobard kingdom up to Magias or Mais, by Meran. Charles also married Suanahild, a Bavarian princess, and thus became the brother-in-law of Liutprand, and the friendship between these sovereigns was firmly established (Hartmann, II, 2, 125).

[2] A. D. 724 (Waitz; Pabst, 469, note 2).

the nation of the Bavarians came for the purpose of devotion to Rome to the foot steps of the holy apostles.[1]

CHAPTER XLV.

When then at Forum Julii (Cividale) the patriarch Serenus had been taken away from human affairs, Calixtus, a distinguished man who was archdeacon of the church of Tarvisium (Treviso) received through the efforts of king Liutprand the government of the church of Aquileia. At this time as we said, Pemmo ruled the Langobards of Forum Julii. When he had now brought to the age of early manhood those sons of the nobles whom he had reared with his own children, suddenly a messenger came to him to say that an immense multitude of Slavs was approaching the place which is called Lauriana.[2] With those young men, he fell upon the Slavs for the third time, and overthrew them with a great slaughter, nor did any one else fall on the part of the Langobards than Sicuald, who was already mature in age. For he had lost two sons in a former battle, which occured under Ferdulf, and when he had avenged himself upon the Slavs a first and a second time according to his desire, the third time, although both the duke and the other Langobards forbade it, he could not be restrained but thus answered them: " I have already revenged sufficiently," he says, " the death of my sons

[1] A. D. 716 (Waitz). He had divided his dominion among his four sons. One of his granddaughters had married Liutprand and another Charles Martel (Hodgkin, VI, 440).

[2] Supposed to be the village of Spital near Villach (Waitz) on the Drave in Carinthia (Waitz). This seems quite uncertain.

and now if it shall happen, I will gladly receive my own death." And it so happened, and in that fight he only was killed. Pemmo, indeed, when he had overthrown many of his enemies, fearing lest he should lose in battle any one more of his own, entered into a treaty of peace with those Slavs in that place. And from that time the Slavs began more to dread the arms of the Friulans.

CHAPTER XLVI.

At that time the nation of the Saracens, passing over from Africa in the place which is called Septem (Ceuta), invaded all Spain.[1] Then after ten years they came with their wives and children and entered the province of Aquitaine in Gaul so as to inhabit it. Charles,[2] indeed, had then a quarrel with Eudo, prince of Aquitaine, but they joined together and fought by common consent against those Saracens. The Franks attacked them and killed three hundred and seventy-five thousand of the Saracens, while on the side of the Franks only fifteen hundred fell there. Eudo also with his followers fell upon their camp and in like manner killed many and ravaged everything.[3]

[1] The first invasion of Spain by Tarik was in the year 711, before Ansprand returned from his exile in Bavaria. It was in 721, nine years after the accession of Liutprand, that having conquered Spain, the Saracens were defeated by Eudo of Aquitaine at Toulouse (Hodgkin, VI, 418, 419).

[2] Charles Martel.

[3] Jacobi (43) believes that Paul has here combined two battles in one, the victory of Eudo over the Saracens at Toulouse in 721 and the battle of Poictiers in 732. The latter battle, however,

Chapter XLVII.

Also at this time this same nation of Saracens came
with an immense army, surrounded Constantinople and
besieged it continually for three years but when the
citizens with great fervor cried to God, many (of the invaders) perished by hunger and cold, by war and pestilence, and thus, exhausted by the siege, they departed. [1]
When they had gone thence they attacked in war the
nation of the Bulgarians beyond the Danube but they
were overcome also by them and took refuge in their
ships.   When they sought the high sea a sudden tempest
attacked them and very many also perished by drown-
ing and their ships were dashed to pieces.   Within
Constantinople, indeed, three hundred thousand men
perished by pestilence.

Chapter XLVIII.

Liutprand also, hearing that the Saracens had laid
waste Sardinia and were even defiling those places where
the bones of the bishop St. Augustine had been formerly carried on account of the devastation of the barbarians and had been honorably buried, sent and gave
a great price and took them and carried them over to
the city of Ticinum and there buried them with the honor

appears to be indicated, for Eudo, after his victory at Toulouse,
had been vanquished by the Saracens, and it would seem that the
remnant of his troops shared with those of Charles Martel the victory of Poictiers (Hodgkin, VI, 419, 420).

[1] Hartmann says (II, 2, 85) the siege lasted one year, A. D.
717–718.

due to so great a father. In these days the city of Narnia (Narni) was conquered by the Langobards. [1]

CHAPTER XLIX.

At this time king Liutprand besieged Ravenna and took Classis and destroyed it. [2] Then Paul the patrician sent his men out of Ravenna to kill the Pope, but as the Langobards fought against them in defense of the Pope and as the Spoletans resisted them on the Salarian bridge [3] as well as the Tuscan Langobards from other places, the design of the Ravenna people came to nought. At this time the emperor Leo burned the images of the saints placed in Constantinople and ordered the Roman pontiff to do the like if he wished to have the emperor's favor, but the pontiff disdained to do this thing. Also the whole of Ravenna and of Venetia [4] resisted such commands with one mind, and if the pontiff had not prohibited them they would have attempted to set up an emperor over themselves. [5]

[1] Probably by the duke of Spoleto (Hodgkin, VI, 444).

[2] Probably not later than A. D. 725 (Hodgkin, VI, 444, note 3).

[3] A bridge on the Salarian way, over the Anio (Hodgkin, VI, 448).

[4] This word is the plural, "the Venices," for there were then two, land Venice, mostly under the Langobards, and sea Venice, under Ravenna. (See opening words of the Chronicon Venetum by John the Deacon, Monticolo's ed., p. 59.)

[5] To understand this controversy we must return to the time of Gregory I. The weakness of the Byzantine empire and its inability to protect its Italian subjects from the Langobards, combined with the growth of the administrative powers of the Pope throughout the extensive domains of the church, gave the papacy

Also king Liutprand attacked Feronianum (Fregnano)

more and more a political character. Gregory extended this influence; he even attempted to make a separate peace with the Langobards, an act which was resented by the emperor Maurice. The people of Italy began to look to the Pope for protection, and there were aspirations for independence from the Eastern Empire and for a re-establishment of the Empire of the West. The usurpation of the exarch Eleutherius and the subsequent rebellion of Olympius which was supported by Pope Martin I, as well as the revolt of Ravenna under Georgius, all show this separatist tendency. Ecclesiastical differences such as the assumption of the title of Universal Bishop by the patriarch of Constantinople, the Monothelete controversy, the *Type*, the imprisonment of Pope Martin, etc., accentuated the irritation of the West. Constantine Pogonatus, indeed, like some of his predecessors, had adopted a policy of friendship with the papacy, and also concluded a definitive treaty with the Langobards, fixing the boundaries of the Langobard and Roman dominions. But after this peace was made, the Langobards became subject to the ecclesiastical jurisdiction of the Pope and it became the interest of the Roman See to play the emperor and the Langobard king against each other in favor of its own greater power and independence. (Hartmann, Atti del Congresso in Cividale, 1899, pp. 153 to 162). When Leo the Isaurian mounted the throne, he was recognized at Ravenna, but an insurrection broke out against him in Sicily, which, however, was soon suppressed. But his heavy hand was felt in Rome in his efforts to collect from church property the means for carrying on his contests against the Saracens. Gregory II, a man of great ability, then occupied the papal chair and resisted his exactions, whereupon plots were laid by imperial officers to depose and perhaps to assassinate the Pope. Then came the conflict in regard to the worship of images, a practice which had gradually grown in the church and which Leo determined to eradicate. In 725 he issued a decree for their destruction. The work was begun with energy at Constantinople, all opposition was stamped out with great severity and a popular insurrection, as well as an attack

Mons Bellius, (Monteveglio) Buxeta (Busseto) and

upon the city by a rebellious fleet was suppressed with a strong hand. In Rome, however, his efforts were not successful, and when in 727 the order for the destruction of the images was renewed, Gregory armed himself against the emperor. The people now elected dukes for themselves in different parts of Italy and proposed to elect a new emperor, but the Pope restrained them, not wishing perhaps to have an emperor close at his side or possibly fearing a greater danger from the Langobards. Italy was distracted by internal struggles, the Pope, aided by the Spoletans and Beneventans, prevailed, and the exarch Paul was killed. Upon his death the eunuch Eutychius was appointed to succeed him. He landed at Naples and sent a private messenger to Rome instructing his partisans to murder the Pope and the chief nobles, but the people assembled, anathematized Eutychius and bound themselves to live or die with the Pope. Then Eutychius turned for aid to the Langobards, and Liutprand, who had at first favored the Pope and the Italian revolutionary movement and had improved the occasion to seize a number of the possessions of the empire, now changed his policy and formed a league with the exarch to subject Spoleto and Benevento to his own dominion and enable the exarch to control the city of Rome. The king first marched to Spoleto where he took hostages and oaths of fidelity, then he moved to Rome and encamped on the plain of Nero close to the city. The Pope came forth to meet him, attended by his ecclesiastics and Liutprand fell before him and took off his mantle, his doublet, his sword and spear, crown and cross, and laid them in the crypt before the altar of St. Peter. In spite of these manifestations of reverence, however, Liutprand insisted upon a reconciliation between the Pope and the exarch which put a limit to the Italian movement toward independence and to the political aspirations of the papacy, and in great measure restored the power of the exarch—although in the controversy regarding the destruction of images, in which the people took a passionate interest, the emperor Leo was never able to impose his will upon his subjects in Italy. In other matters too, local self-government had made

Persiceta (San Giovanni in Persiceto) Bononia (Bo-

great progress during the various revolutionary movements and nowhere more than in the islands of the Venetian lagoons, where the new settlements made by the fugitives from the mainland, had now assumed a semi-independent character under the doges or dukes of Venice, who in Liutprand's time made treaties with the Langobard king (defining the boundaries of each) and (regulating the intercourse between the two communities.) Liutprand also made a treaty with Comacchio, the rival of Venice in the commerce on the Po. It is surprising that these events should have been omitted by Paul, especially as they are referred to in the Liber Pontificalis, one of his sources. It shows the incomplete character of this last book of Paul's unfinished history.

Gregory II died in 731, but his successor Gregory III pursued the same policy in respect to the emperor's edict for the destruction of the images. He convened a council attended by the archbishops of Grado and Ravenna and ninety-three Italian bishops, with other clergy and laity, which anathematized all who took part in the work of destruction. The emperor now withdrew from the jurisdiction of the Roman See all the dioceses east of the Adriatic, as well as those in Sicily, Bruttium and Calabria, and made them subject to Constantinople, and the rich and important papal possessions in the three last-named provinces were confiscated. The portions of Italy still subject to the empire became now divided into three parts—1st, southern Italy and Sicily, more directly subject to the central authority of Constantinople ; 2nd, the duchy of Rome, which, subject to papal influence, gradually became more and more independent ; and 3d, the immediate exarchate of Ravenna, which conducted for a short time a desperate struggle for existence (Hartmann, II, 2, 85–114 ; Hodgkin, VI, 432–436).

After king Liutprand had attained his purpose in regard to the dukedoms of Spoleto and Benevento, his unnatural alliance with the exarch came to an end. A Roman army under Agatho, duke of Perugia, attacked Bologna, which was in possession of the Langobards, and was defeated (Ch. 54, *infra*), and Liutprand

logna) [1] and the Pentapolis [2] and Auximun (Osimo) [3] fortresses of Emilia. And in like manner he then took possession of Sutrium (Sutri) [4] but after some days it was again restored to the Romans. [5] During the same time the emperor Leo went on to worse things so that he compelled all the inhabitants of Constantinople either by force or by blandishments, to give up the images of the Saviour and of his Holy Mother and of all the saints wherever they were, and he caused them to be burned by fire in the midst of the city. And because many of the people hindered such a wickedness from being done, some of them were beheaded and others suffered mutilation in body. As the patriarch Germanus did not consent to this error he was driven from his see and the presbyter Anastasius was ordained in his place.

CHAPTER L.

Romoald then, duke of Beneventum, chose a wife Gumperga, by name, who was the daughter of Aurona, king Liutprand's sister. From her he begot a son whom

captured Ravenna itself (A. D. 732–3), though the city was afterwards re-taken by the Venetians (see Hartmann, II, 2, 132–133).

[1] Tregnano is west of the Panaro (Hodgkin VI, 454, note 1); Monteveglio is west, and San Giovanni in Persiceto is a little northwest of Bologna (id.).

[2] Rimini, Pesaro, Fano, Sinigaglia and Ancona.

[3] Near Ancona.

[4] A. D. 728–729 (Jacobi, 58). It is a place about 25 miles northwest of Rome.

[5] Liutprand took it from the empire, but in restoring it put it into the possession of the pope, who was then at the head of the independent movement in Italy (Hartmann, II, 2, 96–97).

he called by the name of his father, Gisulf. He had again after her another wife, Ranigunda by name, the daughter of Gaiduald, duke of Brexia (Brescia).

CHAPTER LI.

At the same time a grievous strife arose between duke Pemmo and the patriarch Calixtus and the cause of this discord was the following: Fidentius, bishop of the Julian fortress (Julium Carnicum) [1] came on a former occasion and dwelt within the walls of the fortress of Forum Julii (Cividale) and established there the see of his bishopric with the approval of the former dukes. When he departed from life, Amator was ordained bishop in his place. Up to that day indeed, the former patriarchs had their see, not in Forum Julii, but in Cormones (Cormons) because they had not at all been able to dwell in Aquileia on account of the incursions of the Romans. It greatly displeased Calixtus who was eminent for his high rank that a bishop dwelt in his diocese with the duke and the Langobards and that he himself lived only in the society of the common people. Why say more? He worked against this same bishop Amator and expelled him from Forum Julii and established his own dwelling in his house. For this cause duke Pemmo took counsel with many Langobard nobles against this same patriarch, seized him and brought him to the castle of Potium,[2] which is situated

[1] Now Zuglio, a town north of Tolmezzo (Hodgkin, VI, 41, note 2).

[2] Not identified. Giansevero believes it was the castle of Duino.

above the sea, and wanted to hurl him thence into the sea but he did not at all do this since God prohibited. He kept him, however, in prison and nourished him with the bread of tribulation. King Liutprand hearing this was inflamed with great rage, and taking away the dukedom from Pemmo, appointed his son Ratchis in his place. Then Pemmo arranged to flee with his followers into the country of the Slavs, but Ratchis his son besought the king and reinstated his father in the monarch's favor. Pemmo then, having taken an assurance that he would suffer no harm, proceeded to the king with all the Langobards with whom he had taken counsel. Then the king, sitting in judgement, pardoned for Ratchis' sake Pemmo and his two sons, Ratchait and Aistulf, and ordered them to stand behind his chair. The king, however, in a loud voice ordered that all those who had adhered to Pemmo, naming them, should be seized. Then Aistulf could not restrain his rage and attempted to draw his sword and strike the king but Ratchis his brother prevented him. And when these Langobards were seized in this manner, Herfemar, who had been one of them, drew his sword, and followed by many, defended himself manfully and fled to the church of the blessed Michael and then by the favor of the king he alone secured impunity while the others were for a long time tormented in bonds.

CHAPTER LII.

Then Ratchis having become duke of Forum Julii as we have said, invaded Carniola (Krain), the country of the Slavs, with his followers, killed a great multitude of

Slavs and laid waste everything belonging to them.
Here when the Slavs had suddenly fallen upon him and
he had not yet taken his lance from his armor-bearer,
he struck with a club that he carried in his hand the
first who ran up to him and put an end to his life.

CHAPTER LIII.

About these times Charles the ruler of the Franks
dispatched his son Pipin to Liutprand that the latter
should take his hair according to custom. And the
king, cutting his hair, became a father to him and sent
him back to his father enriched with many royal gifts.[1]

CHAPTER LIV.

During the same time the army of the Saracens again
entering into Gaul made much devastation. Charles
giving battle against them not far from Narbo (Narbonne) overthrew them in the same manner as before
with the greatest slaughter.[2] Again the Saracens invaded the boundaries of the Gauls, came as far as Provincia (Provence), took Arelate (Arles) and destroyed
everything around it.[3] Then Charles sent messengers

---

[1] This friendship between the royal houses of the Franks and
the Langobards had been the traditional policy since Agilulf's
time and had been of great advantage to both kingdoms (Hartmann, II, 2, 137).

[2] A. D. 737 (Waitz).

[3] The Frankish writers have related nothing of this. It seems
doubtful whether a new incursion of the Saracens was meant inasmuch as they occupied Arles in A. D. 737 (Waitz).

with gifts to king Liutprand and asked assistance from him against the Saracens and he without delay hastened with the whole army of the Langobards to his assistance.[1] The nation of the Saracens when they learned this, presently fled away from those regions and Liutprand with his whole army returned to Italy.[2] The same ruler waged many wars against the Romans in which he was always the victor except that once in his absence his army was defeated in Ariminum (Rimini), and at another time, when at the village of Pilleum, a great multitude of those who were bringing small presents and gifts to the king and the blessings of particular churches were attacked and killed or captured by the Romans while the king was stopping in the Pentapolis. Again when Hildeprand the nephew of the king and Peredeo the duke of Vincentia (Vicenza) got possession of Ravenna, the Venetians suddenly attacked them. Hildeprand was taken by them and Peredeo fell fighting

[1] Jacobi says (p. 44) that Paul has arbitrarily changed the history of this campaign. The Chron. Moiss. (MG. SS. I 292) states that Charles Martel on the news of the invasion of the Saracens into Provence, by which Arles, Avignon, and other places fell into their hands, marched against them, drove them back over the Rhone, besieged Narbonne, and without raising the siege, defeated a second army of the Arabs approaching for the relief of the city. Paul out of this makes two campaigns. In the first, the Saracens invaded Gaul and were defeated by Charles not far from Narbonne; in the second, they devastated Provence and took Arles, whereupon Charles called upon Liutprand for help and the fame of his name frightened the enemy.

[2] A. D. 737 (Hodgkin, VI, 475).

manfully.[1] At a subsequent period [2] also, the Romans, swollen with their accustomed pride, assembled on every side under the leadership of Agatho, duke of the Perugians, and came to seize Bononia (Bologna), where Walcari, Peredeo and Rotcari were then staying in camp, but the latter rushed upon the Romans, made a great slaughter of them and compelled those who were left to seek flight.

[1] This confused chapter in which Peredeo (unless it be some other of the same name) afterwards comes to life again, has been considered to indicate that Ravenna had been taken by the Langobards and was recovered by the Venetians. These Venetians were still a feeble community. Their chief towns were not on the site that Venice now occupies, but in other parts of the lagoons, at Heraclea, Equilium, and Metamaucus. The present city on the Rialto was not founded until nearly seventy years after the death of Liutprand (Hodgkin, VI, 484, 485), notwithstanding Venetian traditions to the contrary.

The tribunes who had originally ruled the different islands had been superseded by a single doge or duke who may have been originally an official selected by the emperor or the exarch. After the reigns of three doges the infant community remained for five years subject to '' Masters of Soldiery '' who were elected annually; then the dogeship was restored. John the Deacon who wrote near the end of the tenth century says (Monticolo's edition, Chronache Veneziane Antichissime, p. 95), that during the administration of Jubianus one of these Masters of Soldiery (A. D. 731–735), the exarch (probably Eutychius), came to Venetia and entreated the Venetians to help him guard and defend his own city, which Hildeprand, nephew of Liutprand, and Peredeo, duke of Vicenza had captured; that the Venetians hastened to Ravenna; that Hildeprand was captured, Peredeo fell and the city was handed over to the exarch (Hodgkin, VI, 487, 488).

[2] Probably in a preceding period since Peredeo is mentioned (Waitz).

CHAPTER LV.

In these days Transamund rebelled against the king, and when the king came upon him with his army, Transamund himself repaired to Rome in flight. Hilderic was appointed in his place.[1] When indeed Romuald the younger, duke of the Beneventines, died,[2] after he had

[1] It would seem that duke Transamund of Spoleto about the year 737 or 738 had taken the castle of Gallese from the Romans and had thereby interrupted the communication between Ravenna and Rome. Gregory III, realizing how valuable would be an alliance with the duke and how dangerous he was as an enemy, offered a a large sum of money for the restitution of Gallese and for a treaty binding him to make no war upon the Pope. Transamund made the treaty and restored the place, whereupon the duchy of Benevento also joined the alliance. This was contrary to Liutprand's policy of conquest and expansion, and the king, for this and perhaps other causes, treated Transamund as a rebel and traitor, and on June 16, 739 we find Liutprand in possession of Spoleto (Hartmann, II, 2, 137–138). After he had appointed Hilderic he marched on Rome where Transamund had taken refuge, and as Gregory refused to give up the fugitive, the king took four frontier towns, Ameria (Amelia), Horta (Orte), Polimartium (Bomarzo) and Blera (Bieda). Gregory now wrote to Charles Martel, king of the Franks, telling him of the sufferings of the church and exhorting him to come to its aid. But Charles was the friend of Liutprand and refused (Hodgkin, 475–478). Transamund recovered Spoleto in 740 but he now refused to restore the four cities taken by Liutprand and the Pope withdrew his aid (id., 479–480). Before Liutprand set forth to recover Spoleto again Gregory III died and was succeeded in the papal chair by Zacharias, who had an interview with the king, who promised to surrender the four towns, whereupon the Roman army joined him and Transamund was forced to give up Spoleto (see Ch. 57, *infra*).

[2] A. D. 731 or 732 (Hartmann, II, 132).

held the dukedom six and twenty years, there remained
Gisulf his son, who was still a little boy. Some con-
spirators rose against him and sought to destroy him,
but the people of the Beneventans who were always
faithful to their leaders, slew them and preserved the life
of their duke.[1] Since this Gisulf was not yet fit to
govern so great a people on account of his boyish age,
king Liutprand, then coming to Beneventum, took him
away from thence and appointed his own nephew
Gregory as duke at Beneventum, with whom a wife,
Giselperga by name, was united in marriage.[2] Matters
being thus arranged, king Liutprand returned to his own
seat of government and bringing up his nephew Gisulf
with fatherly care, he united to him in marriage Scauni-
perga, born from a noble stock. At this time the king
himself fell into a great weakness and came near to
death. When the Langobards thought that he was departing from life they raised as their king his nephew
Hildeprand,[3] at the church of the Holy Mother of God,
which is called " At the Poles " outside the walls of the
city. When they handed to him the staff as is the
custom, a cuckoo bird came flying and sat down on the

[1] A catalogue of Beneventan dukes preserved at Monte Cassino
shows that one Audelais, probably a usurper, reigned for two
years after Romuald II (Hodgkin, VI, 471).

[2] Gregory ruled Benevento 732 to 739 (id.).   Hilderic's appointment in Spoleto occurred about the time of Gregory's death or
afterwards (Hodgkin, VI, 475).

[3] A. D. 735 (Hodgkin, VI, 473).   The election of Hildeprand
actually preceded the rebellion of Transamund, and Paul has in-
verted these events (Waitz ; Pabst, 478, note 5).

top of the staff. Then to certain wise persons it appeared to be signified by this portent that his government would be useless. King Liutprand indeed when he had learned this thing did not receive it with equanimity, yet when he became well of his illness he kept him as his colleague in the government. When some years had elapsed from this time, Transamund, who had fled to Rome, returned to Spoletum,[1] killed Hilderic and again undertook the daring project of rebellion against the king.

CHAPTER LVI.

But Gregory when he had managed the dukedom at Beneventum seven years was released from life. After his death Godescalc was made duke[2] and governed the Beneventines for three years, and to him a wife, Anna by name, was united in marriage. Then king Liutprand hearing these things concerning Spoletum and Beneventum, again advanced with his army to Spoletum. When he came to the Pentapolis, while he was proceeding from Fanum (Fano)[3] to the City of Forum Simphronii (Fossombrone),[4] in the wood which is between these places, the Spoletans uniting with the Romans brought great disasters on the king's army. The king placed duke Ratchis and his brother Aistulf with the

[1] December, 740. Supported by the army of the dukedom of Rome and by the Beneventines (Hartmann, II, 2, 139).

[2] A. D. 740. Without the nomination or approval of the king (Hartmann, II, 2, 138).

[3] On the Adriatic coast northwest of Ancona.

[4] In the March of Ancona.

Friulans in the rear; the Spoletans and Romans fell
upon them and wounded some of them, but Ratchis with
his brother and some other very brave men, sustaining
all that weight of the battle and fighting manfully, killed
many and brought themselves and their followers from
thence except as I said the few who were wounded.
There a certain very brave man of the Spoletans named
Berto cried out to Ratchis by name, and came upon him
clothed in full armor. Ratchis suddenly struck him,
and threw him from his horse. And when his companions attempted to kill the man, Ratchis with his accustomed magnanimity allowed him to get away, and the
man crawling upon his hands and feet entered the forest
and escaped. Two other very strong men of Spoleto
indeed came up behind Aistulf on a certain bridge,
whereupon he struck one of them with the blunt end of
his spear and hurled him down from the bridge and
suddenly turning upon the other, killed him and plunged
him into the water after his companion.

CHAPTER LVII.

But Liutprand indeed when he reached Spoletum
drove Transamund from the ducal power and made him
a churchman,[1] and in his place he appointed Agiprand

---

[1] After Transamund had been reinstated in the duchy of Spoleto
the Pope called upon him to perform his part of the engagement
upon which Gregory had supported him, namely, to restore to
Roman dominion the four fortified places which had been taken
by the Langobards, but Transamund refused. About this time
(at the end of the year 741) Gregory III died, and was succeeded
in the papal chair by Zacharias. The new pope now asked the

his own nephew. When he hastened to Beneventum,
Godescalc having heard of his approach, endeavored to
embark in a ship and flee to Greece. After he had put
his wife and all his goods in the ship and attempted
himself, last of all, to embark, the people of Beneventum who were faithful to Gisulf, fell upon him and he
was killed. His wife indeed was carried to Constantinople with everything she possessed.

CHAPTER LVIII.

Then king Liutprand, arriving at Beneventum,[1] appointed his nephew Gisulf duke again in the place which
had belonged to him.[2] And when matters were thus
arranged he returned to his palace.[3] This most glorious

king to restore the four places, and offered to support him with a
Roman army in recovering Spoleto. The king agreed, and in the
spring of 742 advanced with his army, as related in the text, deposed Transamund with the aid of the Romans, and then proceeded to Benevento (Hartmann, II, 2, pp. 139, 140).

[1] About 742 (Waitz).

[2] Gisulf II reigned for ten years, outliving Liutprand (Hodgkin,
VI, 472). He conformed to the policy of Liutprand, who had
restored him to his dukedom (Hartmann, II, 2, 141).

[3] After Liutprand had recovered control of Spoleto and Benevento he delayed restoring the frontier cities to the duchy of Rome
(VI, 55, note *supra*), and Pope Zacharias set forth with a train of
ecclesiastics to Terni, where the king resided, for a personal interview, as a result of which the four cities were restored, with other
territory, and a peace was concluded for twenty years. But in
the following year Liutprand resumed his preparations for the conquest of Ravenna, and Zacharias, at the request of the exarch,
journeyed to Pavia to the king, and in a second interview en-

king built many churches in honor of Christ in the various places where he was accustomed to stay. He
established the monastery of St. Peter which was situated outside the walls of the city of Ticinum and was
called the " Golden Heaven."

He built also on the top of Bardo's Alp a monastery
which is called " Bercetum."[1] He also established in
Olonna, his suburban manor, a dwelling to Christ of
wonderful workmanship in honor of the holy martyr
Anastasius, and in it also he made a monastery. In
like manner too he established many churches to God
in different places. Within his palace also he built a
chapel of our Lord the Saviour and he appointed
priests and churchmen to perform for him daily divine
services, which no other kings had had. In the time of
this king there was in the place whose name is Forum[2]
(Foro di Fulvio), near the river Tanarus, (Tanaro) a
man of wonderful holiness Baodolinus by name, who,

treated him to desist.   Liutprand reluctantly consented to restore
the country districts around Ravenna and two-thirds of the territory of Cesena, and to grant a truce until the king's emissaries
should return from Constantinople, whither they had gone for the
purpose of concluding a final treaty.   This interview was one of
the last public acts of Liutprand, whose ambition for the unification of Italy was thus at the last moment apparently renounced.
Possibly the near approach of death and his consciousness of the
impossibility of his schemes of conquest being realized by his successor may have led to their abandonment (Hartmann, II, 2, 144,
145 ; Hodgkin, 491–498).

[1] Or, more correctly, Liutprand endowed this monastery, which
had been built before (Waitz).

[2] To-day Valenza, near Alessandria (Giansevero).

aided by the grace of Christ, was distinguished for many
miracles. He often predicted future events and told of
absent things as if they were present. Finally when
king Liutprand had gone to hunt in the City Forest,
one of his companions attempted to hit a stag with an
arrow and unintentionally wounded the king's nephew,
that is, his sister's son, Aufusus by name. When the
king saw this he began with tears to lament his misfortune, for he loved that boy greatly, and straightway
he sent a horseman of his followers to run to Baodolinus the man of God, and ask him to pray to Christ for
the life of that boy. And while he was going to the
servant of God, the boy died. And when he came to
him the follower of Christ spoke to him as follows: " I
know for what cause you are coming, but that which
you have been sent to ask cannot be done since the boy
is dead." When he who had been sent had reported to
the king what he had heard from the servant of God,
the king, although he grieved, because he could not
have the accomplishment of his prayer, nevertheless
clearly perceived that Baodolinus the man of God had
the spirit of prophecy. A man not unlike him, Teudelapius by name, also lived at the city of Verona, who
among other wonderful things which he performed,
predicted also in a prophetic spirit many things which
were to happen. In that time also their flourished in
holy life and in good works, Peter, bishop of the church
of Ticinum, who, because he was a blood relative of the
king had been driven into exile at Spoletum by Aripert
who was formerly king. To this man, when he attended
the church of the blessed martyr Savinus, that same

venerable martyr foretold that he would be bishop at
Ticinum, and afterwards when this occurred, he built a
church to that same blessed martyr Savinus upon his
own ground in that city. This man, among the other
virtues of an excellent life which he possessed, was also
distinguished as adorned with the flower of virgin chastity. A certain miracle of his which was performed at
a later time we will put in its proper place.[1] But Liutprand indeed after he had held the sovereignty thirty
one years and seven months, already mature in age,
completed the course of this life,[2] and his body was
buried in the church of the blessed martyr Adrian[3]
where his father also reposes. He was indeed a man of
much wisdom, very religious and a lover of peace,
shrewd in counsel, powerful in war, merciful to offenders,
chaste, modest, prayerful in the night-watches, generous
in charities, ignorant of letters indeed, yet worthy to be
likened to philosophers, a supporter of his people, an
increaser of the law.[4] At the beginning of his reign he

[1] Paul died before this history was completed, and no account
of this miracle appears.

[2] A. D. 744 (Hartmann, II, 2, 146).

[3] He was afterwards buried in another church (San Pietro in
Cielo d'Oro). See epitaph in Waitz.

[4] On the first of March of each year during fifteen out of the
thirty-one years of his reign, Liutprand, by the advice of his
judges (and no longer under the sanction of a popular assembly),
issued certain laws to settle matters not provided for by his predecessors. He claims that these laws were framed by divine inspiration, ''because the king's heart is in the hand of God.'' The
laws of Liutprand were written in Latin so barbarous as to be
almost incomprehensible. They show a great change in the

took very many fortresses of the Bavarians.   He relied

social life of the Langobards.   We no longer find provisions in regard to hunting and falconry, but instead, there are enactments providing for the enforcement of contracts and the foreclosure of mortgages.   The fine paid for murder is superseded by absolute confiscation of the offender's property, and if that property is insufficient, the murderer is handed over to the heirs of the murdered man as a slave.   Some of these laws mention the fact that they refer to Langobards only, and one law concerning scribes ordains that those who write deeds, whether according to the laws of the Langobards or *those of the Romans*, must not write them contrary to these laws, thus indicating that at least a part of the population was governed to some extent by Roman law.   (Hodgkin, VI, 392–399).   It would be a necessary result of the peace made at different times between Langobards and Romans that the civil rights of Romans who lived in the Langobard territory should be recognized, which was not the case in the earlier days of Langobard domination (Hartmann, II, 2, 2–4).   Under Liutprand's laws if a Roman married a Langobard woman she lost her status, and the sons born in such a union were Romans like their father and had to live by his laws.   There were many laws against oppressions by the king's agents, and heavy penalties were imposed upon judges who delayed judgment.   The barbarous wager of battle was continued, but somewhat restricted, for it was said, "We are uncertain about the judgment of God, and we have heard of many persons unjustly losing their cause by wager of battle, but on account of the custom of our nation of the Langobards we cannot change the law itself."   There were severe laws against soothsayers and against certain forms of idolatry.   (Hodgkin, VI, 400–407).   A number of the later provisions of Langobard laws must be traced to Roman influence (Hartmann, II, 2–29).

There is a question how far the Langobards supplanted the Romans and how far their institutions superseded those of the Romans.   The great preponderance of the Latin over the Germanic ingredients in the Italian tongue to-day and the survival of

always more upon prayers than upon arms, and always with the greatest care kept peace with the Franks and the Avars.[1]

Roman laws and institutions down to the present time seems to indicate that the Roman population and civilization greatly outweighed that of the Langobards. (See Savigny, Geschichte des Römischen Rechts im Mittelalter, I, p. 398.)

[1] The constant object of Liutprand's policy, at least until his final interview with pope Zacharias, was the unification of Italy under his own scepter, though the means he took for the accomplishment of this object varied with the occasion. For this purpose the friendship of the Frankish king was necessary and this he constantly maintained, aiding Charles Martel against the Saracens without claiming any territorial concessions at his hands. The principal objects of Liutprand's aggressions during the greater part of his career were the duchies of Spoleto and Benevento so far as these aspired to independent sovereignty; also the Eastern Empire, though he allied himself with the exarch when he found it necessary for the purpose of reducing the duchies to submission. The Catholic church and the papacy were protected by him, and he encouraged the movement in favor of the autonomy of Italy against Byzantium, until the pope identified himself with the rebellious dukes. Even then Liutprand's opposition to the papacy remained always of a political, and not of a religious character (Hartmann, II, 2, 125, 126). He encouraged the culture as well as the religion of Rome, and his aim was to rule ultimately over a civilized, as well as a Catholic Italy. He adapted himself to general as well as local currents of popular opinion, as is seen in the fact that he retained in his laws the trial by battle while expressing his own disbelief in its justice and that he gave to Benevento and to Friuli rulers of their own princely lines, after he had subjugated them to his authority. He always recognized the limits of possible achievement, and did not, like his successor Aistulf, contend madly against the inevitable. He was an efficient administrator and an able legislator as well as a courageous

and successful warrior. And yet this really great statesman, like his distinguished Ostrogothic predecessor Theodoric, could neither read nor write (Hartmann, II, 2, 127).

Paul's last book contains many grammatical errors and faults of construction. It was more carelessly written than the preceding portions of the work, and being the last book of an unfinished history, it is itself somewhat incomplete.

It is greatly to be regretted that Paul's work ceases at the very place where, independently of other sources, he could have told his story in great part out of the rich abundance of his own experience. From his position toward the last Langobard princes on the one side and their Frankish conquerors and the church upon the other, he possessed the highest qualifications for writing an impartial contemporary history of the overthrow of the Langobard kingdom, yet for this period, the most pregnant of all in its results on general history, we have only the meager accounts of the Frankish authorities, and the papal writings which are filled with partisan spirit. The most important source for the last half century of the Langobard kingdom is found in the lives of the Roman popes, composed by members of the Roman court, mostly contemporaneous, and collected by Anastasius in the second half of the ninth century. Besides these we have the letters of the popes to the Frankish kings and such authorities as the Chronicle of the monk Benedict of Soracte, the Legend of St. Julia, the legendary Life of Saints Amelius and Amicus, and the Chronicles of Novalese and Salerno (Abel, p. xxiv to xxvi).

Our knowledge of the last days of the Langobard kingdom is therefore very fragmentary and great care is required even in the use of the slender materials we have. No adequate explanation is given in them for the extraordinary fact that a powerful and freedom-loving people, fifty years after it had reached the summit of its power under king Liutprand, was overthrown and became the spoil of its Frankish neighbor.

A closer investigation shows that this was due to the lack of any proper law of succession to the Langobard throne, to the absence of sufficient cohesive power in the monarchy, to the intractable character of the Langobard nobles, to increasing difficulties with the church, and to the civil disturbances and quarrels occasioned by all these causes. After the time of Gregory I, the independence of the papacy and its desire for temporal power greatly increased, while the authority of the Greek empire over its scattered Italian possessions grew constantly weaker. Charles Martel was bound to Liutprand by friendship and by the need of aid against the Saracens, but after Liutprand's death the relations between the Franks and the Langobards became more strained. (Abel, xxvii, *et seq.*) Liutprand's successor, Hildeprand, did not possess sufficient skill either to conciliate the adherents of the Pope or to control his Langobard subjects. Duke Transamund was reinstated in Spoleto, and soon the most powerful Langobard leader in the north, duke Ratchis of Friuli, was chosen king by his dependents, and Hildeprand was deposed after a reign of only eight months. Ratchis, whose diplomatic character had been shown in his career under Liutprand, now concluded a twenty years' truce with Rome, but from some cause unknown to us, difficulties afterwards arose, and he found himself constrained to attack the Pentapolis and to lay siege to Perugia. The Pope came from Rome with a train of followers, visited the camp of Ratchis, and in a personal interview induced him to desist from his undertaking. This subserviency to papal influence, however, aroused the contempt of his own nobles and followers, who in Milan, in June, 749, chose as their king his younger brother Aistulf, a man of headstrong and unyielding character, whereupon Ratchis became a monk in the cloister of Monte Cassino. Aistulf now began a career of conquest, capturing Comacchio and Ferrara, and within two years from his accession, Ravenna, the capital of the exarchate, was in his hands. Then he pushed on to Rome, and thus gave occasion to the coalition between the papacy and the Frankish kingdom, which ultimately led to the overthrow of the Langobard dominion. (Hartmann, II, 2, 146–151.) Owing to the weakness of the empire and to the theological and other differences between Rome and Byzantium, the practical separation of the West from the East was already far advanced, and the spiritual influence of the pontiff over the countries of the West, stimulated by reforms in the church and by numerous pilgrimages to Rome from Britain and other countries, was becoming very powerful. Charles Martel had been succeeded by Pipin, who desired to change his title of Mayor of the Palace (where he reigned in the name of a helpless Merovingian monarch) to that of king, and who wished to secure the recognition of his new title, not only by the chiefs and nobles of his realm, but also by the church and by the Roman empire. Accordingly he sent an embassy to Rome to enquire of the Pope whether it was proper that in the kingdom of the Franks there should be kings who possessed no kingly power, and the Pope answered, as had been anticipated, that it would be better that he who had the power should be the monarch. Pipin now assumed that he was called to the sovereignty by apostolic authority. The Franks assembled at Soissons and chose him as their king, and he ascended the throne in November, 751, while the last Merovingian monarch was sent to a cloister. The papacy had thus rendered the new Frankish king a most important service, and now when it found itself in peril from the Langobards it was natural that a return should be solicited. In June, 752, when Aistulf with his army threatened Rome, Stephan, who had succeeded Zacharias in the papacy, secretly sent a message to Pipin imploring him to send ambassadors to that city to conduct the Pope to the kingdom of the Franks. Not long afterwards an imperial messenger from Constantinople brought word to Stephan that the emperor could send no help, but he commanded the Pope to seek a personal interview with the Langobard king and induce him if possible to relinquish his designs. In the meantime Pipin's ambassadors had come to conduct the Pope to the Frankish king, and in October, 753, Stephan, in company with these, as well as the imperial representatives, proceeded to Aistulf, who had withrawn from Rome and was then at Pavia, his own capital city. He refused, however, to abate his pretentions or to restore any of the territory he had taken from the empire. The emissaries of the Frankish king now requested Aistulf to dismiss the Pope that he might go with them to Pipin. Aistulf fell into a fury at the prospect of his plans being thwarted by a combination with the Franks, but he did not venture to restrain the Pope and thus bring on an inevitable conflict. Stephan proceeded upon his journey, and Pipin, after an assembly of the Frankish kingdom had ratified his policy, agreed to restore, not to the emperor, but to the representative of St. Peter, the territories that had been seized by the Langobard king. Pipin and his two sons, Charles and Carloman, were now consecrated by the Pope, and the Frankish nobles bound themselves under pain of excommunication to choose no sovereign from any other line. The Frankish authorities relate that the king and his sons were at the same time made patricians, which was an imperial rank, and implied a recognition of their title at Constantinople. (Hartmann, 2, 176–187.) This title may have been granted in accordance with a previous understanding with the emperor or his representatives, but if so the empire subsequently derived little advantage from the act.

The league between Pipin and the Pope was thus sealed by the mutual exchange of possession that belonged to neither, since Stephan gave Pipin the crown of the Merovingians, and the king promised the Pope the territories which had belonged to the empire (Abel, xxviii, xxix). The king accordingly set out with his army for Italy ; defeated Aistulf near the foot of the Alps and laid siege to Pavia, whereupon the Langobard king agreed to restore Ravenna and the rest of the conquered territory and to comply with the Pope's demands. But scarcely had the Franks left Italy when he repudiated his promises, and in January, 756 he renewed his attack upon Rome. Again Stephan implored and secured the intervention of the Franks, again Aistulf was defeated and besieged in his capital city and again Pipin "gave him his life and his kingdom," but upon condition that Aistulf should not only restore the captured territory, but should give to the Franks one-third of the royal treasure in Pavia besides other gifts, and pay an annual tribute of twelve thousand solidi. Aistulf did not long survive this last humiliation, he died in December, 756 (Hartmann, II, 2, 189 to 197), from an accident while hunting. His brother Ratchis now forsook his monastery, and was recognized as king by the Langobards north of the Apennines, while Desiderius, a duke in Tuscia, set up his own pretensions to the throne and the Spoletans and Beneventans joined the league of the Pope with the Frankish king. Ratchis appeared to have the advantage of Desiderius until the latter appealed to Stephan, who required from him an oath to surrender the cities belonging to the empire and to live in peace with Rome and faithful to the Frankish kingdom. Upon these terms Stephan agreed to support his pretensions; he now became undisputed king and Ratchis again retired. Faenza and Ferrara however were the only territories he had surrendered when Stephan died and was succeeded by his brother Paul, whereupon Desiderius, far from fulfilling his promises, pushed forward with his army through the papal Pentapolis into Spoleto, treated its duke as a rebel, expelled the duke of Benevento and put his own son-in-law Arichis into the vacant place. He raised difficulties in respect to the boundaries of the places to be ceded, but by Pipin's intervention a compromise was effected by which the Pope renounced his claim upon the territories not yet surrendered, and Desiderius agreed to recognize the Pope's authority over his Italian possessions and to protect him against an attack from his own nominal sovereign the emperor (Hartmann, II, 2, 206–215).

In 768 Pipin died and was succeeded by his sons Charles and Carloman, whose mother Bertrada sought an alliance with the Bavarians and the Langobards, and asked for the hand of the daughter of Desiderius for Charles. In 771 Carloman died, whereupon Charles seized his brother's share of the kingdom, repudiated the marriage planned for him by his mother and sent back the daughter of Desiderius. The widow and children of Carloman were now taken under the protection of the Langobard monarch, and deadly hatred arose between the two sovereigns. Desiderius now seized Faenza, Ferrara and Comacchio and pushed forward into the territories of Ravenna and Rome. Hadrian, who then occupied the papal throne, urgently besought Charlemagne for immediate aid. Charlemagne traversed the passes of the Alps, marched against Desiderius and laid siege to Pavia. In June, 774, the city was taken, Desiderius was led into captivity and the kingdom of the Langobards was destroyed. Charlemagne was afterwards crowned Emperor of the West and the temporal power of the papacy over a region in the middle of Italy was permanently established (Abel, xxvii to xxix). Grievous consequences have followed the division of that peninsula into fragments which have continued almost to the present time; and the dream of Italian unity cherished by Rothari and Liutprand was not to be realized until the days of Victor Emmanuel, Cavour and Garibaldi.

APPENDIX.

SOME SOURCES AND ANALOGS

The *Origo Gentis Langobardorum*

Besides his ecclesiastical sources, Paul the Deacon drew upon continuations of late Roman histories and epitomes, oral traditions, the works of Gregory of Tours and Bede, and the now lost *Acts of the Lombards* by Secundus of Trent (a contemporary of Gregory I). In addition, Paul had before him a short epitome of Lombard history called the *Origo Gentis Langobardorum*. Some idea of the traditions within which Paul worked may be seen in a second document, dating from around 805, called the *Codex Gothanum,* a short work on Lombard history which did not use Paul's *History* and offers some different versions of episodes Paul and the *Origo* also treated. Paul also had available one or more lists (one of which is included below) of the provinces of Italy (II, 15–24). The translation of the *Origo Gentis Langobardorum* used here is that of William Dudley Foulke in the original edition of this book, pp. 327–331. The notes, too, are Foulke's.

I. There is an island [1] that is called Scadanan,[2] which is

[1] The Madrid and La Cava manuscripts in place of "There is an island" have "That is under the consul" which is evidently a corruption (see Mommsen, p. 60, note 2).

[2] "Scadan" says the Modena MS., "Scandanan," the La Cava MS.

interpreted "destruction," [3] in the regions of the north, where many people dwell. Among these there was a small people that was called the Winniles. And with them was a woman, Gambara by name, and she had two sons. Ybor was the name of one and Agio the name of the other. They, with their mother, Gambara by name, held the sovereignty over the Winniles. Then the leaders of the Wandals, that is, Ambri and Assi, moved with their army, and said to the Winniles: "Either pay us tributes or prepare yourselves for battle and fight with us." Then answered Ybor and Agio, with their mother Gambara: "It is better for us to make ready the battle than to pay tributes to the Wandals." Then Ambri and Assi, that is, the leaders of the Wandals, asked Godan that he should give them the victory over the Winniles. Godan answered, saying: "Whom I shall first see when at sunrise, to them will I give the victory." At that time Gambara with her two sons, that is, Ybor and Agio, who were chiefs over the Winniles, besought Frea, the wife of Godan, to be propitious to the Winnilis. Then Frea gave counsel that at sunrise the Winniles should come, and that their women, with their hair let down around the face in the likeness of a beard, should also come with their husbands. Then when it became bright, while the sun was rising, Frea, the wife of Godan, turned around the bed where her husband was lying and put his face toward the east and awakened him. And he, looking at them, saw the Winniles and their women having their hair let down around the face. And he says, "Who

---

[3] *Exscidia* (Modena MSS.). A derivation pointing to the Gothic word *skattigan,* to injure, German *Schaden,* English *scathe* (Hodg., VI, 90). Mommsen considers this a later interpolation to be rejected (p. 60, note 3).

are those Long-beards?" And Frea said to Godan, "As you have given them a name, give them also the victory." And he gave them the victory, so that they should defend themselves according to his counsel and obtain the victory. From that time the Winniles were called Langobards.

II. And the Langobards moved thence and came to Golaida and afterwards they occupied the aldionates of Anthaib and Bainaib and also Burgundaib. And it is said that they made for themselves a king, Agilmund by name, the son of Agio, of the race of Gugingus. And after him reigned Laiamicho of the race of Gugingus.[4] And after him reigned Lethuc and it is said that he reigned about forty years. And after him reigned Aldihoc the son of Lethuc. And after him reigned Godehoc.

III. At that time king Audoachari went forth from Ravenna with the army of the Alani and came into Rugiland and fought with the Rugians and killed Theuvane king of the Rugians, and led many captives with him into Italy. Then the Langobards departed from their own territories and dwelt some years in Rugiland.

IV. Claffo, the son of Godehoc reigned after him. And after him reigned Tato the son of Claffo. The Langobards settled three years in the fields of Feld. Tato fought with Rodolf king of the Heruli and killed him and carried off his banner (*vando*) and helmet. After him the Heruli had no kingly office. And Wacho the son of Unichis killed king Tato his paternal uncle together with Zuchilo. And Wacho

[4] The words "Of the race of Gugingus" are omitted in the Modena MSS. and Mommsen regards them (p. 68) as an interpolation (see also Brückner Zeitschrift für deutsches Alterthum, p. 56).

fought, and Ildichis the son of Tato fought, and Ildichis fled
to the Gippidi where he died.   And to avenge his wrong the
Gypidis made war with the Langobards.   At this time Wacho bent the Suabians under the dominion of the Langobards.
Wacho had three wives: (first) Raicunda, daughter of Fisud
king of the Turingi.   After her he took as his wife Austri-
gusa a girl of the Gippidi.[5]   And Wacho had from Austri-
gusa two daughters; the name of one was Wisigarda whom
he gave in marriage to Theudipert king [6] of the Franks, and
the name of the second was Walderada whom Scusuald king
of the Franks had as his wife, but having her in hatred he
transferred her to Garipald for a wife.   He had as his third
wife the daughter of the king of the Heruli, Silinga by
name.   From her he had a son, Waltari by name.   Wacho
died and his son Waltari reigned seven years without pos-
terity.[7]   These were all Lethinges.

V.   And after Waltari, reigned Auduin.[8]   He led the
Langobards into Pannonia.   And there reigned after him
Albuin, his son, whose mother is Rodelenda.   At that time
Albuin fought with the king of the Gippidi, Cunimund by
name, and Cunimund died in that battle and the Gippidi
were subjugated.   Albuin took as his wife Cunimund's
daughter Rosemund, whom he had captured as booty, since
his wife Flutsuinda, who was the daughter of Flothar, king
of the Franks, had already died.   From her he had a daughter by name Albsuinda.   And the Langobards dwelt forty-

[5] Jacobi, 20, note 4.

[6] Read *regi* with Modena MS. in place of *regis*.

[7] *"Farigaidus"* (Bruckner, pp. 19, 203).

[8] "Of the stock of Gausus" says the list of kings in Rothari's
Prologue (Mon. Germ. Hist. Leges, IV, 2).

two years [9] in Pannonia. This Albuin led into Italy the
Langobards who were invited by Narses (chief) of the secretaries. And Albuin, king of the Langobards, moved out of
Pannonia in the month of April after [10] Easter in the first
indiction. In the second indiction, indeed, they began to
plunder in Italy, but in the third indiction he became master
of Italy. Albuin reigned in Italy three years, and was killed
in Verona in the palace by Rosemund his wife and Hilmichis
upon the advice of Peritheo. Hilmichis wished to be king
and could not because the Langobards wanted to slay him.
Then Rosemund sent word to the prefect Longinus that he
should receive her in Ravenna. When Longinus presently
heard this he rejoiced; he sent a ship of the public service and
they brought Rosemund and Hilmichis and Albsuinda, king
Albuin's daughter, and conducted all the treasures of the
Langobards with them to Ravenna. Then the prefect Longinus began to persuade Rosemund to kill Hilmichis and
become the wife of Longinus. Having given ear to his counsel, she mixed poison and, after the bath, gave it to him
(Hilmichis) to drink in a goblet.[11] But when Hilmichis
had drunk, he knew that he had drunk something pernicious.
He commanded that Rosemund herself should drink, although
unwilling, and they both died. Then the prefect Longinus
took the treasure of the Langobards and commanded Albsuinda, the daughter of king Albuin, to be put in a ship, and
sent her over to Constantinople to the emperor.

[9] The Modena MS. says twelve. Neither number is correct.
They probably remained there about twenty-two years.

[10] *A Pascha,* (Waitz, p. II, 7, note.)

[11] Thus Abel translates *in caldo* (p. 6), or perhaps it is "In a
hot potion."

VI. The rest of the Langobards set over themselves a king named Cleph, of the stock of Beleos, and Cleph reigned two years and died. And the dukes of the Langobards administered justice for twelve years and after these things they set up over themselves a king named Autari, the son of Cleph. And Autari took as his wife Theudelenda, a daughter of Garipald and of Walderada from Bavaria. And with Theudelenda came her brother named Gundoald, and king Autari appointed him duke in the city of Asta. And Autari reigned seven years. And Acquo,[12] the Thuringian duke,[13] departed from Turin and united himself with queen Theudelenda and became king of the Langobards. And he killed his rebel dukes Zangrolf of Verona, Mimulf of the island of St. Julian and Gaidulf of Bergamo, and others who were rebels. And Acquo begot of Theudelenda a daughter, Gunperga [14] by name. And Acquo reigned six years, and after him Aroal reigned twelve years.[15] And after him reigned Rothari, of the race of Arodus, and he destroyed the city and fortresses of the Romans which were around the coasts from the neighborhood of Luna [16] up to the land of the Franks and in the east up to Ubitergium (Oderzo). And he fought near the

[12] Aggo in Modena MSS.

[13] *Turingus*. Perhaps this merely means that he was duke of Turin. "Of the stock of Anawas" adds the Prologue to Rothari's Edict (Mon. Germ. Hist. Leges, Vol. IV, p. 2).

[14] "And a son named Adwald" adds the Modena MSS.

[15] In the Prologue, "Arioald of the race of Caupus." The text here seems greatly corrupted. Paul and the Chronicon Gothanum give Agilulf's reign at 25 years and that of his son Adalwald (here omitted) at 10 years.

[16] Northwest of Lucca.

river Scultenna,[17] and there fell on the side of the Romans the number of eight thousand.

VII. And Rothari reigned seventeen years. And after him reigned Aripert nine years. And after him reigned Grimoald.[18] At this time the emperor Constantine departed from Constantinople and came into the territories of Campania and turned back to Sicily and was killed by his own people. And Grimoald reigned nine years, and after him Berthari reigned.[19]

[17] In Modena.
[18] The Modena MSS. adds "seventeen years."
[19] The Modena MSS. omits the sentence regarding Berthari.

The *Codex Gothanum*

The condensation and translation below is from Thomas Hodgkin, *Italy and Her Invaders,* Vol. V, The Lombard Invasion (Oxford, 1895), pp. 146–150. The notes and editorial comments are Hodgkin's.

The opening and closing paragraphs of the Codex Gothanus (described at the beginning of chap. iii) are so utterly different from the Origo and the history of Paulus, that, instead of attempting to weave them into one narrative therewith, I prefer to give a separate translation of them here.

1. The fore-elders of the Langobardi assert "per Gambaram parentem suam pro quid exitus aut movicio seu visitatio eorum fuisset, deinter serpentibus parentes eorum breviati exissent," [1] a rough and bloody and lawless progeny. But coming into the land of Italy they found it flowing with milk

[1] I cannot pretend to translate this sentence.

and honey, and, what is more, they found there the salvation
of baptism, and receiving the marks of the Holy Trinity,
they were made of the number of the good. In them was
fulfilled the saying, "Sin is not imputed where there is no
law." At first they were ravening wolves, afterwards they
became lambs feeding in the Lord's flock: therefore should
great praise and thanks be brought to God who hath raised
them from the dung-hill and set them in the number of the
just, thereby fulfilling the prophecy of David, "He raiseth
the needy from the dung-hill, and maketh him to sit with the
princes of the earth." Thus did the aforesaid Gambara
assert concerning them [2] (not prophesying things which she
knew not, but, like the Pythoness or Sibyl,[3] speaking because
a divine visitation moved her), that "the thorn should be
turned into a rose." How this could be she knew not, unless
it were shown to her by God.[4] She asserts, therefore, that
they will go forth, moved not by necessity, nor by hardness
of heart,[5] nor by the oppression of parents, but that they may
obtain salvation from on high. It is a wonderful and un-
heard-of-thing to behold such salvation shining forth, when
there was no merit in their parents, so that from among the
sharp blades of the thorns the odorous flowers of the churches
were found. Even as the compassionate Son of God had
preached before, "I came not to call the righteous, but sinners" [to repentance]. These were they of whom the
Saviour Himself spake in proverbs [parables] to the Jews,

[2] 'Cum eisdem movita (?) adserebat.'

[3] 'Sed phitonissa inter Sibillae cognomina.'

[4] 'Nesciens in qualia, nisi divinandum perspicerit.'

[5] I.e. not by oppressors driving them forth from their own
land.

"I have other sheep, which are not of this fold: them also I must bring to seek for the living water."

2. Here begins the origin and nation or parentage of the Langobardi, their going forth and their conversion, the wars and devastations made by their kings, and the countries which they laid waste.

There is a river which is called Vindilicus, on the extreme boundary of Gaul: near to this river was their first dwelling and possession. At first they were Winili by their own proper name and parentage: for, as Jerome [6] asserts, their name was afterwards changed into the common word Langobardi, by reason of their profuse and always unshaven beards. This aforesaid river Ligurius flows into the channels of the river Elbe, and loses its name. [7] After the Langobardi went forth, as has been before said(?), from the same shore, they placed their new habitations at first at Scatenauge on the shore of the river Elbe: then still fighting, they reached the country of the Saxons, the place which is called Patespruna, where, as our ancient fathers assert, they dwelt a long time, and they encountered wars and dangers in many regions. Here too they first raised over them a king named Agelmund. With him they began to fight their way back to their own portion in their former country, wherefore in Beovinidis they moved their army by the sound of clanging

[6] Really Isidore in his Etymologica, ix. 226. I take the reference from Waitz.

[7] 'Hic supradictus Ligurius fluvius Albiae fluvii canalis inundans, et nomen finitur.' Evidently something is omitted, as the Ligurius has not been mentioned before.

trumpets to their own property:[8] whence to the present
day the house and dwelling of their king Wacho still appear
as signs.[9] Then requiring a country of greater fertility,
they crossed over to the province of Thrace, and fixed their
inheritance in the country of the city (*sic*) of Pannonia.[10]
Here they struggled with the Avars, and waging many wars
with them with most ardent mind, they conquered Pannonia
itself. And the Avars made with them a league of friendship, and for twenty-two years they are said to have lived
there.

From this point to the accession of Rothari, A.D. 636, the
text of the Codex Gothanus coincides very nearly with that
of the Origo. It then proceeds as follows:—

7. Rothari reigned sixteen years: by whom laws and
justice were begun for the Langobardi: and for the first time
the judges went by a written code, for previously all causes
were decided by custom (*cadarfada*) and the judge's will, or
by ordeal (?) (*ritus*).[11] In the days of the same king Rothari, light arose in the darkness: by whom the aforesaid

[8] 'Unde in Beovinidis aciem et clauses (classes ?) seu tuba
clangencium ad suam proprietatem perduxerunt.' Quite un-
translateable. See reference to Beowinidis in § 9.

[9] 'Unde usque hodie praesentem diem Wachoni regi eorum
domus et habitatio apparet signa.' A most incomprehensible
sentence: and why introduced here? Four kings are mentioned after this before Wacho appears on the scene.

[10] 'In Pannoniae urbis patriam suam hereditatem affixerunt.'

[11] 'Per quem leges et justiciam Langobardis est inchoata: et
per conscriptionem primis judices percurrerunt: nam antea
per cadarfada et arbitrio seu ritus fierunt causationes.'

Langobardi directed their endeavours to the canonical rule,[12] and became helpers of the priests.

[8 contains the durations of the kings' reigns from Rodwald to Desiderius].

9. Here was finished the kingdom of the Langobardi, and began the kingdom of Italy, by the most glorious Charles, king of the Franks, who, as helper and defender of lord Peter, the prince of the Apostles, had gone to demand justice for him from Italy. For no desire of gain caused him to wander, but he became the pious and compassionate helper of the good: and though he might have demolished all things, he became their clement and indulgent [preserver]. And in his pity he bestowed on the Langobardi the laws of his native land, adding laws of his own as he deemed fit for the necessities of the Langobardi: and he forgave the sins of innumerable men who sinned against him incessantly. For which Almighty God multiplied his riches a hundredfold. After he had conquered Italy he made Spain his boundary: then he subdued Saxony: afterwards he became lord of Bavaria, and over innumerable nations spread the terror of his name. But at last, as he was worthy of the Empire's honour, he obtained the Imperial crown; he received all the dignities of the Roman power, he was made the most dutiful son of lord Peter, the apostle, and he defended Peter's property from his foes. But after all these things he handed over the kingdom of Italy to his great and glorious son, lord Pippin, the great king, and as Almighty God bestowed the grace of fortitude on the father, so did it abound in the son, through whom the

---

[12] 'Ad cannonicam (*sic*) tenderunt certamina.'

province of Thrace(!), together with the Avars, was brought into subjection to the Franks. They, the aforesaid Avars, who were sprung from a stock which is the root of all evil, who had ever been enemies of the churches and persecutors of the Christians, were, as we have said, by the same lord Pippin, to his own great comfort and that of his father, expelled and overcome: the holy churches were defended, and many vessels of the saints which those cruel and impious men had carried off, were by the same defender restored to their proper homes. Then the cities of the Beneventan province, as they deserved for their violation of their plighted oath, were wasted and made desolate by fire, and their inhabitants underwent the capital sentence. After these things, he also went to Beowinidis(?) with his army and wasted it, and made the people of that land a prey, and carried them captive. Therefore also by his orders his army liberated the island of Corsica, which was oppressed by the Moors. At the present day by his aid Italy has shone forth as she did in the most ancient days. She has had laws, and fertility, and quietness, by the deserving of our lord [the Emperor], through the grace of our Lord Jesus Christ. Amen.

An Account of the Provinces of Italy

The list, printed by Waitz from a tenth–century manuscript in Madrid, is from the original edition of this book, pp. 380–382, notes by Foulke.

The first province is Venetia. This Venetia contains Verona, Vincentia, Patavium, Mantua and other cities, but among all, the city of Aquileia was the capital, in place of which just now is Forum Julii, so called because Julius Cæsar had established a market there for business.

The second province is Liguria, in which is Mediolanum and Ticinum, which is called by another name, Papia. It stretches to the boundaries of the *Langobards*. Between this and the country of the Alamani are two provinces, that is First Reptia and Second Reptia lie among the Alps, in which properly the Reti are known to dwell.

The Cottian Alps are called the third province. This extends from Liguria in a southerly direction up to the Tyrrenian Sea, and on the west it is *reckoned* from the boundaries of the Gauls. In it are contained Aquis (where there are hot springs) and the cities of Dertona, Genua and Saona and the monastery of Bovium.

The fourth province is Tuscia. This includes Aurelia toward the northwest and Umbria on the eastern side. In this province Rome was situated, which was *at one time* capital of the whole world. In Umbria are Perusium and Lake Clitorius and Spoletium.

Campania, the fifth province stretches from the city of Rome to the Siler, a river of Lucania. In it the very rich cities of Capua, Neapolis and Salernum are situated.

The sixth province, Lucania, begins at the river Siler and extends with Oritia [1] as far as the Sicilian strait along the coast of the Tirrenian Sea, like the two last named provinces, holding the right horn of Italy. In it cities are placed, *that is,* Pestus, Laynus, Cassanus, Cosentia, *Malvitus* and Regium.

The seventh province is reckoned in the Apennine Alps, which take their origin from the place where the Cottian Alps terminate. These Apennine Alps, extending through the middle of Italy, separate Tuscia from Emilia, and Umbria

---

[1] Evidently a mistake for Britia (Bruttium).

from Flaminea. In it are the cities of Feronianum and Montebellium and Bovium and Orbinum, and also the town which is called Verona.

The eighth province, Emilia, beginning from *the province* of Liguria, extends towards Ravenna between the Apennine Alps and the waters of the Padus. It *contains* wealthy cities: Plagentia, Regio, Boonia and the Forum of Cornelius, the fortress of which is called Imola.

The ninth province, Flaminea, is placed between the Apennine Alps and the Adriatic Sea. In it are Ravenna, most noble of cities, and five other cities which in the Greek tongue are called Pentapolis.

The tenth province, Picenum, comes after Flaminea. It has on the south the Apennine mountains, on the other side, the Adriatic Sea. It extends to the river Piscaria. In it are the cities Firmus, Asculus and Pennis, also (Hadriae) consumed with old age.[2]

Valeria, the eleventh province, to which Nursia is attached, is situated between Umbria and Campania, and Picenum, and it touches on the east the region of Samnium. This contains the cities of Tibur, Carsiolis, Reate, Forconis and Amiternum, and the regions of the Marsians and their lake which is called Focinus.

The twelfth province, Samnium, is between Campania and the Adriatic Sea and Apulia. This begins at the Piscaria. In it are the cities of Theate, Aufidianum, Hisernia and Sampnium, consumed by its old age, from which the whole province is named, and the most wealthy Beneventum, the capital of this province.

[2] Waitz supplies here "Hadriae" from Paul's History.